Narratives from the Women's Studies Family

NARRATIVES FROM THE WOMEN'S STUDIES FAMILY

Recreating Knowledge

Editors

Devaki Jain
Pam Rajput

SAGE Publications
New Delhi ✠ Thousand Oaks ✠ London

First published in 2003 by

Sage Publications India Pvt Ltd
B-42, Panchsheel Enclave
New Delhi 110 017

Sage Publications Inc
2455 Teller Road
Thousand Oaks, California 91320

Sage Publications Ltd
6 Bonhill Street
London EC2A 4PU

Published by Tejeshwar Singh for Sage Publications India Pvt Ltd, Phototypeset in AGaramond by InoSoft Systems and printed at Chaman Enterprises, New Delhi.

Library of Congress Cataloging-in-Publication Data

Narratives from the women's studies family: recreating knowledge/edited by Devaki Jain and Pam Rajput.
    p. cm.
Includes bibliographical references and index.
    1. Women's studies—India. 2. Women—Information services—India. I. Jain, Devaki, 1933– II. Rajput, Pam, 1942–

HQ1181.I4 N365   305.4'071'0954—dc21   2002   2002070529

ISBN: 0–7619–9695–8 (US-Hb)   81–7829–167–3 (India-Hb)
    0–7619–9787–3 (US-Pb)   81–7829–231–9 (India-Pb)

Sage Production Team: Shahnaz Habib, Mathew P.J. and Santosh Rawat

Contents

Section II: Case studies of women's studies centres outside the university

Section III: Individual scholars

विश्वविद्यालय अनुदान आयोग
नई दिल्ली—110 002
UNIVERSITY GRANTS COMMISSION
BAHADUR SHAH ZAFAR MARG
NEW DELHI–110 002
OFF : (011) 23237143
FAX : (011) 23231797
E-mail : narun42@hotmail.com

डॉ. अरूण निगवेकर
अध्यक्ष

Dr. Arun Nigavekar

Chairman

Foreword

Women's studies as a significant discipline—with ramifications that flow not only into all the disciplines within a university but also into the policy, action and implementation of the Constitution of India—has come of age in India. This volume, the first of such efforts to describe as well as understand the value of women's studies, is a project of the Commission, and it gives me great pleasure to present this volume to the public.

The Introduction to the volume reveals the power of the discipline, the commitment of those who have been engaged in building women's studies centres in India (both within the university's domain and outside it) as also the constraints that these pioneers of women's studies faced. These constraints not only constitute those of finance but also have to do with an inveterate resistance towards new sources of knowledge, such as that which women have been uncovering about women and men. The 17 essays contained in this volume exhibit both diversity and unity—diversity in the initiation and characteristics of centres, and unity in the extraordinary energy and creativity that the centres and their pioneers have revealed.

There is now an increasing demand by young as well as intellectual and programmatic agencies for knowledge about women and men, young and old, their contributions and their constraints, in order to build a just and egalitarian society. In that context, I applaud this effort, congratulate all the contributors as well as the editors and take pleasure in writing the Foreword to this book.

New Delhi
Date: 4 July 2002

(ARUN NIGAVEKAR)

Acknowledgements

This volume, which speaks of the being and becoming of the women's studies family across India, is not the result of the efforts of the editors alone. We wish to acknowledge our deep appreciation and gratitude to Professor Armaity S. Desai, former Chairperson of the UGC, who envisioned this volume. Dr Arun Nigavekar, the Chairperson of the UGC, deserves special gratitude for his continued support to this endeavour and for sparing his valuable time to write the Foreword to this volume. We would also like to place on record our thanks to the Standing Committee of the UGC, especially its Chairperson, Professor Kamalini Bhansali, who entrusted us with the task of editing this volume. We hope that their expectations have not been belied.

The contributors to this volume, who are pioneers of women's studies in India, deserve our special thanks for their invaluable contributions that have made this volume possible.

Our acknowledgements would be incomplete without mentioning many other persons who have contributed to the completion of this book. A special mention must be made of Dr Manvinder Kaur (Research Officer, CWSD, Panjab University) and Dr Jyoti Grewal (Visiting Fellow, CWSD), for their painstaking help with copy editing the manuscript, and Ms. Ameer Sultana (Project Officer, CWSD, Panjab University), who was constantly of great help in innumerable ways. C.P. Sujaya, who refereed almost all the essays, is remembered with warmth. We would also like to acknowledge with thanks Kala Ramesh (writer) and Nageena Nikhat Khaleel (Research Assistant) for their help with editing this work, and M.V. Jagadeesh for secretarial support.

We do hope that this book, which encompasses the labours of so many, will deepen the understanding and broaden the acceptance of women's studies among the academia and general intelligentsia as yet another domain in a world abuzz with hopes of democratisation.

Acknowledgements

List of abbreviations and acronyms

AIADMK	All India Anna Dravida Munnetra Kazhagam
AU-CWS	Alagappa University Centre for Women's Studies
AWG	Autonomous Women's Groups
BHU	Banaras Hindu University
CIDA	Canadian International Development Agency
CIEFL	Central Institute of English and Foreign Languages
CSCS	Centre for the Study of Culture in Society
CSIR	Council of Scientific and Industrial Research
CSO	Central Statistical Organisation
CSWI	Committee on the Status of Women in India
CWL	Centre for Women and Law
CWDS	Centre for Women's Development Studies
CWSD	Centre for Women's Studies and Development
DAWN	Development Alternatives with Women for a New era
DMK	Dravida Munnetra Kazhagam
DPEP	District Primary Education Programme
DRDA	District Rural Development Agency
DWCRA	Development of Women and Children in Rural Areas
EC	Executive Committee/Council
EDP	Entrepreneurship Development Programme
EIWIG	Economists Interested in Women's Issues Group
ESCAP	Economic and Social Council for Asia and the Pacific
FCRA	Foreign Contribution Regulation Act
FICCI	Federation of Indian Chambers of Commerce and Industry
HBT	Hyderabad Book Trust
HIVOS	Humanist Institute for Development Cooperation
IACIS	Indo-American Centre for International Studies
IAWS	Indian Association of Women's Studies
ICHS	Indian Council of Historical Studies
ICMR	Indian Council of Medical Research
ICPD	International Conference on Population and Development
ICRW	International Centre for Research on Women
ICSSR	Indian Council for Social Science Research

IDS	Institute of Development Studies
ILO	International Labour Organisation
IPSA	International Political Science Association
IRDP	Integrated Rural Development Programme
ISST	Institute of Social Studies Trust
IWSA	Indian Women Scientists Association
JRF	Junior Research Fellow
MIDS	Madras Institute of Development Studies
MMM	Mahila Mukti Morcha
MS	Mahila Samakhya
MTWU	Mother Teresa Women's University
NAM	Non-Aligned Movement
NCERT	National Council for Education, Research and Training
NCSW	National Committee on the Status of Women
NCW	National Commission for Women
NCWS	National Conference on Women's Studies
NGO	Non-Governmental Organisation
NIMHANS	National Institute of Mental Health and Neuro Sciences
NSSO	National Sample Survey Organisation
OECD	Organisation for Economic Co-operation and Development
PMRY	Prime Minister's Rozgar Yojana
PROWID	Programme for Women in Development
RCWS	Research Centre for Women's Studies
RUWS	Research Unit on Women's Studies
SC	Scheduled Castes
SEWA	Self-Employed Women's Association
SISC	Small Industries Service Centre
SNDT	Shrimati Nathubai Damodar Thackersey University
ST	Scheduled Tribes
STEP	Support Team for Employment Promotion
TISS	Tata Institute of Social Sciences
UGC	University Grants Commission
UN	United Nations
UNDP	United Nations Development Programme
UNESCO	United Nations Educational, Scientific and Cultural Organisation
UNICEF	United Nations International Children's Fund
UNIFEM	United Nations Development Fund for Women

VC	vice-chancellor
VHAI	Voluntary Health Association of India
WDC	Women's Development Centre
WHODSIC	Women, Household and Development Studies and Information Centre
WICEJ	Women's International Coalition for Economic Justice
WID	Women in Development
WSC	Women's Studies Centre
WSDC	Women's Studies and Development Centre
WSRC	Women's Studies Research Centre
WWF	Working Women's Forum

Introduction

Devaki Jain and Pam Rajput

Women's studies is the typical offspring of a movement for justice, recognition and emancipation from subordination. It embraces within itself, academia and action, theory and practice, voices and scripts. It has been a powerful tool for calling attention to the intellectual and ideational skills of women across the world, and to the importance of role distinction between men and women in society at large. This difference was uncovered by women's studies at both material and intellectual planes.

Scholars in women's studies challenge the philosophical underpinnings of human knowledge and critique existing paradigms in all intellectual disciplines. Their basic premise is that the concepts, tools and techniques that are now in use, endorse gender-based discrimination and the denial of equity to women. Their aim is to interrogate these through a perspective that highlights the processes through which women have been made marginal and invisible, as also to formulate new definitions and methodologies that can give the necessary critical edge to future knowledge systems. Their theoretical intrusions are meant to assimilate gender consciousness into mainstream disciplines. Women's studies has been crucial in helping social science to broaden the notion of 'social', thus transcending earlier narrow formulations. The challenge of women's studies has been to change and transform the way that social reality is presented in all the so-called 'mainstream' disciplines.

Women's studies has inspired the engendering of documents and reports, whether at the global level, as in the case of the World

Development Report or the Human Development Report; at the national level, as in the case of the National Planning documents; or at the local level, in designing and implementing projects. Sometimes the perception could be entirely mechanical or instrumental—that unless women's separate roles and strengths are identified and accommodated, a project or production would not be utilising its resources as efficiently as it should. In the case of population discourse, for instance, it is argued that inputs targeted at women, such as education, will directly bring about outputs like lower fertility. Sometimes, the perception could be more moral—that it is unjust to ignore the condition, role and contribution of women. Whichever the perception, it became a 'gender line'—a colour that was woven inextricably into the social fabric. Just as in the operational so too in the intellectual sphere, women's studies is synonymous with the women's movement, challenging the dichotomy between thought and action both in its persona as well as in its impulses.

Women's studies has had a very special history in India. The growth of this discipline was propelled by an interest in equity and justice, and drew inspiration from the grass-roots level experience of women's organisations. Women's studies, as perceived by the Indian women's movement, is a potent instrument that plays a deliberate and active role in the battle to change people's mind-sets and values. In the last four to five decades, it has provided information and ideas for policy, programme design and innovative implementation to universities, the government as well as other agencies.

In the Indian landscape, there is an interesting diversity within women's studies. Sources of research, information, documentation and action vary widely, ranging from individuals located in mainstream research and development institutions and university departments to directors of specific women's studies centres that were opened within universities and were supported by the University Grants Commission. The range also includes women's studies units in colleges that are not necessarily part of the UGC scheme, as well as centres that have been funded by the Indian Council of Social Science Research, and finally those that have mushroomed in the NGO sector as participants in social and political movements, including the women's movement. This variegated membership profile is the strength of the Indian women's studies movement, and its most lively expression is found in the Indian Association of Women's Studies, which encompasses this entire network of individuals and agencies.

The Indian Council of Social Science Research (ICSSR) and later the National Policy of Education (NPE 1986, which was updated in 1992) identified women's studies as a 'critical instrument of social and educational development'. The Policy, stressing the need for education of women, laid down that 'education will be used as an agent of basic change in the status of women. The National Education System will play a positive interventionist role in the empowerment of women.... Women's Studies will be promoted as a part of various courses and educational institutions encouraged to take up active programmes to further women's development'.

One of the major outcomes of this was the entry of the University Grants Commission (UGC) into this field and its enunciation of guidelines for the promotion of women's studies, which clearly reflect the objectives of the women's studies movement, through the setting up of women's studies centres in various universities in India in the mid-1980s. Initially four, their number has now grown to 32.

Around the late 1970s, a number of autonomous women's studies centres such as Aalochana, Anveshi, Vimochana and Institute of Social Studies Trust (ISST) also became engaged in research related to women, while the Centre for Women's Development Studies emerged from the ICSSR network. These centres—both UGC and non-UGC—are doing front-line work, documenting and analysing women's issues and experiences, and formulating new pedagogical approaches and methods. They have contributed to the visibility of women's concerns, tried to combine erudite knowledge with socially relevant theories and action, created a space for women's studies in the patriarchal set-up of the university system and succeeded in opening a dialogue in multi-disciplinary collaboration. They have helped develop a Third World focus on gender issues, which is significant, considering the specificity of social structures such as caste, kinship and various other cultural matrices. From its embryonic origins in the mid-1970s, women's studies has now become a national movement.

It was the recognition of the need to document the growth of women's studies in India which led to the conception of this volume, which is one of several others being published by the UGC on the occasion of 50 years of India's independence. The committee also decided that a workshop should be organised in order to present and critique the papers, so that the volume would have the benefit of experts in the field. This workshop was held in Chandigarh in April 1999, hosted by the Women Studies Centre and supported by the University Grants Commission and Indian Association of Women's Studies.

This volume is a collection of essays by various individuals from the Indian women's studies family who were, by and large, the initiators of the centres about which they have written. In a pioneering attempt to document the histories of these centres, the Standing Committee on Women's Studies of the University Grants Commission invited these authors to recall their specific histories against a broad, open-ended outline. These essays were commissioned especially to enable posterity to comprehend the purpose, issues and background (both external and internal) against which the centres had been started. The hope was that such a recall would also be useful for those who were beginning to make inroads into women's studies.

Many valuable, creative individual contributions to the knowledge base and activity base of the women's studies movement could not be included within the bounds of this volume, at least not in sufficient numbers. A similar problem arose with regard to the 'autonomous' centres, as we have termed those organisations that mushroomed in response to the women's movement impulse independent of any financial assistance from the government. Thus, in the overall representation of women's studies centres in India, we have two from the autonomous group, three individual scholars, one ICSSR-supported centre and 10 from the UGC family.

In some ways, this characterisation is invaluable. As we learn about the genesis, evolution, triumphs and tribulations of the centres in these 17 retrospections, there are many common characteristics that bring them into one whole. This phenomenon of the similarity of experience—what can be called in more conventional terms as 'unity in diversity'—has been one of the most enriching and important aspects of developing this collection.

The variations and 'jagged edges', on the other hand, are an indication of the heterogeneity of the locations and the particular nuances of the local situation or environment. This lack of uniformity detracts from what some would call a 'smoothened finished product', but then the editors have consciously tried to retain the story 'as it is' and narrate it in the words of those who actually suffered the birth pangs and nurtured the centres through the crucial years.

Looking back at this volume, the editors realise that this is only the tip of the iceberg. The larger family of women's studies has had the benefit of contributions from women writers, poets, mediapersons, video film-makers and practitioners of the performing arts and the plastic arts, as well as the masses of ordinary women and men who have, in their own little ways, been making a difference for themselves and the country. This larger group has a legitimate place in any volume that claims to document women's studies in India. We do realise that their absence here is a lacuna. Nevertheless, we can only see this volume as the first of what could not only be many more volumes, but also differently constructed volumes that gather together the contributions of the large population of those who have contributed to enabling women in their crusade for justice, peace and development.

In what follows, we first explain the similarity of experience and then the variations in the themes of the contributions to this volume. We trace these variations to various types of causalities, structures and impulses in the environment. By defining their roles and discussing the issues that needed consideration, we attempt to illustrate the substantial contribution of the women's studies family as gathered within this volume, and reflect on the past with an eye on the future.

The oneness

The most striking aspects of all the narrations in this volume are the contributors' commitment to the broader cause of justice and to reordering the status of women, as also their recognition of the roles that women's studies can play in socio-political movements for transformation. These essays bear testimony to their determination, their capacity to evoke support from the environment (both external and internal), and their ability to get the business going against all odds. There is another remarkable similarity in the forms of support that have been extended even by women not directly associated with the women's studies movement. Each writer has invariably acknowledged other women—whether they are team members within the organisation, or belong to the larger academic community or operate outside it. This acknowledgement of humility and the expression of collectivity is a common chorus and ethos across the board.

Women enable and are enabled

Yet another striking, if disturbing, feature, is the virtual absence of male participation in the women's studies movement, except in rare cases such as in the founding of a women's university by a male social reformer or educationist, or in the presence of a male vice-chancellor in the advisory committee of a women's studies centre.

Women both within and outside the university, on the other hand, have gravitated towards the women's studies centre as a place where they receive not only knowledge but also support. This phenomenon holds true for centres and individuals outside the UGC circuit as well.

Most of these characteristics are universal and go beyond the boundaries of India. Women have supported women's endeavours and struggles for equality or against discrimination from the very beginning of the movement, as revealed when we trace the history of the United Nations from 1946. It was women who lobbied for the recognition of women's rights when the first charter on human rights was drawn up. Again, it was women who fought for a Commission on the Status of Women in the United Nations. This is an unfortunate comment on the social history of gender relations.

The phenomenon of women enabling women is also universal. In many universities across the world, the women's studies nucleus has also had to provide 'support services', including counselling, shelter and legal redress against violence. Thus, many universities have had to open a second window which deals specifically with grievances, violence against women, sexual harassment and counselling.

These kinds of experiences point to the well-known fact that even today, in the 21st century, women suffer from discrimination and a sense of oppression, and need spaces where they can bond on the basis of their gender identity for psychological and political support. The other side of the coin is that it is natural that women's bonding cuts across the divides of academia and action, as well as across generations, disciplines and organisational identities.

Flowing into the mainstream

The struggle for acceptability in mainstream disciplines in the groves of academe is another point of similarity. Whether it is the university structure, the individual departments, the disciplinary forums or socio-political and economic forums, women's studies as a meaningful specialist subject has been marginalised. This peripheral status is manifest in different ways in different spaces. An individual scholar in a large male-dominated space like the National Law School first undergoes a personal metamorphosis after studying gender laws and then experiences a struggle in introducing the latter as an important analytical frame for the entire spectrum of courses. Another writer who is, in fact, part of a women's studies centre within a department in a university discovers that while her own discipline has accepted the engendering, other disciplines will still not accept this as legitimate.

Outside academia, that is, amongst those working in the broader socio-political realm—in women's resource centres, for example—there are instances of marginalisation by political and social agencies who may see them as 'breakaway' as they call attention to a specific division of the struggle. Individual writers and scholars engaged in the articulation of women's voices have not been fully accepted by these forums either. Hierarchies of power, hierarchies of legitimacy in thought and hierarchies of prioritisation including in terms of financial allocation, have diminished the importance of those engaged in this domain.

Thus, across the board, we observe fighting spirit and support for it on one side and the frustration of not being able to join the mainstream on the other—though it must also be recorded that quite a few do just that and perhaps even changed its direction and momentum.

The double bonus

Each individual writer has made a double journey. The first is the internal journey, where the person herself grows into what can be informally called a 'feminist' or a women's activist. Simultaneously they have built the women's studies centres. This is linked to another kind of internal experience, of perhaps those who came earlier on the scene. In their case, analysis points out the importance of the political premise, how their involvement in the needs of the environment made them grow, made the centre 'relevant'—but concludes that intertwining seems to fade away as the centre 'settles in'. They further suggest that when that happens, the centre and its work both lose their individual growth-making impulses.

Coping with scarcities

Raising finances for work has been a universal challenge for all the centres. While there are differences between those who belong to a scheme such as the UGC's and those who do not, money has certainly been the 'root' of many problems. Along with the paucity of funds, there is also the scarcity of experienced persons who can design courses as well as teach them. Here, too, the spirit of mutual support and the willingness to accommodate has been responsible for collective growth. The few stalwarts move around and are much appreciated. Documents, books and library lists are shared, photocopied and mailed (this was before the advent of e-mail), bibliographies are prepared, document rooms are converted into reading rooms and public libraries and networks are created with little resources. The spirit is that of a movement and not a typical academic space. It can be suggested, cautiously, that this is very much the women's experience—to maximise on minimal inputs. We have heard of women's coping and survival strategies, not to mention the limitlessness of maternal altruism. Nevertheless, we suggest this cautiously as it is not the intention here to endorse this form of 'exploitation', 'suffering' or 'sacrifice', the various words used to refer to this phenomenon, each connoting a different ideological premise. However, past experience does provide a link and raise the feminist question.

Most of the university centres have had to cope with indifference, eternal queries and dissociation with the spirit behind their initiatives, all these together leading to endless delays in cash actually reaching the centres. It is here that the directors have had to be very inventive, using strategies and mechanisms that would have done global entrepreneurship proud! Feminine stereotypes could be turned on their head by this experience. To be inventive at a time of scarcity is a trait that is unique to women.

From nowhere to somewhere

The struggle to establish the centre is also associated with finding space. Each writer tells her unique story, which becomes part of a single larger story—'from cycle shed to power house', 'from a file to a light house', and so on. Each of these efforts, whether it is for a room of one's own, or to be part of a space which represents the theme and purpose of women's studies, speaks of the enormous importance of physical location, its significance from the perspective of inclusion. This sentiment is also universal, the global experience not only of women's studies centres but of all women who work for the women's cause, whether in a newspaper office, in a university or in administration. Where they are made to sit and what kind of relationship their centre has to the main building invariably have a political significance.

The all-in-one package

Catalysts, networkers, activists, policy makers, teachers, counsellors, marchers, agitators, documenters, itinerant travellers—the writers in this volume have been all of these, whatever be the origin and structure of the centre which they initiated, and whatever be the aim they started out with. It is practically impossible for them to stay within the limits of a single role—the outside constantly knocks on their doors, and the woman question is such that any person who enters this field has to take on all these roles to play even one role effectively. As in other situations, such elasticity creates its own problems. What is the central identity? A research scholar, an activist, a lobbyist or a mobiliser? Such questions trouble the staff and the leadership as they have significance for fund raising and in the quest for legitimacy in either academia or the public action space. Inclusion often requires clarity of identity and so the amorphousness could become another reason for exclusion and marginalisation. The 'all-in-one' package, on the other hand, has its popularity and can be legitimised as the ethic of being part of a movement and not a discipline.

The issues

Weaving in gender

One of the persistent and yet unresolved questions that confront all those who are in a powerless or subordinate position in any power scenario is how to make their voice, knowledge, wisdom, value, concerns and power audible, visible and accommodated, if not emancipated. Many terminologies have appeared in the process of articulation. For example, 'mainstreaming' is a term that is used in dialogues on women and development. Another is the description of the voice as 'subaltern' and the theories unfolded by that analytical frame. An earlier reference was to the 'big' and 'little' traditions, when referring to cultures. The 'highroad' as different from the 'bylanes' is another and there are many more.

As is wont to happen, these modes of description or valuation are also challenged. Mainstream is not mainstream at all if it is defined in terms of the majority view, or by any measure of numbers. It may be the language of power, but if mainstream refers to the flow of opinion and thought, what is then considered mainstream is actually minority and marginal. Much of this naming can be critiqued this way, as naming connotes hierarchies and the hierarchies are already embedded in forms of traditional power including patriarchy amongst others.

This issue however haunts the proponents of women's studies. Which is more effective—to bring a gender line into all the disciplines or to have a separate unit for women's studies? Women's studies gets ghettoised as 'for women, by women' and marginalised because of the hierarchies in the knowledge enterprise. Its market value as education that leads to the best of employment opportunities is also part of the hierarchy.

The uncovering of knowledge by women's studies, however, reveals errors in theorisation. These errors are due to lack of note of gender differentiation and ignorance of the perspectives and ideas drawn from the feminine experience. Each academic discipline needs to transform itself with this new knowledge for the sake of accuracy, if not justice. So the pointer is to what can be called penetration.

On the other hand, the separate identity has value, as it provides a space for women, and endorses and enhances the ethic of strength in women's solidarities and collectivities. Separatism can be a necessary identity/condition for building equity from a position of collective strength. This position is endorsed by those involved in battles for justice from caste and race discrimination.

Leadership and succession

Another haunting question is that of leadership, and links with the question of transition. There is much agonising on this subject in most, though not all, of the introspections in this book. Once again, this agonising is not limited to India alone, or to the zone of women's studies. Since leadership also connotes power, and dealing with power is one of the major preoccupations of both the person and the organisation, this is a serious dilemma. A pathway out of this gridlock has to be found and that is also an item for future consideration.

Most of the writers emphasise on team collectivity and an inclusive approach both in terms of immediate colleagues as well as other allies. Most look forward to a continuity of spirit with the next generation. Most conduct orientation programmes which impart training as distinct from the teaching that has to take place in centres located in the university. The bonding for a common cause or commitment and the shared consciousness of identity often supersedes generational and other gaps.

But most also express disappointment and even admit failure in building what they perceive as the continuity of the idealism and dedication with which they started the centres. While retrospecting, one of the remedial ideas that is discussed is longer tenures for the initial builders. The argument is that long-staying leaders are able to create more durable foundations for a purpose-driven centre, as compared to situations where due to various rules or other reasons, there is constant change of leadership. Another remedy is groomed succession, where the successor is part of the early ethos and carries forward the same culture. A third is using certain well-defined criteria in selecting successors, which includes involvement with the women's movement, an inclusive public-space orientation and a political commitment to the struggles for justice and democracy. It is also necessary for this person to support the mutually reinforcing interaction of research and activism.

Another aspect of transition is that transformation with change in leadership, has often shrunk the spaces and dimensions of the work done by the centres. Succession has certainly been smoother where there has been an internal grooming over the preceding period. But long-term domination by one person also takes its toll. People leave, and organisations get emptied because of the continuity, as not everyone can accept single leadership and its particular characteristics.

These dilemmas bring us to an important question. Is it necessary to evolve a feminist approach to organisation and leadership?

Since collectivity seems such an important ethic in the movement, the issues of what leadership is, how to mute individuality and how to promote collective leadership have been hotly debated within the bounds of the women's movement and have often riven organisations.

Is there a case for working out a system, which is inclusive? Is it necessary to evolve a feminist approach to organisation and leadership? This is how continuity, not only of personnel but also of ideology, ethics, principles, purposes and methods can insure against 'undesirable' change. This is again an area where feminism and the idea of feminist studies might give cohesion.

Feminists are known for challenging the inherited theories of knowledge, analysis and practice. Whether it is theology, psychology, social anthropology or history, we have been uncovering errors in the information base, in the understanding and reconstructing of these sciences. We need then to challenge the attitudes hidden in conventional notions of leadership.

The other bank looks greener

There has always been not only a distance, but also unease, stemming from a sense of the other being more privileged, between the two families or cohorts of women's studies centres—those within the UGC and those outside it.

Those outside, whether they are individual scholars or documentation and research centres, perceive that the UGC-funded centres are financially more stable and do not face the challenges of having to find salaries every month, pay rents and endure a continuous struggle for funds. The fact that university payscales apply to those who are in the UGC centres also means that their remunerations are at a much higher level than in the small centres. This particular comparison does not apply to individual scholars in large R&D institutes such as the Centre for Social Sciences, the Madras Institute of Development Studies, the Centre for Development Studies, the Indian Institutes of Management or the Indian Institute of Public Administration, where there are eminent feminist scholars making invaluable contributions to the field of women's studies. These scholars are also part of a government-aided programme and therefore receive the remuneration of Readers and Professors on a regular basis.

However, on the other hand, the UGC family perceives the individual scholars and the small centres as having greater flexibility and often, better access to larger funds and larger networks.

It is possible that since they are also in the vanguard of public action and on the fringe of the women's movement, if not in some sense in its mainstream, the visibility of individual scholars and small centres is greater, and therefore their capacity to attract funds and disperse funds faster, gives them an edge over the UGC family. The UGC family has also suffered a great deal both due to the irregularity of support as well as the extraordinarily impeded conduits through which they receive whatever support they do. Many of the narrations talk of the great pain they experienced in relation to the UGC bureaucracy, and one or two even mentioned that they have had to advance funds from their personal salaries to keep the organisation alive. Many had to close down during the period when the UGC was reconsidering whether women's studies centres should be supported at all.

This particular brand of financial exigency is not experienced in the non-UGC centres but economic hardships are a very real problem to those outside the UGC family. Since there are not many narrations from those spaces, an inference cannot be drawn with justice. The two case studies which do discuss this aspect in non-UGC centres cannot provide the required balance. The cultural and psychological distance between the centres has also impeded, in a way, the desire for drawing these different structures into one movement. It is often suggested that the departments and centres for women's studies in the universities do not invite their activist-sisters in the neighbourhood and vice versa.

Academic responsibilities within universities as well as the require-ments for both academic research as well as written inputs and out-puts often push the university-based groups into pathways that make sharing of space difficult.

On the other side of the coin, the vanguard institutions find the UGC-aided centres and individuals sometimes conservative, some-times tethered. Yet, many of the narrations show happy cohabitation and mutual support. In fact, the case studies reveal that having been members of a non-UGC centre was a source of inspiration to many under the UGC aegis, and that many of those who retire from the UGC family have jumped across to a non-UGC centre.

A major difference however lies in the activity profile. Research methodology, workshops, refresher courses in women's studies, teach-ing and preparation of curriculum and source material, formal scholar-friendly libraries—these are all features of UGC centres, but not part of the non-UGC baggage. When the non-UGC centres and individual scholars plunge into an issue or a research curiosity, they can carry it all the way through without having to fulfil overarching obligations to university procedures.

Taken together, all the agencies have made invaluable contributions to the women's movement by providing backup support with information, policy notes and forums. The further melding of the two would depend to some extent on an ironing out of procedural and financial bottlenecks. One of the case studies mentions a proposal that had been made to the Planning Commission to provide a grant-in-aid pattern of assistance to some of the more established non-UGC, non-ICSSR centres, so that the constant pressure of survival that they faced could be reduced, and their skills be used both in the public space as well as within the women's studies network.

In the approach paper to women's studies prepared for the Ninth Plan by the UGC Standing Committee on Women's Studies, a con-ceptual framework was drawn up whereby it was decided to bring in all these agencies under one umbrella through the concept of network-ing. Those centres funded by the UGC would have an inclusive ap-proach by having advisory committees, steering committees, partner-ships and joint ventures with these other agencies in their endeavour to make women's studies a meaningful exercise in the journey towards justice, equality and peace.

This approach has been widely acclaimed by the women's constituency, as this mutual reinforcing was long overdue. Individual scholars and well-advanced 'autonomous' women's studies centres have had a great impact both in providing information and in influencing policy. University-based women's studies centres are uniquely placed to contribute a new dimension to the whole process of higher education by integrating gender differentiation, gender perspective and feminist studies into teaching and by linking theory and practice.

Contributions to substances

The women's studies movement has made some major breakthroughs in the content of research as well as in the methodologies employed. Scholars have researched fields as diverse as dairy-farming cooperatives and software industries. Institutions such as the family (for example, in a nation-wide study on the girl child), education (like the one that looked at the disparity between women and men in education or the sexism in education) and religion (looking at how women featured in Buddhist texts) came in for scrutiny. Various structures, be they political (for example, women contesting in local elections), economic (paid and unpaid labour), cultural (rereading works of poet-saints) or social (prevalence of matriliny in Kerala), have been probed. They have also travelled a long way in researching contemporary topics such as globalisation, and HIV/AIDS.

Through these studies, the centres not only evolved more accurate ways of measuring women's contribution to society, but also legitimised what were otherwise considered 'non-formal' sources of information like oral history, personal narratives, etc. Besides individual research, many of the centres also encouraged joint and interdisciplinary ones— different ways of doing research. All this was part of the larger attempt to move women's issues from the periphery to the centre.

This striving to reconstruct knowledge from the vantage point of women led to an overturning of many established norms and labels. To illustrate, the dichotomy between personal and public which held that domestic violence is a private affair was questioned; the myth that women were ill-equipped to handle finances was definitely debunked by studies of women's economic activities and women-headed enterprises. Women are often construed as passive victims but closer investigations showed quite clearly that women participated vigorously in various struggles. This process of enquiry resulted in the questioning of old categories and definitions such as the notions of 'productive' and 'resistance'.

The centres also worked to shape policy at various levels. Some developed models to increase productivity, to supply drinking water and addressed many other such practical needs, retaining a focus on the concerns of women. Others scrutinised the impact of particular projects—awareness programmes, dairy-farm projects, credit schemes—all through a feminist lens, and suggested substantive modifications in the policies as they stood.

The effort to bring about curriculum change was pursued in myriad ways. These included the 'sprinkler approach' of infusing feminist consciousness into various disciplines, be it psychology, education or law; as well as the 'integrationist' approach which draws other disciplines into the women's studies ambit. The centres had to also undertake to frame new courses in the discipline. Refresher courses, changing the syllabus at the undergraduate level and working to introduce a human rights course at the school level, are all instances of the changes in the construct and content of the curriculum. This was a particularly tough proposition for many centres because they were often in uncharted territory.

The knowledge base of the women's movement was also greatly enriched by the many publications—books, reports and the 'grey literature' (newsletters, pamphlets and so on)—that were produced by the women's studies centres. These were also vastly different from traditional academic books, not only in content but also in form, style and in the way they were collected and organised to spawn institutions such as documentation centres, reading rooms and open libraries. As a result, we have essays on women and nature, the representation of women in art, simple booklets on women's health, women and law etc. Book exhibitions were organised and extensive bibliographies prepared. The case studies also outline that the kind of training that women's studies centres (along with other constituents of the women's movement) promoted was participatory in nature.

All in all, what is very evident is that the centres created an impact as much by doing things differently as by doing different things.

Looking back

Today, the political impulses, concerns and ethos are different from those of the 1970s and 1980s when most of these centres were born. However there is as much excitement, knowledge, creativity and arenas of struggle as there were in the early days.

There are not only many more of those engaged in gender concerns and people's movements, but there is also much greater strength in communication due to the advent of e-mail. There are more educated young people and many more men and women entering technical and managerial professions than before, as opportunities in the service sector have expanded much more quickly than in the other sectors of manufacturing.

Politics is no less interesting now than it was twenty years ago, though it is often suggested that it has grown worse. But it is also true that there is greater connectivity, which makes those who are engaged in such efforts in the university and outside 'more visible'. Important differences include larger numbers, the trend towards specialisation and the affirmation of difference. This has been the mood of the women's movement worldwide, namely, the celebration of difference, the localising of feminisms and the drawing of attention to micro levels of action as being more meaningful than the earlier preoccupation with macro and global.

This atmosphere has naturally influenced the momentum, mood and actions of the women's studies centres as well, as they respond to the students, the market and the overall environment.

There are several lively examples of how terminologies such as 'mainstream', 'main discipline', and 'pure scholarship' have been mocked or altered by feminists. For example, it is often heard, 'Who wants the polluted mainstream?' or 'We prefer the gurgling downstream'. Trying to locate the informal sector, a group renamed it as the 'first sector' since the largest number of workers are in that sector, apart from the fact that in the production process, it preceded the so-called formal sector. In other words, rather than joining it, feminists have claimed the mainstream as their own. This is one of the significant outcomes of research and debate in the forums and networks of the women's studies movement. Constant reality checks have made the movement's learning process very down-to-earth.

The experience of the centres described here seems to suggest that both integration with and separation from the mainstream are necessary. Integrate the knowledge into the databases of various disciplines as that is where the potential for transformation from the top lies. But retain the separate identity for building strength drawn from collectivity, and for building a power base from the 'bottom', so to speak.

In discussing leadership and transition, writers also give examples of exclusion as an experience in the aftermath of succession, again raising the question of failure in understanding the ethic. There is also a suggestion that some of the new leadership adopted stereotypes set by the male world of power and management, thus distancing themselves from the feminist styles. While it is understood that leadership has to change so that new ideas are given space for fulfilment, the question raised is whether in the other spaces and communities in which women work and strive, as for instance in the movements, there is the need to cushion leadership, as also whether there is space for leadership of many kinds. Here one kind of leadership may not be a threat to another. The discussion seems to suggest a need to understand 'leadership' as well as redefine it as an ethic. There is also need to undertake transition with greater circumspection, not to mention the inclusiveness of the feminist ethic.

The experience seems to suggest that there is work to be done within the women's studies family, strengthening their capacity to relate to and transform the inherited knowledge. This would suggest more attempts at theorising. In addition, we need to undertake some exercises which will enable women's studies to move to feminist studies—or ways of defining or enveloping the research in a philosophical, ethical or ideological warp which can be called feminism. An 'ism' can be an enabling torchlight as well as provide the rigour of principles, which in turn gives legitimacy to an idea or an advocacy.

Power is expressed everywhere, in location, in quantum of funds and in forms of inclusion and exclusion. The experiences narrated in this book are vivid examples of the prevalence and practice of hierarchies which have been challenged when feminist scholars reorder knowledge theories.

There is experience here that points to the need to change management modes, financial procedures and structural distances. While there are interesting diversities, what is striking is the unity, and for securing the future of women studies and its companion—the women's movement—we need to strengthen the connectivity and purpose, sustain creativity and build a theoretical and philosophically derived identity or definition.

Characteristics which are common to all the experiences narrated in this volume, stimulate reflection as well as point in that direction.

A quick overview

The fact that **Maithreyi Krishnaraj** is writing about the first women's studies centre in the country gives her account a distinctive tone. When the Research Unit for Women's Studies came into existence at the SNDT University, Bombay, it was conceived as having 'an all-India scope', and as being a 'clearing house' for other centres in the country.

Maithreyi's narrative scans the history of events that led to the establishment of the centre and also includes a detailed account of how the locational and other aspects of the centre's existence evolved over time.

The other important part of Maithreyi's paper deals with the complicated process of transition from one head/director to another, and how such a shift can be particularly difficult when it is from a founding director who has been very much responsible for the 'birthing' of the institution to younger heads who are not part of the same context.

Maithreyi concludes her paper wondering what the new role of the centre will be in the new scenario with so many centres functioning already. She concludes saying, 'We can end this on a note of hope. The political situation in the country being as unstable as it is now, the centres may have to opt for more self-help, more cooperative work, more sharing'.

Pam Rajput's account of the transformation of the Panjab University's Centre for Women's Studies and Development from a 'cycle shed' to a 'powerhouse' is particularly moving as it is set, unlike any of the other pieces in this collection, against a background of extremist militancy resulting especially for women, in repression, fear and physical violence. 'Punjabi women', Pam writes, 'bore the double burden of being Punjabis and of being women'.

This paper draws attention to the fact that in spite of a historically progressive scenario of women participating in and influencing every aspect of life, there exists a 'carefully fortressed patriarchal and feudal society where women are treated as inferior beings' and customs such as female foeticide, purdah and child marriage are very much prevalent.

Against this background, the women's studies centre's attempts to build visibility and find a physical location for itself take on a special significance. The journey of the unit to becoming a powerhouse engaged in the task of academic change along with activism outside the campus is described with a sprinkling of wry humour.

Chaya Datar asks whether, if all disciplines within the education system became gender-sensitive, the significance of women's studies would be negated. She goes on to add that the ultimate aim of women's studies is the formation of a society where 'women's problems' and 'women's issues' need not be a separate category.

Chaya's paper not only looks at various aspects of the working of the women's studies centre at the Tata Institute of Social Sciences, but also examines in some detail the uneasy relationship between social work and women's studies. She also looks at the effects of the cross-fertilisation between the two.

Susheela Kaushik of the Women's Studies and Development Centre at University of Delhi points out that this nomenclature was deliberately chosen for the centre, so as to include both academicians and social activists.

Susheela describes at length the internal problems of a women's studies centre, particularly in relation to human resource management at various levels including the post of director.

She also points out that the success of her centre is due in large part to its location as an independent unit, equidistant from other departments.

Susheela's account looks at the activities of the Women's Studies and Development Centre and at its collaborative efforts in the area. Her paper ends on a note of warning; she points out that though the years of struggle and uncertainty have passed, and women are being appointed to more and more enquiry committees, academic panels and so on, they are yet to emerge in positions of authority. She also warns that women's studies is vulnerable to the kind of backlash that hit the feminist movement some years ago and suggests that the women's studies community should watch out against spreading itself too thin.

Surinder Jetley's piece begins with an interesting observation— that her own and the other writers' 'personal' accounts may not be all that personal after all, for 'it is really the same process through which most of us came into women's studies, that is, through our own empirical research and personal involvement in women's issues.'

Apart from interesting observations about the geographical and ideological location of the Women's Studies Centre of the Banaras Hindu University, Surinder draws attention in her paper to prevalent faulty perceptions of the 'appropriate' candidate for women's studies, both at the level of teachers and at that of the director. In both cases, sensitivity to women's issues figured very little in the process of selection and it was only after continuous appeals that this aspect was considered.

Surinder also talks about the aspect of personal transformation in the course of exposure to women's studies and looks at the strengths and weaknesses of the Women's Studies Centre at Banaras Hindu University.

The philosophical ending of this paper draws attention to an aspect of women's studies that not many of the other papers have dwelt on— the fact that the very existence of women's studies indicates the existence of gender insensitivity and gender discrimination.

The School of Women's Studies at Jadavpur University has come a long way from its beginnings, which **Jasodhara Bagchi** compares to 'having to start a garden in the middle of a desert'. Thereafter, it collaborated with the Indian Association of Women's Studies and the Indian Science Congress and was part of an Indo-French-Russian colloquium. The list of visitors to the School is just as impressive. Like a number of other women's studies centres, the Jadavpur School also went through an initial stage of not having a place of its own—it operated out of Jasodhara's tiny cubbyhole in the English department, and it was through this department that women's studies made its entry.

Talking of the school's failures, Jasodhara also describes an instance of sexual harassment of girl students by a male professor. Unfortunately the Teachers' Association decided to back the professor in a spirit of trade unionism.

Jasodhara concludes that the School of Women's Studies at Jadavpur University has become a major presence in academia by crossing disciplinary boundaries and revising unyielding canons.

Bharati Ray's account of the establishment of the Women's Studies Centre of Calcutta University begins with the statement that 'functions and ceremonies hardly make a centre'. She follows this with an account of how this particular centre was steered and pushed into its present shape and location.

An interesting aspect of this particular centre is that its decision to have the centre function as a catalyst in drawing participation from other departments in the university actually worked (and works) wonderfully well, which is not often the case. An equally striking aspect of the work of the Women's Studies Centre of Calcutta University is the networking it has meticulously established with schools, colleges, NGOs and even governmental agencies, as well as with scholars, activists, researchers and the women's movement.

The Alagappa University was the first general university to introduce women's studies as an autonomous discipline and to have the only UGC-approved Centre for Women's Studies (AU-CWS). **Regina Papa** tells us that it was the late M.G. Ramachandran who paved the way for the entry of women's studies into Tamil Nadu. She also describes the background by giving a gripping account of the cultural and social aspects of life in the state, and the significance of the Dravidian movement.

While elaborating on the need to consider both 'intrinsic' and 'extrinsic' demands on the course, giving equal weightage to both the theoretical and the practical, Regina Papa also talks of the many misconceptions regarding women's studies, in particular, of the myth that teaching it is usually seen as not requiring any particular skill. She points out that women's studies scholars are seen as primarily attached to other disciplines while being interested in women's issues.

Regina's account describes the many crises that every women's studies centre has to pass through before it gains acceptance as a serious subject that is worthy of study, and ends with the poignant words that while a full sack is a burden, an empty sack simply won't stand.

The Women's Studies Research Centre at the Maharaja Sayaji Rao University, as **Amita Verma** tells us in her paper, was established as a consequence of certain developments that took place at the university during 1979–89. The detailed account of the actual process is valuable in giving us an idea of the tedium and the pains involved at every step. Amita Verma's paper deals with such aspects of the working of the centre as the teaching programme, staffing, research agenda and students. Amita's paper also describes the networking and advocacy efforts of the centre and explores the dilemma of activism versus scholarship as manifested in the WSRC and gives some answers, many of which are very encouraging, to the question whether women's studies has made a difference on the campus.

The paper ends on a note of personal reflection, with Amita Verma dwelling on how she overcame the criticism that she was neither part of the active women's movement nor a feminist scholar and was therefore unsuitable to head a women's studies centre. It is also here that she talks of how the years of involvement in the WSRC have brought about a personal transformation. Amita's paper ends on a note of hope and affirmation, when she points out the need for various women-centred organisations to strengthen each other.

Rameshwari Varma tells us that the Women's Studies Centre of the Mysore University began with a 'dramatic surprise', when the vice-chancellor announced its informal establishment at the inauguration of a seminar on, of all things, agricultural marketing!

Rameshwari takes us through the first steps of the process of establishing the centre, in some detail. She examines the implications of location and approach—what are the advantages and disadvantages of locating the centre within a larger institute, what are the pros and cons of the interdisciplinary approach in curriculum design and so on. She also looks into both internal and external pressures that are exerted on women's studies centres and discusses the impossibility of putting into practice the feminist mode of non-hierarchical functioning in the midst of a well-established system. Finally, Rameshwari details the impact of the centre on its various constituencies both within as well as outside the university and the different kinds of support which the centre has been receiving from these constituencies.

Devaki Jain, looking back at the growth of the Institute of Social Studies Trust (ISST) and the various influences that shaped its character, says that it 'just happened, brick by brick'; it had neither an architectural plan, nor any initial financial backup; there was not even 'a suggestion of what it was all about and what it was going to unleash'. Devaki traces step by step how a structure actually evolved for ISST out of its involvements and the processes necessitated by those involvements.

ISST's initial years are very different from its later life in 'fast forward' mode. The early years are characterised by slow but sure steps and by strategies that came into being through actual work being done. It was also a period of intense involvement at all levels of work within the organisation. The later years bring with them a number of break-downs that reveal the need for rules, regulations and finances that would stabilise the organisation. She also points out that ISST's history/experience suggests that the women's movement as well as development agencies, including the government, require a service station which can provide researched, data-based reports and reference material, as well as tackle problems after studying these reports. Devaki's paper also looks into questions of power and feminist ways to handle both power and the practicalities of work.

Anveshi Research Centre for Women's Studies was founded in 1985 by a small group of women activists who felt that 'our activism had clarified for us the need to study, document and analyse the manifold dimensions of the Indian situation as it impacted on women'. The most interesting aspect of this paper is that it highlights a point raised by a number of other papers in this collection—i.e., how much should (or should not) a women's studies centre be involved in the movement. Anveshi's efforts have 'succeeded in creating a more permeable border between theory and practice and a space for exchange between the academy and a new range of publics'. The paper describes Anveshi's initiatives over the years, which include publications, workshops, seminars etc. that were complemented by actual involvement in issues, such as its interaction with the Dalit movement.

The paper ends on a cheery note, with the hope of being able to offer scholarships to researchers and activists, providing travel grants to Third World scholars and participating in the dissemination of ideas and information on theoretical and popular issues.

Kumud Sharma dwells at length on the conflicts within women studies as a discipline, between the purist and the interdisciplinary points of view. Kumud writes, 'we often feel that we speak in two voices— one for academic discourse and the other in an activist idiom and expression'. She points out that the tensions between academicians and activists persist and wonders which identity one represents; who can speak for whom?

Another aspect of Kumud's paper reflects a common concern of many of the papers in this volume. Are independent women's studies centres more policy-oriented and less academically-oriented as they are often accused of being? The ability of such centres to respond to issues, both contextually and strategically, varies and depends on human resources and competence in building institutional linkages and in-house capacity. The role of apex bodies like the ICSSR and UGC in supporting, funding and promoting women's studies research and teaching is also looked at.

Kumud's paper concludes by pointing out that there are many issues confronting the women's studies community and that it is necessary to work out a common agenda for debate and mobilisation. She
also points out that if women's studies is to retain its dynamism and
avoid ghettoisation within academia, it needs to grow on a broad base
without diluting its main drive or getting trapped in narrow ideological moulds.

V.S. Elizabeth of the Centre for Women and Law begins her paper
with the confession that she feels out of place among the writers in
this collection, all of whom, unlike her, have a long association with
either women's studies or the women's movement.

As the paper unfolds, however, what becomes evident, as Elizabeth
herself points out, is that you need only to be aware of what is happening in the world to see that there is no equality of gender, not even,
appallingly, in the eyes of the law.

Her narrative interweaves the personal with the official and attempts
to find and use a set of effective tools to explore and redress gender
injustice. Elizabeth takes us on a tour of the initiatives from lawyers
and law towards this end, citing a number of cases that underscore the
obvious fact that the law is blind to gender justice.

She details the work of both the Centre for Women and Law, which
she currently heads, as well as that of the National Law School of India
University, where she teaches. Perhaps what lends depth to Elizabeth's
paper is that she also talks of how to link the past with the current
scenario, as her basic training is that of a historian.

Leela Gulati begins her account from a situation that many women
are only too familiar with—being relegated to a 'housewife' status, and
the struggle to re-enter the academic scene. Leela herself was inspired
in her attempts by the work of Ester Boserup, who, despite not working professionally, had made a significant contribution to the understanding of women and work across a range of countries.

It is thus that Leela begins her own work and writing, much of which
has to do with female work participation and profiles of poor women.
It is from this context that she voices her concern about the ethics of
fieldwork, the relationship of researcher to research subject and especially the ethical and moral issues of the study of very poor people.

The paper ends with Leela wondering how the frontiers of such work
can be pushed from a descriptive to a more analytical level and concludes

that these questions can be best answered by upcoming young scholars who are better qualified and trained, and more articulate and sensitive. **Uma Chakravarti's** paper begins with the tantalising observation that feminist scholars have been less forthright in evaluating tendencies manifested within the women's studies movement than in their criticism of mainstream academia.

Uma looks at the university as a reflection of the wider universe, taking us through the various reactions expressed within the university to changes taking place across the country. This section traces the effects of the Naxalbari uprising, the influence of Jayprakash Narayan as well as the consequences of the Emergency. The Emergency was experienced with a peculiar intensity in the University of Delhi, leaving a legacy of teacher and student activism for many years thereafter.

This paper also describes Uma's own work as a historian. It talks of her attempts to link class and gender, since she was concerned about the internal stratification *within* women who, she says, have never constituted a homogenised category for her. She points out that sisterhood is not a given; it has to be forged as a conscious political affiliation which refuses to be complicit in any oppressive arrangement.

Uma's paper ends on a rather piquant note when she says that perhaps what needs to be done is to mainstream gender, making it impossible for anyone to study anything without exploring its gender dimensions.

The journey that this volume has taken reveals what was said at the beginning of this introduction, namely that women's studies has been one of the most valuable torchlights to illumine the path of social and political analysis within and outside academia. India's special contribution to this increasingly powerful discipline is embedded in real life experiences of women at the ground level. The commitment of the women's studies movement in India to the removal of poverty, both of men and women, and to the effacing of practices and instruments of social injustice, comes through clearly, regardless of whether the centre described in this volume is located in the heart of the university or on the fringes of the women's movement.

From the very beginning of the recorded history of India's civilisation, women have been articulate in engaging with the whole range of intellection—whether it is philosophy or the understanding of social relations. The intellectual Gargi and the spiritual Akka Mahadevi have challenged society and eminent male thinkers on their understanding of the female of the species. They have asked to be recognised and understood as minds, and not merely as bodies; in other words, they asked for the differentiation, which is usually physiological, not to become a disqualification. Women's studies as reflected in these essays, continues this tradition of seeking a change in this perception, this mindset.

The enormously complex relationships within Indian social organisation such as family, caste, village community, class and occupation have also been scrutinised to show that these institutions can be as oppressive to women as they can be enhancing and enabling to all members of that social group. Thus, family—which has become a symbol of caring and comforting institutions, and is linked by binding relationships—is now not so clearly identified with the culture of equality. Yet, in this volume, we use the term 'Narratives from the Women's Studies Family', to posit that the family as a concept can *still* be seen as a coming together of individuals under the common identity of kinship. Women would suggest that their 'new families' are composed of friends, persons with whom they identify themselves towards the common goal, as indeed is the ideal description of the sociological family posited on blood relations. This is one example among many others in this book of how women are reinterpreting the language and the terminologies that describe the world around them, both to show their difficulties as well as their potential.

Without this attempt of bringing the narrations into one composition, we would not have been able to receive the enrichment of this family. In introducing this volume, we hope that others within the movement, as well as outside, would join the effort made by those who have contributed to this volume, to make the world a better place to live in for all.

1

From women's education to women's studies

The Long Struggle for Legitimacy

Neera Desai, Vina Mazumdar and Kamalini Bhansali

The passage from acceptance of the legitimacy of education for women to the recognition of women's studies as a critical instrument in the educational process, has been long and protracted. The process has been marked by recurring challenges and struggles and reluctant concession of legitimacy, immediately followed by resistance or apathy. Obstacles in this context are raised by the following dominant ideologies:

1. social construction/perception of gender roles in civil society;
2. educational systems that create structural rigidities/resistance;
3. politics and economics of educational policy; and
4. determination by market forces in all activities, whether pertaining to mind or body.

This paper attempts to forge a link between women's access to education and the acceptance of women's studies as an agency of transformation, both in academics and in the everyday perception of women's issues. In order to invoke the various debates and actions which have influenced the introduction of women's studies in higher education, this paper is broadly divided into four sections. The first section covers a very large span of nearly 150 years culminating in the establishment of the premier women's studies organisation—Indian Association of Women's Studies in 1981. The second begins with a description of the struggles for legitimisation of women's studies against the background of macro developments—national and international—and its relationship with the growing women's movement. The third section examines the issues involved in the acceptance of women's studies by India's apex education body—the University Grants Commission—and in growing developmental activities outside the university system. The final section highlights the new agendas for women's studies centres as outlined in the revised guidelines of the UGC's Ninth Plan policy, which underscores the need to reach out to wider sections of society through association with other organisations working in the same direction and the need to sharpen the quality of research and teaching.

Opening the gates of education for women

The entry of women into the formal education system not only signals the willingness of society to provide facilities for the same, but also touches upon the issue of the perception of gender roles in society. As has been recorded, in the early decades of the 19th century, women were almost completely excluded from the formal system of education and it was believed that girls could acquire all that was necessary, as education, in their domestic surroundings.[1] It was a period of deep-rooted prejudice against women's education, encapsulated in such homilies as 'educate a girl and you give a knife into her hands', and 'education will entail widowhood upon a girl'. It is, therefore, not surprising to find that when the government of Bombay undertook an inquiry into the condition of indigenous education in the 1820s, the district reports did not record even a single instance of girls attending school in the province. The earliest efforts to educate girls were made by Christian missionaries. In the city of Bombay, the first school for girls was started in 1824. Of course, most of the girls attending mission school were either Christians or from the lower castes.

During the first half of the 19th century, the discussion on education was characterised by a fierce debate between the Bombay and the Bengal groups, the former in favour of education through the vernacular languages and the latter preferring English as the medium of instruction. Though this controversy abated with Macaulay's Minute establishing English as the medium of instruction (mainly aiming at preparing clerks for the British Raj), none of these debates had any direct impact on the question of women's education.

In their attempts to reform tradition-bound Indian society, reformers did stress the education of women—in fact, the woman's question or concern with improving the status of women became a central issue in various social reform movements. However, most of these reformers did not envisage education for women as an equal right with men, or as a human right. Rather, as Narmad, a reformer from Gujarat put it, 'By educating the women, the men will benefit'. The idea was that women were to be educated so that they could be better companions to men. In spite of the overwhelming moral tone in the arguments favouring women's education, there were a few thinkers like Jyotiba Phuley, Vidyasagar, Karve, Savitribai Phuley and Pandita Ramabai, who believed in imparting education to women as a matter of justice in itself. Savitribai said, 'Education alone can banish ignorance and inhuman behaviour and make us human beings.'

The entry of women into the formal education system raises a number of questions. Though stray efforts by Phuley and other non-Brahmin educationists were made in the 19th century, the intertwining of caste and gender is quite visible. Those who were able to obtain higher education were mostly from the upper castes, thus underscoring the link between access to education, class and gender. However, at times, the plea for women's education was also made on the basis of knowledge per se. It was asserted that for women, the significance of education was in broadening the mind and developing their capacity for handling crises— the thought of providing skills came later. Pandita Ramabai, drawing up a sort of curriculum, included the knowledge component along with certain skills useful in fulfilling the role of housewife and mother.[2] Thus, the entry of women in the field of education brought up these issues, many of which continue to disturb even today, though in different forms.

The women's movement and women's education

The first phase of the women's movement in India began in the 1920s. The Women's Indian Association and the National Council for Women are the two significant precursors of the premier institution, All India Women's Conference (AIWC), established in 1927. The emergence of the AIWC is directly linked to the demand for education.[3] It was resolved that at each conference of the AIWC, a memorandum on female education would be presented. At the first meeting of the Conference, besides women from the royal families and titled upper classes, education- ists and social reformers as well as women associated with the nationalist movement also attended. They conceived of an optimum education based on their perception of a woman's status in society and favoured an education system which combined the fullest development of an individual's latent capacities with an emphasis on the ideals of mother- hood.[4] The ambivalence is quite evident. Soon enough the AIWC realised that education alone could not effectively eradicate social evils and thus included social transformation in its agenda. Initially, the leadership was composed of royalists supportive of colonial rule, and they naturally eschewed any discussion on political issues. However, with the membership of the organisation becoming wider, a number of women with nationalist as well as leftist leanings became active and considerably affected the organisation's stance. This transformed it into a vanguard women's organisation of the pre-Independence days.

An important gender issue during this phase was that of separate schools and curriculum for girls. AIWC was always in favour of a com- mon curriculum for both sexes and its position on education was markedly different from that of the official committees and commis- sions on education as well as that of most male social reformers.[5] The rationale for separate curricula was based on a mixture of fact and myth, such as differences in societal roles, the average school life of girls being shorter than boys, the intellectual inferiority of girls, lack of aptitude and physical weakness of girls etc. In addition to all this, it was argued that the qualities inculcated in girls through education should not make them bold and independent, while at the same time women's organi- sations were promoting the notion of equality.

Thus, by the time India became independent, not only had the sig- nificance of education for both men and women been recognised, but with the growing need in middle-class families to supplement the fam- ily income, the employment potential of higher education was also ac- knowledged. The nationalist movement played a crucial role in bringing women out of the confines of their homes and providing opportunities to participate in the task of creating a better society. The Gandhian move- ment, on the one hand, emphasised mass education and on the other, provided opportunities to Scheduled Caste and Scheduled Tribe girls for attaining at least primary education through the establishment of

Ashramshalas (residential schools). Another significant fallout of the freedom movement was that in the interim period when the movement was withdrawn for various reasons, many women rejoined the educational stream, completed their studies and in many cases built their careers.

Issues in women's education in independent India

Once Independence was attained, the task before the Indian government was not only to promote education but also to widen its reach and use it to inculcate the value of building a better society. The Constitution of India, which was introduced in 1950, included a number of important provisions that had a direct or indirect bearing on women's welfare. Article 45 imposed direct responsibility for providing education on the state. 'The state shall endeavour to provide, within a period of ten years from the commencement of this Constitution, for free and compulsory education for all children until they complete the age of fourteen years.' (That this has still not been achieved after five decades is a different matter). Article 16 promulgated non-discrimination in public employment on grounds of sex, and Article 15(3) empowered the state to make special provisions for the welfare and development of women and children—this provision has been invoked to justify special allocations and relaxation of procedures/conditions in order to expand girls' access to education at different levels.

Considering the importance given to education as an essential instrument of the nation-building process by leaders of the national movement from the 19th century onwards, it is surprising that a comprehensive review of the entire education system was undertaken only two decades after Independence. Previous reviews had been sectoral. The University Education Commission or the Radhakrishnan Commission was the first review body, which submitted its report in 1949, followed by the Secondary Education (Mudaliar) Commission in 1952–53, the National Committee (Durgabai Deshmukh) on Women's Education in 1958–59. The recommendations of the Hansa Mehta Committee on Differentiation in Curricula for Boys and Girls in 1964 were endorsed by the Indian Education Commission (1966)—well known as Kothari Commission—which was followed by the National Policy on Education in 1968. The next National Policy on Education came only in 1986 with its plan of action. Both documents were revised further in 1992.

After Independence, the first major step taken by the leaders of the Nehruvian era was establishing a University Education Commission headed by Dr Radhakrishnan. It is very significant that the Commission devoted a full chapter to women's education, discussing its various dimensions. However, the all-male membership appeared to have advanced little more than the views held on women's role a few decades ago. The following statement is quite revealing: 'The Commission believes that a well-ordered home helps to make well-ordered men. The mother who is inquiring and alert, well informed and familiar with subjects such as history and literature, and who lives and works with her children in the home, will be the best teacher in the world of both character and intelligence.'[6]

This kind of observation in 1949 indicates the persistence of the traditional wife–mother role of the woman in ideology although the reality was fast changing. This further indicates the non-recognition of the reality of unequal gender relations within the household. The Commission seems to waver between the position of identical curriculum and purpose of education for both men and women and that of emphasising the home-making role as the primary one for women, calling for the inculcation of special skills. The ambivalence is obvious throughout the entire chapter on women's education.[7]

Though the Commission mentions that there cannot be educated people without educated women, and emphasises that opportunities should be given to women to receive education, it considers the basic objective of education as passing on tradition to the next generation. While elaborating on the education of women as women, it adds that women are as able as men to perform the same academic work, with no less thoroughness and quality, but adds that it does not follow that men's and women's education should be identical in all things.

In spite of the conviction that the greatest vocation of a woman is that of a homemaker, and concern for women's proficiency in that role, the Commission had to mention that 'a woman's world should not be limited to that of one relationship'. It was forced to take note of the development that women were entering the world of work. Therefore, it ended the section on women's education by remarking, 'the educational system at all levels should prepare men and women for such varied callings.'[8]

As the first document on education to come out after Independence, this report persistently swings between the specific wife–mother role of a woman and the need to equip her for a wider participation in the external world. The remarks of one of the women who gave evidence to the Commission are very telling. She says, 'the modern educated Indian woman is neither happy nor contented, nor socially useful. She is a misfit in life. She is highly suppressed and needs opportunities for self-expression. The new education must provide this opportunity.'[9]

The First Five-Year Plan realised the significance of education for women and the need to adopt special measures. From this phase onwards, there seems to have been a decrease in ambivalence regarding women's education, though the underpinning of the familial role persists. The First Five-Year Plan mentions that the general purpose and objective of women's education cannot be different from that of men's education, but also stated that there are vital differences in 'the way in which this purpose has to be realised...'.

The Secondary Education Commission (Mudaliar Commission) of 1952–53 appears to have been less preoccupied with gender differences. On the issue of girls' education the Commission reiterated, 'In a democratic society, where all citizens have to discharge their civic and social obligations, differences, which may lead to variations in the standard of intellectual development achieved by boys and girls, cannot be envisaged.'

The National Committee on Women's Education, popularly known as Durgabai Deshmukh Committee on Women's Education (1958–59), was one of the most significant committees appointed to look specifically into the question of women's education. Recognising the slow progress of women's education, the focus by this time had shifted from higher education to school education. The major purpose of this Committee was to look into the difficulties that hindered the progress of girls' education and to make recommendations to the government about how this could be brought at par with that of boys'.

The Committee (Hansa Mehta) on Differentiation of Curricula for Boys and Girls was appointed in 1962. After reviewing historical developments during the previous 150 years of official policies and public attitudes regarding co-education, the Committee took an unequivocal stand against differentiation. In its view, the responsibility for the existing gap between the education of boys and girls lay in the continuation of traditional attitudes and values which regarded girls as inferior to boys in physique, intellect and aptitude, and the perpetuation of such ideas through the existing practice of prescribing subjects for girls that reinforced the conventional division of tasks and roles between men and women. Besides recommending co-education at the elementary and secondary stage, and full freedom to opt for co-education or segregated education, the most significant recommendation of this Commission was that home science and vocational courses should be provided for boys and girls.[10]

The Education Commission (1964–66), popularly known as Kothari Commission, which examined in depth the role and goals of education in the process of national development towards a secular, socialist and democratic society, endorsed the views of the Hansa Mehta and the Durgabai Deshmukh Committees, and observed: 'In the modern world, the role of women goes much beyond the home and the bringing up of children. She is now adopting a career of her own and sharing equally with men the responsibility for the development of society in all its aspects. This is the direction in which we shall have to move. In the struggle for freedom, Indian women fought side by side with men. This equal partnership will have to continue in the fight against hunger, poverty, ignorance and ill health.'[11]

The Commission had the mandate to look into education at all stages and from various dimensions, but in spite of a mandate of this scale, it is disappointing that merely two pages were given to women's education and only a few paragraphs for women's higher education! The Report started by mentioning that though the general feeling was that women had entered the portals of university education and therefore one did not have to worry about the same, there was a need for special efforts to expand higher education among women.[12] But the Commission made only two suggestions to enhance women's higher education—the provision of financial assistance and hostels!

Taking the dualistic stance that higher education should be both liberal and technical, the Commission mentioned that universities must encourage individuality, variety and dissent within a climate of tolerance, seek new knowledge, and inculcate fearlessness in the pursuit of knowledge. On the other hand, education was also expected to provide society with competent men and women. The liberal stance of the Report is evidenced by the message that it would be wrong to restrict the girls' choice or to compel them to take particular courses, and that the more academically inclined girls desirous of pursuing careers in research or teaching at the college or university level, or in professions such as medicine or technology, should have all the opportunities and incentives for doing so.[13]

All committees and commissions on education, whether headed by men or women, Gandhian or non-Gandhian, failed to articulate the relationship between women's equality, their participation in national development and the pattern of education itself. No thought was given to the possibly adverse consequences of the educational process on social values and the construction of gender, and how gender equality as a value could—or needed to—affect the educational process.[14]

A major change was, however, taking place in Indian society with a rapid growth in the number of educated women. This, in a way, hid a severe contradiction, for though the number of women in higher education was growing at a fast rate, the spread of literacy itself was dismal. Educated women represented a mixed bag of aspirations governed by conflicts of identity, internalisation of set values and a desire for social approval.[15] At the same time, they also symbolised the national progress that was accomplished in the two decades after Independence and provided leadership in various segments of public life. With a woman prime minister, the final seal was stamped, demonstrating the achievement of Indian women in the public arena.

When the Committee on the Status of Women in India (CSWI) was constituted in 1971 by a Resolution of the Ministry of Education and Social Welfare, the Government received unexpectedly startling findings on the condition of Indian women. The appalling findings of the Report reopened the women's question for the government, academia and women's organisations. It is, therefore, imperative to refer to the emergence and impact of the CSWI Report on the women's movement and women's studies.

A team of academics, social workers, non-governmental personnel and members of Parliament prepared the report titled 'Towards Equality'. The report is an eye-opener to the stark inequalities between men and women, 'summarised by chilling statistics of imbalanced child and adult sex ratios that indicated significant differential in male-female mortality. The subordination of women was now officially on record, to be cited by anyone wishing to address women's issues.'[16] The Report was to significantly affect government policy in the context of promoting women's welfare towards achieving empowerment. On the other hand, the findings crucially influenced a section of Indian academia in their research and teaching, to move from the old approach of women's role as related to the well-being of the family towards looking at women's condition as an input in the process of development and as one of its most critical issues.

Years later, Vina Mazumdar, the member-Secretary of the CSWI, articulated the gravity of the crisis in women's status, deflating the bubble of complacency. 'The one definite outcome of those shocks was an acute sense of unrest about the roles we ourselves as teachers, researchers and political social activists had played.'[17] Ironically, soon after the report was discussed in March 1975, when various countries were preparing for the International Woman's Year Conference to be held in Mexico in June 1975, the Prime Minister Mrs Indira Gandhi declared a state of national emergency, virtually suspending democratic rights. Control over criticism of the government became a great obstacle for social and political workers, many of whom, including women activists, were put behind bars.

In sum, from acceptance of the notion of gender equality by the Commissions on Education to the CSWI findings, concern about women was shifting from equipping them with skills to fundamental issues pertaining to their subordinate status. Of course, the initial agenda concentrated on employment, work and literacy and to some extent, health. The woman's question was swinging between the concerns of middle-class women and those of working class women, and the need to politicise women's issues. Dowry, violence, rape and wife-beating were yet to become issues.

The emergence of women's studies

The urgency for improvement of women's status in developing countries emanated from the process of development, but it took considerable time to realise that the process of development itself had an adverse effect on women's lives and roles in society.

The World Plan of Action for the Decade gave a high priority to research activities, analysis and data collection regarding all aspects of the situation of women, since adequate data and information are essential for formulating policies and evaluating progress about attitudinal as well as basic socio-economic change. It was found to be necessary to get systematic information on the existing conditions, and also to look into the causes of discriminatory practices, attitudes and beliefs which impede women's contribution to development policies. Simultaneously, the GoI had also drawn up a Draft National Plan of Action for Women, where emphasis was given to research, which could identify problems and help in bridging the information gap.[18]

ICSSR, and particularly the late J.P. Naik, had personally facilitated the functioning of the CSWI in a number of ways. However, a more conscious, deliberate and committed action came up when ICSSR constituted an Advisory Committee on Women's Studies (specifically using the term women's studies instead of research on the status of women). As mentioned in the booklet, 'the main objective of the programme of women's studies is the generation and analysis of data with a view of uncovering significant trends in patterns of social and economic organisation which affect women's position in the long run.'[19] Probably for the first time, it was categorically stated that 'all over the world the social sciences are male centred and male biased.' The ICSSR programme changed the direction of researchers in women's studies. Thus far in social sciences, studies on women had been focusing on the middle class; the new stance emphasised the study of women belonging to the poorer or the 'less visible' sections of society. It also stressed that the purpose of the studies was to renew the debate on the woman's question.

SNDT Women's University probably pioneered the use of the term 'women's studies' for academic and action-oriented activities connected to women's issues. Looking back, it seems that this could only happen in a women's university searching for an identity for itself. The university had its roots in social reform, and specialised in organising educational programmes to suit the diverse needs of women. It was also a place where innovations and experiments were encouraged.[20]

A Round Table Discussion on the 'Future Trends in Women's Higher Education and the Role of the SNDT Women's University' held in 1973—where the seeds of future programmes were sown—explored the viability of a women's university in the transformed Indian socioeconomic scenario. Besides emphasising the need for a women's university to meet the requirements of this section of society, the one-day meeting concluded that a research division should be established where focused research about women could be undertaken. The group recommended the founding of the Women's Research Centre.[21]

Thus, a new chapter was begun in the history of both SNDT Women's University and the higher education system, in which women's lives and experiences acquired the status of legitimate areas of academic concern, with a special focus on poor, uneducated women. This seemed an important way to make education relevant. Along with other women's studies organisations, SNDT Women's University played a pivotal role in building the Indian Association for Women's Studies and forging links between women's studies and the women's movement.

Legitimising women's studies: The context of macro-development

The interrelation between the women's movement and women's studies is a very complex one. Whereas in the pre-Independence phase, all aspects of women's education were a vital concern with the women's movement, thereafter both education and the educational system were absent from its agenda. Earlier the movement had kept in view the transformative role of education, its egalitarian potential and its value in building professional careers.

One feature of the early decades of the post-Independence phase was the invisibility of debates on women's issues. Since the mid-1970s, women's studies has had to face the question, 'what was happening to the women's movement in the two decades after Independence?' CSWI data suggests that the regression in women's conditions in health, employment, political participation and social vulnerability could not have taken place within a period of a few years. Why were these protracted processes not detected by women's organisations, which were so active and visible during the nationalist phase? Having won de jure equality within the Constitution, why did the movement lose its role as a vigilance or a pressure group? In fact, some of the pioneer women activists had so much implicit faith in the general acceptance of the principle of equality that it led them at the time to not accept reservation for women as an instrument for political participation.[22]

On the political front, women—of the Left and the far Left—had participated in mass movements as well as in armed struggles. However, various researches and narratives by women's studies academics and activists have highlighted the fact that gender issues were marginalised in party documents.[23] For the first generation beneficiaries of the equality clauses in the Constitution, life in independent India began with hope. Kamaladevi Chattopadhyaya's words are worth noting: 'The past is dead, the present is a chain but in the future lies hope.' She lived at a time when it was possible to dream of a socialist future. Similarly, Vina Mazumdar says: 'All of us had vivid memories of colonial rule and the freedom movement. Some had been fully active in the struggle. Those of us who were younger had only partial experience as students, during the last phase. We were the "Daughters of Independence", the first generation beneficiaries of the equality promised by the Constitution. We were free to choose our post-Independence lives—our careers, beliefs and to some extent aspirations.'[24]

Other than this concern with personal and professional lives among the highly educated, more visible women, there was decreased visibility of the women's movement. Complacency was generated by the Nehruvian dream of a socialist society, co-optation of the most vocal section into positions of power, and state welfare policies/programmes which drew many women into what they saw as 'constructive' work or 'welfare of the poor'. Participation in these programmes gave many of them a sense of satisfaction. The other question which needs to be examined, is whether the phenomenon of a common enemy during the colonial period submerged the political differences that surfaced sharply in the post-Independence period.

One of the first feminist groups was Progressive Organisation of Women (POW), based in Hyderabad. The ideas of equality and feminism were made explicit in their manifesto. The two primary structures of women's oppression which they identified were sexual division of labour and reinforcement of oppression by culture.[25] The Emergency affected this organisation severely.

The focus on women's issues and efforts to draw the attention of the state and the community became prominent only after the mid-1970s. The critical point was the Mathura rape case, which triggered off a series of actions on the part of women's groups. Violence against women in the form of rape, dowry deaths and wife-beating dominated the agenda. In all these struggles, initially the connection between the activists and academics was tangential. By mid-1980s, the relationship was much stronger.

After 1977, the women's movement developed quite differently from the earlier movement. Autonomous women's groups preferred to remain outside political parties, because of ideological reasons. These groups were attacking oppression, exploitation and patriarchy. While feminist groups were mobilising women on the issues of rape, dowry deaths and domestic violence, and urging the state to intervene in providing justice to women, some of the other national women's organisations were demanding more attention to women's concerns in the Sixth Five-Year Plan. The emphasis on women's contributions to the family and the national economy had been made possible by the researches initiated by the CSWI findings and the strategies worked out by a series of working groups of the Planning Commission (1977–80) and various Ministries.

Till 1981, when IAWS came into existence, women's studies programmes were very few in number. Individual scholars were engaged in research on the issues of work, family and patriarchy, delving into history to understand earlier social processes, the role of reformers etc., while activists were beginning to politicise women's issues. Violence was treated not as an issue of individual behaviour, but understood in terms of power. Violence was not merely physical but also a pressure on the minds and personalities of women. It was expressed in many forms—dowry murders, rape and media projection. Health issues were found to have many more implications than mere physical illness. By the end of the 1970s, a convergence was shaping up between the women's movement and women's studies. Women's issues were becoming visible in state programmes as well as in academia.

The 1980s symbolised the peak of the struggle for legitimisation of women's studies and its dual agenda: (*a*) to transform dominant ideologies and mindsets that consciously or unconsciously remain resistant to gender equality and (*b*) to expand the social concern against injustice, marginalisation and oppression of women by harnessing the services of the educational system. The National Conference on Women's Studies held in 1981 in Bombay sought to stimulate/initiate this process by generating a wider awareness of the problems of women as well as by demonstrating the capacity of women's studies as a critical instrument for change. Concluding its chapter on education, the CSWI had observed:

> The deep foundations of the inequality of the sexes are built in the minds of men and women through a socialisation process which continues to be extremely powerful. Right from their earliest years, boys and girls are brought up to know that they are different from each other and this differentiation is strengthened in every

way possible—through language forms, modes of behaviour, of labour etc. They begin to learn very early what is proper or not proper for boys and girls and all attempts at deviation are noticed, discouraged and sometimes punished. The sissy and the tomboy are equal objects of derision. There is nothing wrong in this if it were merely a question of distinction. However, it soon gets inextricably tied up with the traditional concepts of the roles of men and women and their mutual relationships that are based on inequality. The process of indoctrination affects the development of individual personalities.

The only institution, which can counteract the effect of this process, is the educational system. If education is to promote equality for women, it must make a deliberate, planned and sustained effort so that the new value of equality of the sexes can replace the traditional value system of inequality.

Reviews of curricula in different disciplines by the National Conference indicated that omission of women's concerns from course contents perpetuates: (a) the tendency not to ask relevant questions in research, (b) the use of biased analytical tools of different disciplines and (c) the unquestioned ideological acceptance of women's subordinate position in society. To prevent women's issues from lapsing into invisibility under the myth of equality it is necessary to incorporate gender as a category in all research and curriculum planning.[26]

The second important feature of the 1980s was the increasing interest taken by various international agencies, especially UN agencies, in promoting both research and institutional development, for women's studies in developing countries. The third development during the decade was the gradual increase in government responses to the debates initiated between the years 1975 and 1980. However, the last half of the decade saw a gradual worsening of the political situation in India and it is doubtful if the successful expansion of women's studies that took place in India during this decade would have happened without the increasing activism and fighting spirit demonstrated in the formation of the Indian Association for Women's Studies, and the contributions of some outstanding senior leaders like Prof J.P. Naik, Dr Madhuri Shah and Dr Phulrenu Guha.

The National Conference received funding, in addition to that given by the UNICEF and the Ford Foundation, from the ICSSR, the UGC and the Government of India. A substantial response from universities, research institutes, women's colleges, women's organisations, trade unions and other groups, raised the number of participants to over 400. At the international level, women's studies welcomed the Indian venture as a major development. Increasing requests from non-Indian scholars to become members of IAWS and invitations to Indian scholars to participate in women's studies conventions abroad indicated growing exchanges in the field.

The UN Mid-Decade Review Conference held in 1980 in Copenhagen, provided a strong mandate to various UN specialised agencies to give greater attention to women-focused activities in developing countries. Agencies like the UNICEF, the ILO, the UNESCO and the FAO, responding to this mandate, welcomed the Indian National Conference on Women's Studies as a pace-setter.

Support to women's studies: Entry of UN agencies

One of the first widespread efforts at supporting women's studies in India came from the Regional Office of the Social Science Advisor to UNESCO in Asia and the Pacific when it decided to hold an expert-group meeting on women's studies and social sciences in Asia in October 1982, in collaboration with the ICSSR and CWDS.

The report of the meeting was comprehensive, inclusive of various issues, such as the definition of women's studies, critique of social science research, curriculum and objectives of the discipline, and trends in research. The report mentioned that research at the time was increasingly being carried out by local scholars, mostly women, and that indigenisation was leading to questions about the basic assumptions governing research and the need for a critical re-examination of existing theories related to the status of women. It also noted problems, such as recognition and definition of women's studies, poor funding, inadequate means of communication among researchers, non-utilisation of research findings for policy and the urban bias in research.

Further, this meeting also came up with a set of recommendations, framing the objectives of women's studies in the region, which would include promotion of better and balanced understanding of different societies, how they responded to change, assisting men and women in understanding the roles actually played by men and women, empowering women in the struggle for equality and rendering invisible women visible. Interestingly, emphasis was laid on the importance of ethics, autonomy and control, and on monitoring social science data and findings to ensure that they were not utilised to distort social reality.

The process of interaction between women's studies scholars and activists in various Asian and developing countries during this period was further strengthened by the role played by the Asia-Pacific Centre for Women and Development, established under UNESCAP. The Regional Office of the Social Science Advisor to UNESCO at Bangkok also undertook several follow-up actions. It sponsored several comparative studies within the region by women scholars from different countries, organised small workshops to encourage further interaction between scholars involved in these studies and provided small institutional grants for preparation of teaching material for under-graduate students. One such major venture was the preparation of textbooks for undergraduate students by a group of women's studies scholars under the leadership of the Research Centre for Women's Studies in SNDT Women's University. Another small institutional grant enabled the Centre for Women's Development Studies to initiate the first women's studies journal in India titled *Samya Shakti*.

Since its 1976 adoption of a Convention on Rural Labour, the International Labour Organisation increased its concern for information on rural women's situation, encouraging many studies as well as action projects to strengthen employment conditions and organisation of rural women workers. It was hoped that these activities would not only expand the body of knowledge but in the process would change the assumptions about the non-working, dependent, illiterate, 'voiceless' millions of women, and eventually influence the course of both research and action by women's studies practitioners. Fledgling institutions (RCWS–SNDT University, ISST, CWDS etc.) and the Indian Association for Women's Studies were all engaged in these ventures. At the same time there was a rapid growth of autonomous women's organisations.

Coalition of 'academic' and 'social' conscience

The first demonstration of the convergence of social and academic conscience was the widespread agitation against the Supreme Court verdict, acquitting the two policemen accused in the Mathura rape case.

Initiated by four law teachers in 1979 through their open letter of protest to the Chief Justice of India, the agitation spread across Gujarat, Maharashtra, etc., finally reaching Delhi and forcing the Prime Minister, Indira Gandhi, to request the Law Commission to undertake an urgent review of the Rape Laws.[27] This demonstration, more than anything else, encouraged the national organising committee of the National Conference to obtain a mandate in 1981 for the formation of the Indian Association of Women's Studies.

The natural and inevitable tension between the demands of analytical rigour and theoretical development has often been mistaken for a tension between academics and activists. The real foundations of the tension lie within two distinct academic ideologies and traditions: (*a*) the concept of academic neutrality (or a laissez-faire tradition manifested in the notion of 'value-free sciences') and (*b*) the older ideology, of knowledge as the pursuit of truth.

The growth of nationalism/anti-imperialism during the colonial period had played a significant role in opposing political control over Indian universities. Despite persistent efforts to suppress this in the post-Independence period by various national governments, both the Radhakrishnan Commission (1948) and the Kothari Commission (1966) defended university autonomy and academic freedom as essential for building a democracy and enabling universities to act as the 'conscience of the nation'.

The visible dynamism of women's studies attracted people who were concerned with revitalising university education by bringing it closer to social issues. Women's studies thus became another dimension of penetrating the ivory-tower isolation of universities and their increasing alienation from national problems like underdevelopment or maldevelopment, poverty and inequality. Problems of growing violence—criminal, social and political—that disturbed many in the universities and called for institutional and social intervention, were projected by the women's movement jointly with such scholars. There was a distinct increase in the number of such 'academic activists' who used their scholarship and professional skills to intervene in what they felt to be unjust situations/decisions as demonstrated in the Mathura case.

A few progressive and concerned persons within the government also welcomed such efforts on the part of academics. They participated through research, evaluation and advocacy in the search for solutions to critical issues emerging in the course of economic and social change and accelerated by planned or unplanned development, environmental degradation, poverty escalation, population explosion and failure in various areas of human development.

However, such individual efforts did not commit or involve the institutions which they were a part of. It must also be noted that to quite a few academics who were searching for an active participatory social role, the hidebound structures of the university system proved to be too restrictive even for interdisciplinary research. Many of them quit their professions as teachers to become development studies research-ers or social activists affiliated to research institutions or NGOs. This approach was articulated fairly clearly by the National Seminar on Org-anisation and Perspectives held in 1985 in Delhi. In this context, the centres for women's studies were to serve as the nuclear source of in-formation and ideas which would eventually stimulate the university community to play an active, self-motivated role in the entire process of change. That was why they were not designed as departments, and were not visualised as undertaking an independent course of teaching women's studies towards a degree, but rather as playing a catalytic role. This was emphasised at the National Seminar and reiterated in the National Policy on Education by the statement that women's studies would be encouraged within existing institutions, disciplines and courses.

Acceptance of women's studies by UGC

A significant landmark after the release of the report 'Towards Equality' in 1974 was the holding of the National Conference on Women's Studies in April 1981, at the SNDT Women's University in Mumbai. The main purpose of the conference was to stimulate a concern for women's issues by promoting women's studies. The deliberations at the conference produced a lot of material by way of arguments, suggestions and reco-mmendations for launching a movement for women's studies.[28] The sup-port of the UGC to this venture was evidenced by the encouraging presence of Dr Madhuri Shah, then Chairperson of the UGC, who inaugurated the Conference. As a follow-up in 1983, the UGC sent a letter to all the vice-chancellors calling their attention to the need for universities to involve themselves in women's problems through their research, teaching and extension activities. An advisory committee was appointed to assist the UGC in screening the various proposals received from the universities in response to this letter. The response was not satisfactory, as there seemed to be a lack of understanding of the envisioned focus. Dr Madhuri Shah commented that the universities had not applied their minds to the issues of restructuring of courses or curriculum development as a part of taking note of the new knowledge. Only a broad-based movement to develop women's studies within the general educational system could initiate a process to prevent future injustice in the context of the marginal position of women in education.[29] These comments were a green signal to the IAWS to step up its activities in organising discussions on women's studies. All these efforts culminated in a seminar co-sponsored by the UGC, the IAWS and the University of Delhi in April 1985 on Perspectives and Organisation of Women's Studies Units in Indian Universities. The objectives which emerged were both 'academic and social'. They formed the basis of the directives later formulated by the UGC in its guidelines.[30]

The debate did not remain confined to a limited group but was carried to a Non-Aligned Ministers Meeting held in July 1985, to UNESCO and the World Conference of the Women's Decade in 1985, and to a National Seminar in Preparation for Drafting the National Policy on Education (NPE) in 1985–86.

The minutes of the first meeting of the UGC Committee on Women's Studies, held on 23 December 1985, considered the recommendations. The National Seminar on Education for Women's Equality, held from 3–5 November 1985 at New Delhi, was particularly relevant for the UGC, as it was convened by the Ministry of Education in connection with the formulation of the National Policy on Education which was finalised in 1986. The Committee specially drew attention to the recommendations made by the National Seminar on the need for promotional units/cells to monitor measures implemented to improve the role of education in facilitating women's equality and development at the central, state and institutional levels, and in the Ministry of Education, UGC, NCERT, NIEPA, etc. Supporting the above recommendations, Dr Madhuri Shah pleaded with the government that women's studies should be incorporated in the New Education Policy. The evidence of political will would persuade universities to treat this matter with greater seriousness.

The UGC responded to the national policy mandate when, in its meeting, the committee endorsed the above with a recommendation to establish 'a cell in the UGC, and units with the universities and colleges selected for this programme to play catalytic and coordinating roles in the promotion of women's studies.' The committee was of the view that women's studies had to be recognised as a critical input and support system for several other policy thrusts that were already being promoted by the UGC, such as promotion of human rights, population education, adult education and science for the people, and to the introduction of extension as the third dimension of university activities. Hence, early in the planning stage, the committee recognised women's studies as a catalytic agent for change in the academic system as well as its relationship to human rights, mass education and empowerment and its activist role in the field.

The UGC was mandated by the committee to commence new centres in seven identified universities. Further, the committee also accepted a draft of the undergraduate syllabus, prepared at the request of the UNESCO by the SNDT Women's University. The criteria used to identify the university centres was not spelt out.

However, out of seven centres, only four have survived. (These were the ones at universities of Kerala, Panjab and Delhi, and the Banaras Hindu University, while NEHU, Ranchi and Surat university centres did not start at all.) Promotion of material in regional languages, human resource development of key functionaries in Indian universities, intensive training of university and college teachers and revision of postgraduate curricula for incorporating the women's studies dimension in different disciplines, were stressed. It refrained from listing research priorities, as these already existed through various seminars, but it placed a 'high priority on research for development of human resources and teaching-learning materials'.[31]

In the following year, 1986, the NPE also came out with its recommendations on 'Education for Equality', wherein it declared that 'the National Education System will play a positive interventionist role in the empowerment of women.' In this direction, it stated that 'Women's Studies will be promoted as a part of various courses and educational institutions be encouraged to take up active programmes to further women's development.'[32]

UGC's first guidelines for women's studies

In 1986, the UGC issued guidelines to universities, which provided a definition, objectives and some framework for programmes and financial assistance. The guidelines emphasised the dimensions of teaching, training, research and extension. Two models were suggested, namely women's studies cells within the departments of colleges and centres for women's studies as independent units, with the status of a department in the university. In response to the above guidelines, 22 centres were established in the universities and 11 cells in colleges by the end of the Eighth Plan.

The announcement of the National Policy on Education in January 1985 and the formulation of the Guidelines on Women's Studies by the UGC in 1986 represented the first phase of the legitimisation of women's studies in the formal educational system. A striking feature of the Indian situation is the similarity between the arguments of women's studies advocates and those of the Indian Education Commission (1964–66), especially regarding the role of university education. The Education Commission too, had emphasised that the university was 'to act as the conscience of the nation' and recommended involvement in the study and evaluation of social processes for critical assessment of society.

The second significant feature of this phase was the insistence, from the beginning, that to enable universities to play this role vis-à-vis gender issues, a perspective or an ideology was required which would be articulated in every discipline, in every institution and at all levels. The third significant feature was the constant emphasis on the combination of three sets of activities—teaching, research and community action—which was seen as vital for the development of women's studies.

The centres for women's studies were designed to act as catalysts for promoting and strengthening women's studies. They have been instrumental in incorporating women's studies in different courses, have facilitated research on socially relevant subjects, have provided consultations to scholars, and have helped in evaluating projects, documenting experiences and networking within and outside the university system. Centres like SNDT, Delhi, Jadavpur and Panjab have led others. Inspite of these achievements, many challenges remain to be overcome.

Shifting contexts, challenges and pressures before women's studies

If the 1970s were dominated by a political crisis symbolised by the national Emergency and the public reaction to it, the 1980s were dominated by a complex series of political challenges to the systems, institutions and attitudes that had originated in the freedom struggle. To a considerable extent, these complex responses also reflected the downswing in the global economy after two decades of the 'golden age'. Economic recession began to weaken the ideological conscience of the younger generations (and universities) in the developed countries of the world, and strengthened political shifts towards narrower, self-motivated, right-wing groups. This process was visible in several parts of both the First and the Second World blocs in industrialised countries, causing a negative impact on the United Nations system and the efforts of the Third World bloc to fight for a new international economic order. The Third World countries, weakened by the increasing burden of international debt, internal poverty, inequality and strife—leading to political instability—provided a backdrop for various contradictory socio-political movements as channels of popular discontent. Some of them had their roots in democratic ideologies but adopted militant violence as their instrument. Some of them increasingly demonstrated the fascist leanings that developed during the two decades preceding the Second World War. There was also a progressive, secular, ideological trend, fighting against various odds. In India, the upsurge of demo-cratic movements which characterised the end of the national Emergency also caused the expansion of various types of movements.

The wide economic and political inequality, and the rapid growth of identity politics during the 1980s, with the emergence of ethnic and communal movements, posed problems for the women's movement and women's studies practitioners. The movement's opposition to communalism and commitment to democratic ideology were never in question, but the expansion of women's studies, from its initial origins in the social sciences, to the field of literary and cultural studies, brought about a conflict in choosing research priorities. The political reality of India's linguistic, religious and cultural plurality was also reflected in the educational and linguistic equipment of these scholars, who took up cultural studies through literature, social anthropology and explorations into earlier or contemporary history. All this accelerated an unconscious preoccupation with the sources of knowledge accessible to individual scholars. Since the larger number came from the majority community, and the highly educated sections, i.e., the upper middle classes, the output of research during the latter half of the 1980s gave rise to some misgivings among women activists and scholars belonging to the minority communities. To some extent, a similar phenomenon was affecting women's studies at the international level under the increasing influence of post-modernist intellectual challenges.

The 1980s, in some ways, reflected not only the peak of the movement's success in forcing through changes in government policy and legislation, but also the beginning of its failures. Significant changes in some criminal laws, particularly those relating to rape and dowry-related violence—once considered a victory—were increasingly viewed as failures in the face of poor enforcement and rising figures of violence against women. The success in incorporation of two paragraphs on 'education for women's equality' in the NPE in 1986, had to be weighed against the total apathy of the state and state agencies in disseminating these ideas to the various sections of the educational system. This failure was pointed out both in the Ramamurthy Committee Report (1990) and the Revised Programme of Action for the policy adopted by the Parliament in 1992. The failure to protect Muslim women's rights through the enactment of the Muslim Women's Protection of Rights on Divorce Act, 1986, was followed hardly a year later with the resurgence of widow-burning and the failure of the Commission of Sati (Prevention) Act, 1987, forced through Parliament to pacify women's protests.

Against the backdrop of the shift in economic policy during the 1990s, the only silver lining was the introduction of the 73rd and 74th Constitutional amendments, with one-third reservation for women in the local self-government bodies and due representation for the constitutionally recognised and historically oppressed groups—Dalits and Adivasis, Scheduled Castes and Scheduled Tribes.

The huge investment of time and energy by the activists and the women's studies movement in researching and organising rural women for over a decade bore fruit by the end of 1992. The enthusiastic response of rural women to the panchayat elections was astounding. This new awakening among women at the grass roots, especially in rural areas, also demonstrated itself during the literacy campaigns in many districts and in the protest movements that erupted in many states against the states' policy of drawing revenue out of alcoholic drinks. This forced many political parties to adopt a pro-prohibition stand in the Assembly elections that followed.

Further, the women's studies agenda has expanded its horizons because of its proximity to larger movements fighting wider issues. On the one hand, it gives young scholars access to critical information which they would not have been able to reach, had they remained confined to local struggles. On the other hand, international exposure also brings in its wake career opportunities with consultants in international donor agencies posing irresistible temptations to young professionals struggling for survival even as jobs in research and development agencies within the country are becoming scarce due to declining resources.

Some institutions, particularly those within the university system, have found it difficult to groom young scholars as a part of the succeeding generation. However, the shift from research to action has been relatively easy with the development of action-groups at the grass-roots level, which espoused gender as an important dimension of their activities. At the same time, it must be noted that a reverse shift is difficult because of the emphasis on academic qualifications in universities and research institutions. If women's studies is to become more effective, institutions must be willing to give due weightage to academic potential arising from creative problem-solving and involvement with grass-root realities.

The 1990s also witnessed a major shift in the economic policy of the Government of India under pressure from the IMF and the World Bank, resulting in the abandonment of its constitutional commitment to socialism and a welfare state.

Educational institutions found themselves at the receiving end of both changes. On the one hand, many of them became battlegrounds for warring political ideologies, which frequently found expression in attacks on academic freedom and the secularist, tolerant traditions of many institutions. On the other hand, the financial crisis and the pressure to reduce fiscal deficit drastically reduced the availability of resources for educational institutions. Institutions of higher education, and research in non-technological areas were the resultant victims. Women's studies, which had not yet been given a priority status for R&D funding, was the inevitable casualty.

The decline in national as well as UN funding pushed women's studies scholars and institutions into dependence on other donor agencies within and outside India, providing a handle for negative propaganda from that section of political and academic opinion which wanted to ignore the intellectual challenges posed by the women's studies movement. On the positive side, this pushed women's studies into widening its areas of concern in its search for new allies. The preoccupation with women-specific issues in the 1980s was followed by a growing interest in religion, culture and politics, structural adjustment and globalisation, and the environmental and ecological crisis—the last had been passionately articulated by peasant women's struggles even before the appearance of environmental scientists on the horizon.

The international context of these changes had positive and negative fall-outs. There was evidence of some loss of strength among the women's movements in the developed countries and of hostility faced within their national contexts. On the other hand, NGO participation in the Beijing conference demonstrated an enormous increase, both by way of regional representation as well as that of the class/community/occupational background of participants. It also demonstrated improvement in (*a*) the assessment of the global economic and political order, (*b*) willingness to listen to and accommodate a variety of perspectives from women belonging to different cultures and traditions, and (*c*) increasing solidarity within the various movements and the manifestation of this solidarity in women's studies.

As developments, such as the above, illustrated the crucial role of women's studies, the UGC in 1991 constituted a Review Committee to examine the functioning of various centres and cells.[33] The committee found wide variations in the functioning of the centres. Where there was strong leadership, the centres achieved outstanding success, but in many cases activities were limited, especially where support from top management or committed directors was not available. The review committee suggested that women's studies centres which performed better should be strengthened and the non-performing ones closed if they failed to prove themselves. It was further recommended that the number of women's studies centres be reduced after ensuring that all regions in the country were covered. Other recommendations were related to academic, administrative and organisational matters.

As the cells were found to be non-functional, the review committee recommended their closure. As an alternative strategy, the centres were advised to network with the affiliated colleges. Scholars inside and outside the university system criticised the recommendations, particularly those related to closure and limiting the number of centres. The reports were reviewed again and the centres whose closure was recommended were given a fresh lease of life and new review committees visited them again to make their final recommendations. It was recommended that where performance had improved visibly and where the vice-chancellors intervened to assure that all the lacunae would be rectified, centres should be permitted to continue. However, in the colleges, all the cells were closed, except one. Fortunately, the revised PoA (Plan of Action) 1992 encouraged the expansion of the university centres through more opportunities for collaborative work. It focused on women's studies as a critical input to promote better understanding of women's contributions to social processes, their aspirations and conceptual obstacles which made them 'invisible' in many areas of scientific inquiry. The programme, the PoA emphasised, must aim at investigating and removing structural, cultural or attitudinal causes of gender discrimination, and empower women to participate in all areas of development at national and international level.

New thrust in women's studies: Revised UGC guidelines and the new approach: 1998

The Standing Committee of Women's Studies was reconstituted as the Standing Committee on the Development of Women's Studies in 1996 after Dr Armaity S. Desai took over as the chairperson of UGC, with Prof Kamalini Bhansali as the chair of the standing committee.

By the end of the Eighth Plan, the established centres had started gaining legitimacy, but with legitimacy, accountability became more crucial. In addition, new challenges had emerged due to forces like globalisation and privatisation. These had to be kept in mind when contemplating the focus of women's studies in the new century. UGC centres were functioning within the framework of earlier guidelines. However, centres outside the university system had entered new territories. Thus, the need to expand the constituency of women's studies was strongly felt. This called for new ideas and strategies, which, without discarding the old, would provide more space to women's studies.

Keeping these trends in mind, various attempts at revising the guidelines were initiated for incorporation in the Ninth Plan (1997–2002).

The UGC Standing Committee substantially revised the guidelines, and for the first time, a whole section was given in the UGC Ninth Plan in the chapter 'Universities and Social Change'. A new approach towards bringing the different constituents of women's studies together through networking was initiated. The major innovations in the 1998 UGC guidelines are given below.

Structure of the guidelines   The guidelines were in two parts. Part one consisted of the approach paper, which described concepts, goals and roles on the one hand, and strategies and approaches on the other. Part two gave directions for putting the ethos of the approach paper into action. The process of preparing the revised guidelines was meant to be participatory. Having prepared a new framework, the Standing Committee started dialogues with the directors of various women's studies centres. It also became more broad-based, drawing members from university and non-university research organisations and national agencies concerned with women. There was greater flexibility in financial matters, and the organisational aspects were specified in greater detail with new strategies to overcome bureaucratic delays. It was accepted that the programmes would be continuously monitored to ensure accountability and quality.

Expansion of the UGC family   Today, a broad spectrum of organisations in the country are engaged in women's studies. There are centres attached to universities and funded by the UGC, non-governmental women's organisations, registered societies, grass-roots organisations and individual scholars. In the Ninth Plan, a broader view is taken of the women's studies centres and scholars. To achieve mutual reinforcement and partnership and to nurture fledgling centres with support from established ones, networking and clustering among UGC centres with different capabilities as well as between UGC-sponsored and independently established centres, was encouraged. Networking with the departments and colleges, teaching, training, research, documentation, advocacy and field-based action were to be the main thrusts.

Enabling strategies   Since the existing women's studies centres were heterogeneous in character and history, a system of phasing was proposed as an evolutionary process on the basis of the capabilities of each centre. The phases are classified as Phase I, Phase II and Phase III, with Phase I constituting the initial period. The scope of each phase was specified and experienced centres were expected to nurture new ones in their journey.

Doing things together   For the first time, the role and responsibilities of the UGC Standing Committee on women's studies were defined. Innovations were introduced through collaborations with organisations like the National Commission for Women, the Department of Women and Child Development, Government of India, the Planning Commission, the IAWS and the Commonwealth Secretariat, UK.

Some of the important projects discussed with the Department of Women and Child Development and the Planning Commission and meant to be undertaken by the women's studies centres included statewise gender community profiles, gender sensitivity programmes in colleges and universities and developing a grid of women resource centres under the National Resource Centre. Due to lack of funds, the programmes could not be taken up.

As an outcome of a workshop jointly organised in New Delhi by the UGC and the Commonwealth Secretariat, London in 1997 for women in higher education management, the UGC (with the assistance of a group of academics and scholars who formed the sub-group of the Standing Committee on the Development of Women's Studies) contextualised training material prepared by the Commonwealth Secretariat to suit the Indian higher education system. Eight manuals on different aspects of management of higher education, including a bibliography and a database, were brought out under the series 'Women managers in higher education: a training programme'.

The Standing Committee on the Development of Women's Studies took a bold decision to document the experiences and development of women's studies, both in the university system and outside it, and thereby arrive at a vision for the future. As a preparatory step, a UGC–IAWS workshop on women's studies was held at Panjab University, Chandigarh during 15–17 April 1999.

Having given women's studies a major thrust, in line with the NPE and the Programme of Action, the UGC needed to set up a cell. This had been suggested by the first Standing Committee. However, from 1986, it has been operating with the slender resources of the UGC. It was decided that UNESCO be requested to provide a chair in women's studies to the UGC, to guide the development of women's studies centres in tune with the Ninth Plan guidelines, under the overall guidance of the UGC Standing Committee. Although the UGC approved the establishment of the chair, the proposal could not be put into action due to administrative concerns; otherwise, it would have given a greater impetus to the programme.

Recognising the success of the women's studies centres when they collaborated actively in the Girl Child Project, a similar collaborative study between the UGC, the NCW and the Department of Women and Child Development (DWCD), for prevention of child prostitution and rehabilitation of sex workers, is on the anvil.

New centres In addition to proposals submitted by existing centres, several proposals were considered for the establishment of new centres and evaluated through site visits and dialogues. During the Ninth Plan, 11 new centres were established. Orientation programmes for new centres were planned and refresher courses in women's studies were offered at specific women's studies centres.

Though all care has been taken to ensure that the women's studies centres play a meaningful role, the biggest hurdle to the programme has been the lack of commitment on the part of state governments to give permanency to these centres, inspite of the repeated efforts of the UGC chairperson.

In sum, it may be stated that the Standing Committee on the Development of Women's Studies has taken an important step towards invigorating women's studies. It remains to be seen how effective the new approach to women's studies centres proves to be in the university system and outside.

Conclusion

The development of the women's studies programme at the UGC owes much to the two chairpersons of UGC, Dr Madhuri Shah and Dr Armaity Desai, for their vision, determination and courage to initiate change. Dr Madhuri Shah gave legitimacy to women's studies by incorporating it in UGC policies and structures and, as a result, introduced reforms in the higher education system and its programmes.

Dr Armaity Desai gave a fresh perspective to women's studies by widening the agenda of the programme, strengthening the roles of its participants and giving greater academic credibility to the programme. We also record with appreciation the contribution of successive chairpersons and members of the UGC Standing Committee on the Development of Women's Studies for their leadership and commitment to the women's studies programme and their help in making a positive impact on higher education.

This overview is intended to remind readers of the roots of women's studies—in the debates on women's education, and the social purpose of education. Inadequate attention to the latter, not only by the state and by the education system, but also by the educated intelligentsia of the decades following Independence, had aggravated the problems that women's studies was expected to undo. To play this role effectively, women's studies needed not only legitimacy, but also academic credibility and influence. Resentment from the entrenched establishment was inevitable and, in our opinion, to be preferred to apathy, which is more effective in marginalising. In areas where academic credibility has been achieved, indifference is not very visible. Expansion into other issues has now brought in new allies and more credibility—both inside and outside the university system.

We have sought to focus not only on the challenges that face women's studies, but also on the social role and purpose of education in trying to develop new levels of political, economic and institutional consciousness, and in setting a new vision and agenda for the future.

Notes

1. See Desai (1977a).
2. See Forbes (1998).
3. See Desai (1977a). In 1926, the Director of Public Instructions, while giving away prizes at the Bethune College remarked, 'You have asserted yourselves in the field of politics. How long is it to be before you assert yourselves in the field of secondary and higher education?'
4. See Forbes (1998).
5. See Chaudhari (1992).
6. See Ministry of Education (1950).
7. Ibid.

8. Ibid.
9. Ibid.
10. See Ministry of Education (1962).
11. See Ministry of Education (1966).
12. Ibid.
13. Ibid.
14. See Mazumdar (1991).
15. See Desai and Anantram (1982). Also see IAWS (1998).
16. See IAWS (1998).
17. See *Indian Journal of Gender Studies*, Vol. 5 (1).
18. See ICSSR (1977).
19. Ibid.
20. See Desai (1972).
21. The report of the Round Table discussion documents this. Also refer Bhansali (1997).
22. See Desai and Patel (1985) and IAWS (1998).
23. See Sen (1990) and Stree Shakti Sangathana (1987).
24. See IAWS (1998).
25. See Patel (1985) and Radha Kumar (1998).
26. See UNESCO (1983).
27. See open letter written by Upendra Baxi, Lotika Sarkar and Raghunath Kelkar from the Law Faculty of Delhi University, and Vasudha Dhagamwar from Pune University in 1979.
28. See the report of the First National Conference.
29. See Research Group on Women's Studies (1985).
30. See minutes of the first meeting of the UGC Committee on Women's Studies, held in December 1985.
31. See Desai (1999).
32. See Ministry of Education (1992).
33. See University Grants Commission (1993).

References

Kamalini Bhansali (1997), *My Karmabhoomi: Three Decades at SNDT Women's University*, Mumbai: SNDT Women's University.
Karuna Chanana (ed.) (1998), *Socialisation, Education and Women*, New Delhi: Orient Longman.
Maitreyee Chaudhari (1992), *Indian Women's Movement: Reform and Revival*, New Delhi: Radiant Publishers.
A.S. Desai (1999), Opening Remarks [of Chairperson, UGC] at UGC-IAWS

Workshop on Women's Studies, 15–17 April, Panjab University, Chandigarh.

Neera Desai, (1972), *A Struggle for Identity Retention: A Case Study of SNDT Women's University.* Bombay: Research Unit for Women's Studies, SNDT Women's University.

Neera Desai, (1977a), 'The Pattern of Higher Education of Women and Role of a Woman's University', *Journal of Higher Education,* Vol. 3 (1).

——— (1977b), *Woman in Modern India* (2nd ed.), Bombay: Vora & Co.

——— (ed.) (1988), *A Decade of the Women's Movement in India,* Bombay: Himalaya Publications.

——— (1993), 'Women's Education in India' in Jill, Conway and Bourque Susan (eds.), *The Politics of Women's Education: Perspectives from Asia, Africa and Latin America,* Michigan: University of Michigan Press.

Neera Desai and Sharayu Anantram (1982), 'Middle Class Women's Entry into the World of Work', Proceedings of the Indian Statistical Institute Golden Jubilee Symposium, New Delhi.

Neera Desai and Vibhuti Patel, (1985), *Change and Challenge in the International Decade,* 1975–85, Bombay: Popular Prakashan.

Geraldine Forbes (1998), *Women in Modern India.* Cambridge: Cambridge University Press.

Ministry of Education (1950), *Report of the University Education Commission* (Radhakrishnan Commission 1948–49), New Delhi.

——— (1959), *Report of the National Commission on Women's Education* (Durgabhai Deshmukh Committee 1958–59), New Delhi.

——— (1962), *Report of the Committee on Differentiation in Curricula for Boys and Girls* (Hansa Mehta Committee), New Delhi.

——— (1966), *Report of the Education Commission* (Kothari Commission 1964–66), New Delhi.

——— (1985), *Report of the National Seminar on Education for Women's Equality,* 3–5 November, New Delhi.

——— (1992), 'Programme of Action', National Policy on Education, 1986.

Indian Association of Women's Studies (1998), *Perspectives on Indian Independence through Women's Eyes: Selection from a National Seminar on the Early Years of Indian Independence.* New Delhi: IAWS.

Indian Council of Social Science Research (1977), *Programme of Women's Studies,* New Delhi: ICSSR.

Maithreyi Krishnaraj (ed.) (1995), *Remaking Society for Women: Visions—Past and Present,* Delhi: IAWS.

Vina Mazumdar (1991), 'Higher Education, Women and Development', *University News,* Vol. 29(2), pp. 13–15.

Vibhuti Patel (1985), *Reaching for Half the Sky: A Reader in Women's Movement.* Baroda: Antar Rashtriya Prakashan.

Radha Kumar (1998), *The History of Doing* (3rd impression), New Delhi: Kali for Women.

Illina Sen (1990), *A Space Within the Struggle*, New Delhi: Kali for Women.

Stree Shakti Sangathan (1987), *We Were Making History: Life Stories of Women in the Telangana People's Struggle*, New Delhi: Kali for Women.

University Grants Commission (1986), *Guidelines on Women's Studies*, New Delhi.

——— (1993), *Report of the Jaya Indiresan Review Committee: Women's Studies Centres and Cells*, New Delhi.

——— (1996), *Policy Frame and Programmes of the Proposals for the Development of Higher Education in the IX Five Year Plan*, New Delhi.

——— (1998), *Guidelines on the Development of Women's Studies*, New Delhi.

Research Group on Women's Studies (1985), *Report of the Seminar on Perspectives and Organisation of Women's Studies Units in Indian Universities*, New Delhi: Department of Political Science, University of Delhi.

UNESCO, Office of the Regional Advisor for Social Sciences in Asia and the Pacific (1983), *Women's Studies and Social Sciences in Asia: Report of Meeting of Experts*.

Section I

Case Studies of University-based Women's Studies Centres

2
Blazing a quarter century trail

Research Centre for Women's Studies, SNDT Women's University

Maithreyi Krishnaraj

According to the wise, when an age needs a saviour, an avatar is born in the right place. It was a promising moment when the first women's studies centre was established in 1974—the sixty-eighth anniversary of the first women's university in India. Concerned academics in the university, moving with the times, forged a partnership with the authorities, which is somewhat unique in the history of Indian higher education.

This, then, is the story of the first women's studies centre and of those who brought it into existence, nourishing it from a fledgling to a full-bodied being. This first generation 'women's studies centre' is now 25 years old, a veteran of a quarter century. It is not easy to encapsulate in one brief essay, the struggle of being and becoming. Memories, events, people, hopes, fears, failures and joys throng the picture, jostling for attention. What does one select, what does one omit? To draw a clear path through these meanderings is a forced attempt but one has to somehow see the wood for the trees. Besides, the narrator cannot be separate from the narrative as she herself was one of the actors. If it is her voice that you hear, you can only hope that she tells you what she saw, as honestly as she can. In the telling, her 'doing' women's studies and what it meant is a skein that cannot be untwisted from the centre itself and what it did or how it did it.

The establishment and growth of the Research Centre for Women's Studies at SNDT Women's University is intimately associated with the genesis of the university itself—the historical context in which it was born, the purposes it served, the philosophy it espoused and the persons who were associated with it from its inception to the present day. Therefore, the history of this women's studies centre cannot but help begin with an earlier parental biography.[1]

The first women's studies centre in this country was unique because its birth took place in a women's university through the initiative of the university itself—not through an individual or a group of persons from a department lobbying for it either with the support of the concerned university or alternately resisting the recalcitrance of authorities. The university saw women's studies clearly as an adjunct to women's education (the present-day terminology of empowerment had not evolved then). When notions of women's roles undergo reconceptualisation, the content and direction of women's education also gets realigned. Part of our story is precisely how and why women's studies arrived at SNDT in the mid-1970s.

In examining a 25-year period, one inevitably looks back on the basis of whatever 'wisdom' one has gained since then and reads back into history from the present. I joined the department only a few months after it was set up and since then, have lived in it and grown with it. The questions 'did it do its job well' or 'what kind of job did it do?' are interlinked with the expectations one had then and one has now from a women's studies department. Individual achievement may or may not coincide with a department's success. My analysis is based on documents and opinions, of authorities within and outside, as reflected in some of these documents, as well my personal understanding of events as they occurred; it is also based on how my own contribution and that of others fitted into this enterprise.[2]

Search for a philosophy

Child marriage and the plight of Hindu widows preoccupied social reformers in the late 19th century. D.K. Karve started the Anath Balikashram in 1899 to impart education to Hindu widows and steer them towards economic self-reliance. Dr Karve was anxious that as a wife, a woman should be a true companion to her husband. He talked explicitly about the need for removing disparity between men and women; he also stressed upon the woman's responsibility as a mother, entrusted with the rearing of children, for which she needed instruction on health, nutrition, hygiene, child development, etc. This view of a separate and special role for women in order to be a complementary partner to man, and to aid the nation in the capacity of mothers, resonates through many voices and even today, its echoes have not dissipated.[3] The dissenting voices came half a century later.

Dr Karve established the Indian Women's University (Bharatwarshiya Mahila Vidyapeeth) at Hingne in Pune with four students. Distinguished persons such as D.R. Gadgil, who was the secretary, were involved in the provisional committee. Dr Annie Besant wanted it to be an all-India institution. Rabindranath Tagore and Mahatma Gandhi approved, although the records reveal that Gandhi did not like the fact of English being a compulsory subject. The first chancellor was Dr Ramakrishna Gopal Bhandarkar and the first vice-chancellor was Dr R.P. Paranjape. This tradition of distinguished educationists and prominent public figures being associated with the university continued for a long time right up to the late 1980s.

When Sir Vithaldas Thakersey first visited the university, his visit was not prompted by idle curiosity but by his firm belief in the need for women's education. The donation that he made to the university established its foundations. His wife, Lady Premlila Thakersey associated herself with the institution from the year 1920 and, after her husband's death, became totally involved in it. The university shifted to Bombay, later acquiring a bigger building, and its degrees were recognised from 1937 onwards. Many national leaders were present in the 1939 Convocation, including Shri Vishweshwaraiya, Dr Radhakrishnan, Sarojini Naidu and Dr M. Jayakar. In 1947, the state government granted the university its charter and Dr Premlila Thakersey became the first vice-chancellor (henceforth VC).

The perspective of our national leaders on women's education was both class-biased and conservative, as revealed by the reports of the various education commissions. Statements of different national leaders as well as the university's own leaders, made at different times, reveal the ambiguity that informed women's education.[4] The courses of study were designed to suit the requirements of girls, viz. domestic science, general psychology, child psychology, hygiene and arts. Thus between 1916 to 1951, the university was basically interested in a liberal education for women and played the role of social reform by bringing women out of their orthodox homes.

> The most striking point about this phase is that the University fought against the social and political forces...with regard to the objectives of education, the medium of instruction or facilities for the students, it did not follow the normal accepted path.[5]

Over the years, the notion of women's education for 'desh seva' got more clearly emphasised, with people like Dr Paranjape, the first vice-chancellor, talking of the need to bring women 'on the same intellectual level as men and make them better fitted to carry on national work.' After 1951, India's independence made new demands on women—women's participation in elections, in holding political office and in the workforce, meant that women had to be equipped for these roles. The family too was changing.[6] The university had to establish parity with other coeducational institutions, and many of its special features were not unique any more. There was no longer any clear-cut role-specificity for women. As preparation for jobs became a new demand, the university began introducing many professional courses. The university's historic mission was over; faced with the increasing enrolment of women in coeducational institutions of higher education which were also offering a wide variety of curricular choices, and increasing numbers of women going into employment, there arose a need to justify the existence of a separate women's university.

In seminars and symposia organised during the golden jubilee celebrations of the university in 1966, many prominent persons stressed the importance of education for women. Dr Zakir Hussain declared that the time had passed when one had to defend education for women, but he still thought of them as homemakers.

> Whatever else these educated women would do, they would be housewives and mothers on whom would largely rest the responsibility of running an enlightened home and of moulding the future generations of the country.

Dr D.S. Kothari, Dr K.G. Saiyuddin and others reiterated the need for women to acquire intellectual competence and critical understanding, and a sense of commitment and identification with the community. J.P. Naik spoke of freedom, dignity, equality and justice. In 1966, he made the suggestion, radical for its time, that women's roles as mothers must be recognised as a social one and their re-entry into public life and the workforce must be made possible without penalty as in the case of returning soldiers. He said their contribution to the nation was as significant as that of soldiers who returned from defending the country.

Favourable factors

The perceived functions of education for women had no doubt widened, but without challenging women's role as being primarily domestic. What sets SNDT apart is this continuous anxiety to review and rethink its priorities, an anxiety to modernise without giving up its social reform moorings. The National Council on Women's Education was set up in 1960, chaired by Dr Premlila Thackersey. The Council stressed the need for a research unit on women's education which would compile data, discover new areas for action in different aspects of women's education, prepare guidelines, keeping in touch with women's organisations within the country and abroad. One can see how, slowly and surely, the wind was blowing in the direction of women's studies.

Sulabha Panandikar drew attention to the greater role of women in employment but even she did not surrender the contingent clause.

In the context of changing social needs, this University has kept before itself, the ideal of making women fill their place in society. It is accepted nowadays that women too have to be prepared for careers, apart from being good wives and mothers.[7]

The lone voice among these was Neera Desai's.[8] She pointed out that the pursuit of all these laudable objectives was not as unproblematic as everyone made it seem. The values a girl was supposed to imbibe through education, such as self-respect, rationality, objectivity, application of knowledge for a desired social change and a new selfhood as a citizen irrespective of any other consideration contradicted with the actual situation of girls in their homes and in society, where the primary role of a woman was above all else that of wife–mother and where any deviation was acceptable only if their primary roles were not jeopardised. The ideal of emancipation through education was very tough in practice; within the family and society, it led to deep conflicts because the survival of the family unit is premised so strongly on women subordinating their individual aspirations for the family good. Dr Desai posed the question, 'what are we expecting our girls to do—compromise on ideals or aggressively resist opposition and face the repercussions of their action?' It is this very dilemma that confronts us today, in teaching women's studies to women students—that we conscientise them with notions of justice and equality for the sexes without generating the support systems that will enable them to resist practices that go against these principles.

In December 1973, the university held a Round Table discussion on the university's future role. This was a momentous event. A research committee had been formed to survey entrants to various colleges of the university. Another study investigated the views of faculty members and university authorities. The issue posed to the Round Table was this—should the university change its goals, add new ones or redefine its goals? What emerged from this research was that the popular image of the university as second grade was unfair.[9] The distinct advantages of a separate space for women where women students could have more options, freedom and where leadership could be more easily nurtured, seemed to far outweigh the disadvantages of separateness.[10]

What was noticeable during this stage was the effort to retain and strengthen both the academic and social action components, as well as to modernise and keep pace with developments outside. All this was reflected in the expanding curricular options and the introduction of technical, professional courses along mainstream lines.[11] The working paper presented for discussion mentioned aspects like imparting knowledge and developing personality, but emphasised above all that the purpose of women's education was 'to develop a sense of social purpose and competence to play one's role in social and national development.'

A number of distinguished educationists attended the Round Table, held two years before the International Women's Year and a year before the Report of the Committee on the Status of Women, and among the recommendations made was that a research unit be set up to study the problems of women, that vocational and service options be opened up to them and a documentation centre on women's issues established. It was suggested that SNDT Women's University could make a valuable contribution to intellectual life and to uplifting the status of women by dealing with areas and issues concerning various facets of a woman's life. For the first time there was a shift to 'women' themselves as subjects of study, a shift from women's education as grooming (pun unintended) for defined roles to exploration of the problems and issues that affect women—a shift that necessarily led to women's studies.

While social reformers challenged the religious orthodoxy that kept women out of education, they did not conceptualise gender equality or empowerment as the crux of any emancipatory ideal[12]. Moreover, their focus was on urban, upper-caste members of the society. The setting up of the women's studies unit was the outcome of an inherited tradition, now struggling to articulate a new vision that women's education would raise the status of women by examining their own condition. A theoretical view of systemic women's subordination was not yet on the horizon, but women's studies was already being identified as an instrument of change. The university, in its anxious quest for an identity, had arrived at an answer. Women's studies would now be a special mission of the women's university. Prominent academics of the university had a big hand in propounding this vision and giving it form, making the mission a matter of teamwork between the university authorities and senior academics. Among them were Neera Desai, Dhairyabala Vora, Shakuntala Mehta, Kumud Patwa and educationists such as Kamalini Bhansali (then the Registrar), Sulabha Panandikar and Sharada Diwan (then the vice-chancellor). This remarkable partnership has been a special feature of the university, from the time of Lady Thakersey, its first vice-chancellor.

Today, looking at women's studies centres in universities in different parts of the country, one notices their more regional preoccupation. The SNDT unit was conceived as having an all-India scope (there is a frequent appeal that it should be a clearing-house on women's studies in India). It was easy for a unit situated in a premier metropolis to take on a national agenda. Bombay has special facilities, easy access to books, journals, scholars, visitors, government agencies, communications, parties and diverse communities. It has been the arena for many movements including the nationalist movement, Left movements, Dalit politics, and reformist inspirations. As such, legitimacy is not a difficult goal here as it might be for, say, a department in the interior provinces, where conservatism would be stronger.[13]

Laying the first stone

On 15 June 1974, the university's executive council met to scrutinise a proposal for setting up a research unit on women's studies. Shri Udaybhai M.D. Thakersey and family members of Shri Hakubhai Kapadia made an endowment of Rs 1,20,000 in aggregate for scientific research studies on women to be carried out at SNDT Women's University. This full endowment was formed into a fund known as 'Smt Motibai Madhavjee and Shri Madhavjee Damodar Thakersey Women's Studies Research Fund' and the unit set up with the fund was to be known as 'The Research Unit on Women's Studies' (RUWS).

The Syndicate decided that the unit would be totally autonomous. It was to be physically located in the department of sociology and share its facilities. The head of the department of sociology, Dr Neera Desai, was invited to take charge as the honorary director.

The scope, functions and programmes of the unit were stipulated as under.

- To identify and undertake studies pertaining to women's status and role in society.
- To collect information about women in various fields.
- To document and build up reference material on women.
- To liaison with individuals and institutions in India and abroad for meaningful communication on this subject.
- To plan collaborative projects, when possible, with other institutions.

At that point of time, material, data and research studies had not gone very far. What is significant is that RUWS saw itself as serving the whole country. Various non-governmental documentation centres and Departments of Women and Children were to come up much later in every state and at the national level. However, at that time the unit was more or less the lone voyager in this new unmapped territory. Since it was not possible to begin research without an idea of what was available, the emphasis was on making available data on the status of women in diverse fields. Therefore, collaboration with other departments and institutions was deemed critical. The need for 'scientific' studies was also stressed and women's studies was perceived as contributing to intellectual life. Questions of methodology, perspective and frameworks would emerge more clearly only in later years. Women's studies came not as a god-given gift or a happenstance but as the result of hard work, ingenuity, imagination and the enterprise of many persons. The university had cast a pioneering role for itself once again.

The building blocks

The management structure of RUWS points to the deep involvement and commitment of the university, which closely monitored the functioning of the unit. The Syndicate appointed an advisory committee which included eminent educationists. The vice-chancellor chaired the committee and its secretary was the registrar. The advisory committee's terms of reference were to advise the unit in planning research, to indicate priorities, to review the work of the unit and to sanction its needs, to frame rules regarding stipends for research workers and to recommend names of directors/advisory committee members. The university managed all accounts directly, and annual budgets were sanctioned from a research fund that was set up with the donation.

One of the important resolutions taken by the first advisory committee was that since the National Committee on the Status of Women, appointed by the Ministry of Social Welfare had collected a lot of primary and secondary material, the Union Minister of Education be requested by the vice-chancellor to transfer this material to the unit, so that the unit could store it properly and use it meaningfully. Thus, RUWS began work from July 1974.

Tentative first steps: 1974–81

Four main objectives figured (and continue to do so) in the work and goals of RUWS—to identify and undertake studies pertaining to women's status and role, to collect information, to build up documentation and reference material on women and to encourage and organise women's studies as a topic.

Information cell

The idea that RUWS should be a major information base and develop into a national clearing-house finds an echo in every advisory committee meeting held during this phase. The first effort in data compilation was a state-wise statistical profile of Indian women—the first ever in India. Then came a bibliography of works on women, which included theses, journal articles and books. Two other bibliographies also came out at that time—one by the AIWC and another by the National Library, Calcutta. These early efforts at documentation made information on the contemporary situation of women available to scholars. Today there are government agencies that bring out 'gender' statistics, while statistical methods have become more sophisticated with the work done by national and international feminists and the modifications brought about by ILO, UNRISD, UNSNA and UNDP.

Even in those early years, attempts were made to acquire data from various sources. Correspondence files are full of letters to the Census, Bureau of Statistics, the Directorate General of Employment, to government data-producing agencies, to various Ministries for their annual reports, to education departments for their digests of statistics and requests for journals relating to education. Various departments in Bombay University and many foreign institutions were contacted with requests for information. What emerges is a picture of the enormous effort to make the unit a national resource centre. ESCAP was approached for a grant for developing such a resource centre. The idea of being a clearing-house of information was also taken very seriously and every outside query was answered and data supplied. Information was sent to government departments, like the Ministry of Social Welfare. Information on the unit and copies of its publications were sent to the Feminist Press and Educational Resource Centre, the State University of New York. An international outreach was created, especially to the USA where women's studies was well-developed.

Research agenda

RUWS had proposed education, marriage and family and employment as three critical areas of research, but the early emphasis on education did not continue, although some work was done and the two other areas also remained largely unexplored except for a small study on married women students.

Research on students of the university was the first project undertaken—a comparison between employed women students and others, and an evaluation of continuing education programmes at the university. Another small-scale project was the unit plan undertaken with a UNICEF grant to remove sexist bias among primary school teachers, co-ordinated by Dr Madhuri Shah and Kamlesh Nischol. The exercises and slides created for that study are still used by many departments.

There were also two major research projects at this point of time. One was the study on the career progress of women scientists in the newly-formed Indian Women Scientists Association (IWSA) which revealed that although women were as qualified as their male counter-parts, they tended to stagnate in their jobs after some years; that they were concentrated in the public sector (more in teaching and research and less in industry); and that their career progress was reduced to mid-level achievement, partly because of family demands but equally because of organisational hurdles. I conducted this research and CSIR permitted me to use part of it for a Ph.D thesis. A book resulted from the study, *Essays on Women in Science*.

A second research project was a study of the impact of modernisation on a village in Bassein taluka, which was one of the first few studies to identify the impact of industrialisation on agriculture and on women's lives in India. It was also the first study in India to isolate female-headed households and conduct in-depth interviews with them. This brief exploration of female-headed households, which was published under the title, *Hidden from View*, has been frequently quoted.

Studies on women in food-processing and garment industries were also taken up. The study of women in the garment industry in Bombay showed that the stereotype of the garment industry being woman-dominated was simply not true, and that the women were on the margins, stitching saree falls and sewing buttons for male tailors. I have argued that surveys should look at both men and women to derive an understanding of gender-based discrimination. A unitary focus on women cannot distinguish gender discrimination from other variables.[14]

Action research: A big leap

An integrated rural development project for villages in Udwada District in south Gujarat was proposed. The initial survey to identify the needs of the women there was conducted by the research unit. One of the research assistants of the unit coordinated the project, which later found a supporter in the lady Collector of Valsad at the time. This small step, later to blossom into a full-fledged rural development project over the years, was of momentous consequence in giving a new dimension to the activities of the department. It linked extension services for women in rural areas firmly with women's studies in ways that were innovative, imaginative and instructive in many ways. It was a fine example of a community-based training model, implemented through local personnel with co-ordinated inputs from several departments of the university. This demonstrates how an 'action arm' can be fruitfully generated, to restore social relevance and accountability to academics.

Establishing links within the university and outside

During the early years, there was great concern that RUWS should slowly become a regional centre for guiding doctoral research and efforts should be directed to promoting women's studies research in regional languages and in other institutions within the university and outside. There was much collaboration with ICSSR on many fronts.

RUWS's modest financial assistance for small research projects on rural women and women in the lower social strata saw us forging partnerships with researchers, scholars and women's groups. These included an affiliated college of the university to study working women in Sangli district and a teacher from Ruia College for a study of women in the unorganised sector in two slums of Bombay as well as the publishing of a research study undertaken by the Marathi department on widow remarriage in Maharashtra.

Spreading wide

RUWS had visitors from all over, among who were Gloria Steinem, Germaine Greer, Florence Howe, Scarlet Epstein, members of ESCAP, scholars from Pakistan and parts of Asia. We were often conducting research amidst a flurry of activity—seminars, conferences and visits. Dr Neera Desai was invited by the American government for a consultation at Houston. Some scholars sought affiliation, and Doreen Jacobson was one of them. CSIR sent their national fellow to us for a year.

Going through the correspondence files of 1974–82, it is remarkable to note to what extent the registrar and all the vice-chancellors promoted the visibility of the unit. The unit's publications were sent to all those who had contact with the university and as a result, within a couple of years, the unit began receiving visitors. Contacts were established with many organisations within and outside India (as far as Australia, New Zealand, Canada, UK and the USA). The brochure and publications (which were very few at the time) were also sent to many government organisations at state and national levels. In the university reports presented during convocations, special and laudatory references were always made to the pioneering work of the unit, in the tones of a proud parent. Above all, women's organisations were invited to all discussions, meetings or seminars. The International Women's Year (1975) was full of excitement. Women's organisations of all political hues participated in our deliberations and we too attended conferences organised by the autonomous organisations.

The International Women's Decade was a thrilling period of sisterhood, of hope for the women's movement, regardless of ideology and different brands of politics. There were many meetings and seminars within SNDT in collaboration with the government. The milieu was of an emerging, vibrant women's movement, cutting across class distinctions, making our work at RUWS meaningful and profoundly satisfying. There was a certain ethos then which made our task seem missionary—to promote women's studies for women's betterment; in a way, the connotation of women's studies was wider than academic research.

Maybe we took on too many things. We often heard later that the 'research' at our centre was not of 'high quality'. Without appearing to

justify failures, one must attempt to emphasise out what we saw at that
time as our priority areas—to build reference material and to spread
the message of women's studies. Without this first layer, individual scholars could not have blossomed as they did. At that time we were gener-
alists by compulsion, attending to many aspects—research, critique
of disciplines, action programmes, documentation, building networks,
stimulating interest in women's studies both within the university and
among the activists. As pioneers we could open doors at many levels
but not journey deep into their passages.

Publications

Apart from research reports, bibliography, statistical profiles etc., some
papers submitted to the National Committee on the Status of Women
were brought out in book form. The papers on politics edited by Vina
Mazumdar was published by Allied Publishers, Delhi and titled *Symbols
of Power*. Translations of the synopsis of the National Committee's report
brought out by ICSSR in Marathi and Gujarati were published. Regional media analyses were undertaken. These were the first few authori-
tative texts used in teaching women's studies courses at SNDT. Also
RUWS was exploring the possibilities of starting a women's studies
journal with ICSSR support.[15]

Rear view

The formative years have yielded both positive and negative lessons.
A laudable practice at RUWS, which went against normal procedural
traditions in universities, was that the research staff always attended
advisory committee meetings along with the director. As a result, the
administration was personalised and the higher authorities were
approachable.[16] Perhaps the most important factor was that RUWS
was a cause dear to those in the top echelons of the university who saw
it as a new, exciting frontier. This meant at times that the authorities
had their own strong views on what our priorities should be, which would
conflict with what they were. While all the vice-chancellors were committed

to women's studies and gave abundant support, their perceptions also varied according to their professional backgrounds. Our social science approach was not familiar to some, and often it was not easy to convey that while we believed in action, community work and field-level research, we were equally convinced that academic work was a necessary prelude to informed action.

The personal background of senior staff in the early years also contributed to a particular orientation—the belief in teamwork and respect for each other's individuality. Competition was not absent but was subdued. All of us did many tasks including manual work because we had very little infrastructure. Dr Neera Desai, the Honorary Director, was from the national movement and had a commitment to peoples' struggles. I had lived through the nationalist fervour of pre-Independence days as a child and if not directly involved in it, had retained some values from that generation. During my post-graduation in the Delhi School of Economics, I had been exposed to the tremendous optimism of planned development and had had illustrious teachers like Dr K.N. Raj, Dr B.N. Ganguli and Dr V.K.R.V. Rao. They were nation-builders and had a deep sense of social purpose and social justice. These influences along with my study abroad during the eventful 1960s of active civil rights and the feminist movement[17] gave me an opportunity to read and discuss many issues, all of which had in a way groomed me for women's studies.

Despite its national sweep, the university had a history of teaching in regional languages and catering mainly to women students[18] from two distinct communities—Marathi and Gujarati. This double agenda generated dilemmas of reconciliation later on. Our resources were spread too thin. The unit was not a specialised centre for the western region but it did a little of everything—working at regional, national and international levels. It was also inspired by the wish to play a role in the national scene as a way of carving its unique identity as the spokesperson for women. In fact in the initial years, the unit and later the centre attracted more national and international attention than regional.

In retrospect, over the years we did suffer from several drawbacks, as certain traditions became a handicap. The camaraderie was not always an asset; when the department expanded and many new people had to be inducted, rules and procedures became necessary, expertise and academic accomplishment grew to be crucial, people who were 'important' in the early phases but lacked academic skills and training felt marginalised in the company of newcomers with more academic credentials. The relaxed atmosphere at times came in the way of efficiency and professionalism, which research or any serious academic work requires. The 'personal is political' theory sometimes went to illogical extremes; if staff regularly came late and were pulled up, there would be tears and accusations that a women's studies department ought not to be so unkind to women staff. Once we had an activist on the staff who was routinely outraged by even the simplest of regulations. It was difficult to convince activists that functional hierarchies were part of a university set-up and we could neither behave like an action-based women's group nor was it necessary. Middle-aged women graduates, who had taken a break because of marriage and motherhood, would turn up every day to demand work because they had heard that we were a women's organisation. Most of them wanted to have work they could take home, sometimes so that they could be home to give proper lunch/dinner to sons in their thirties!

Women students and teachers would drop in to say they wanted to do 'research on women' but had no notion of what they wanted to do. We were seen as a women's resource centre rather than as a study centre. One of the problems which women's studies continues to face in its struggle for academic legitimacy is that it is seen as a dimension of social work, redressing women's problems which are viewed as 'social problems'.[19] When Dr Yashpal, former UGC Chairman came to visit, he dismissed our efforts by saying, 'What is the use of studying? You should go and fight against dowry'.

Does anyone ask an economist why he is 'studying' poverty, instead of going out and fighting it?

To some extent, the newness of the field of women's studies also meant that it lacked constructive peer critique, which is so crucial for intellectual advancement. We paid a double price. As the first practitioners, our mentor status inhibited our own growth for we became the dispensers of wisdom. True, the academic community in the country took no notice of women's studies scholars until the late 1980s, when articles by individual scholars began appearing in mainstream periodicals. Often, these scholars, who now receive academic acclaim, were building upon the achievements of the women's studies units/ centres, that had opened up issues, made documentation and empirical work available, and fought for legitimacy.

Dr Neera Desai set up a tradition of participatory approaches. As associate director, I found it creative to formulate proposals for grants, to write perspective papers for the centre, to be given the chance to organise programmes, to plan acquisitions for documentation, to suggest new directions, and to advise and guide the younger staff. The contributions of colleagues were acknowledged by the centre, with no appropriation of the work of junior members. All the research staff were invited to meet visitors or hear distinguished guest speakers. The whole research team attended conferences and seminars. The junior members in later years were given several opportunities to learn. All of us worked extra hours as and when the occasion demanded it because we were all made to feel that it was 'our work'. I am placing emphasis on the management style (at the women's studies centre and at the university), because institution-building calls for leadership and vision, the ability to cement team relations, and build human capability. The collective style was followed by all of us in the department, which is why the academic-activist controversy did not affect us—we had from the start evolved the tradition of involving activists in research; they became partners and received credit for co-authorship.

Towards identity: The 1980s

It was in 1981 that the Executive Council of SNDT gave its approval for making the Research Unit on Women's Studies (RUWS) a permanent department of the university. The university took over the responsibility of providing the core staff. At that point of time, we had Neera Desai as Honorary Director, and Laj Deshmukh (who left soon after), Jyotsna Sanjanwala and myself as research assistants. We had a clerk and a peon to ourselves and a university employee to help with accounts. In 1982, the two research assistants obtained senior scale as research associates and, along with the clerk, became permanent, fortuitously at a time when the research fund from the private donation was practically exhausted. In the meantime, we had applied for a Ford Foundation grant.

The need for some historical research as well as for work on concepts was evident. Promoting women's studies in other departments and among activists continued, along with building documentation. In our research programme, we tried to follow, if not always in equal measure, Madhuri Shah's suggestion that three aspects should be covered—fundamental research, applied research and advocacy research.

On 17 October 1981, the Ford Foundation grant came through.

I was then appointed as Reader. As the unit's activities had expanded considerably and Dr Neera Desai had to manage her parent department, I was made associate director to assist in the planning and execution of the programmes of RUWS. This was perhaps the most creative period for many of us, certainly for me. Once again the university had strengthened the department before UGC help came. The Ford Foundation grant and the first major UGC grant that came when Madhuri Shah became the UGC chairperson (a fortuitous event for women's studies) placed us in a financially secure position.

RUWS moved to an independent place in the Juhu campus in 1982. Another big step towards autonomy was the separation of the accounts of the unit. By a resolution on 14 September 1982, it was stipulated that the Ford grant be transferred to the Juhu campus, and that detailed accounts and auditing would be done by the unit. Any new projects sanctioned from outside would be credited to the unit's account.

For half the sky?

In 1981, RUWS along with Dr Mazumdar of CWDS and Dr Hemlata Swarup, organised the first women's studies conference. This historic conference (hatched in conspiracy by Madhuri Shah, Vina Mazumdar and Neera Desai) gave birth to the Indian Association of Women's Studies. Out of the first two conferences grew the preparation of a women's studies directory—a 'who's who' which the RUWS compiled. Unfortunately this could not be updated.[20]

Those were the halcyon days when we had friendly femocrats aligning with women's studies people—C.P. Sujaya, Nirmala Buch and Padma Ramachandran to name a few, who were instrumental in pushing women's agenda within the government.

The women's movement gained impetus. In 1982 there was a conference of autonomous women's groups, which mooted the idea of a periodical, and Manushi arrived. Kali for Women, the feminist press followed. Books on women began to appear in quick succession—for instance, Vikas started Shakti as a branch. Devaki Jain mooted the Economists Interested in Women's Issues Group (EIWIG). CWDS was established. Women's groups became strong in all the states. SEWA (Self-Employed Women's Association), WWF (Working Women's Forum) and Annapurna Mahila Mandal became the premier institutions for women's empowerment. Thus, the scenario changed rapidly and even though women's studies was not a part of the general university system, women's issues attained visibility.

Spreading wings

Around this time, an ambitious proposal for an advanced centre with full facilities including a building, a guesthouse, funds for research and documentation and visiting faculty, was rejected by the UGC. The first major grant from the UGC to convert the unit into a full-fledged centre came only in 1984, more as an addition rather than as a beginning, as a recognition of the work of ten years.

When the UGC support for faculty posts ceased, the state would be requested to fill in (and most often obliged). The junior research fellowship was not continued but all other positions were taken up by the state government, thus ensuring continuity, thanks to the perseverance of the university vice-chancellor, Dr Jyoti Trivedi. Regional centres today, however, find it difficult to get the support of their state governments, and are cutting down on assistance in the changed political and economic situation.

In January 1986, the UGC chairperson, Dr Madhuri Shah sent the following communiqué.

> The Commission has agreed to the strengthening, consolidation and expansion of the programme of women's studies in Indian universities during the seventh plan. With this in view, the Commission has identified your university to play a leadership role in curriculum material, human resource development and research in the promotion of women's studies.

From being a unit, we had become a centre and now, a lead centre.

Climbing higher: 1982–91

The initial Ford Foundation grant was the first big opportunity to design our programmes the way we wanted to, and some real expansion occurred as a result. Our understanding of the women's movement, of women's issues and research priorities improved. In a perspective paper we wrote entitled 'Change and Challenge', we analysed the direction which women's studies ought to take, which, as it turned out, was quite prophetic.

There are many puzzles and contradictions in Indian women's positions, their perceptions and their struggles. There also appears to be 'a great divide' in the women's movement of pre-Independence era and post-independence era. What were the forces that impelled the earlier militancy and what have been the inhibiting forces that could explain the post-Independence inertia? Are these contradictions because of shifts in policies or did their seeds lie in the formulation of earlier struggles? For the last hundred years, great social, economic and political changes have taken place. Can we understand the contemporary situation of women and their growing journey to equality without this understanding?

In this, the role of significant institutional changes that have altered women's position and women's consciousness need study. The efforts of women themselves in mobilising support for change and initiating change are as important as the broad forces that operated in the larger society.

Three areas of study were identified—women's work in the 19th century, women's organisations, and women's education. The first study produced some useful material from factory reports, census and gazetteers but a consolidated analytical account did not emerge.

The second study was on four pioneer women's organisations that were set up 75 to 100 years ago. This did not result in a book, as it should have. The third was a study of the history of home science education in India. This too did not become a finished product suitable for publication. Part of our problem was paucity of senior academically trained persons in various disciplines. This lacuna stems from inadequate graduate training for independent thinking and good writing in our universities.

We also commissioned work on feminist concepts; many scholars and activists were invited to participate and the series, which became very popular, was developed through workshops and a series of discussions. There were three volumes. Volume 1 contained 'Patriarchy and Matriarchy' by Gail Omvedt, Volume 2 had 'Sexual Division of Labour' by Vidyut Bhagwat, 'Domestic Labour' by Chaya Datar and 'Production–Reproduction' by Gita Sen and Volume 3 had 'Sex and Gender', 'Concept of Status' and 'Notion of Power' by Maithreyi Krishnaraj.

Our link with other scholars and activists was strengthened through a small grant for research out of which 24 projects were completed, with many of them published as articles later. Those undertaking research were given guidance and seminars were held on their findings. An important piece of work which we commissioned was a study of landmark judgments on women's cases, later published as *In Search of Justice*.

A grant from the UNESCO enabled us to prepare a textbook for women's studies, *Women and Society in India*, which remains the only comprehensive introduction to women's issues and is still being used in all women's studies courses.[21] Other important source books that were brought out included a women's studies directory (which included activists), a bibliography on the Indian women's movement, abstracts of Ph.D theses from Bombay institutions, a directory of women's organisations and an index of journal articles. Translations were undertaken in Marathi and Gujarati, journals in these languages from the 19th century were scrutinised, and bibliographies and abstracts prepared. On the other hand, a South Asia collaboration to develop systematic documentation on women and development remained an ambition that was not realised.

The First Ford Foundation grant helped to expand the library by planned acquisitions of feminist journals, important Acts, policy documents and reference books, including a women's thesaurus from the National Council of Research on Women, New York in addition to the collections of seminar papers, conference papers etc. Our newspaper clippings files were widely used by many. We sent our working papers and other occasional papers to over 25 research organisations in the country and requested exchange of material. This helped in identifying who was doing what. A quarterly newsletter has been coming out since 1980. Financial support in the first few years came from the university, and the centre took over later as its resources improved.

Preparing women's studies teachers

Under the second Ford Foundation grant, more expansion took place and the accent was on staff training and holding workshops on methodology. It was supplemented by UGC funds for teacher orientation and distributing material.

Teacher orientation programmes in the form of winter institutes tried to spread the message of women's studies perspectives. The first one resulted in the book, *Women's Studies in India: Some Perspectives*. In that programme, giving the inaugural address, Dr Vina Mazumdar stated the three essential ingredients of women's studies as follows:

- Acceptance and recognition of Indian society as a plural society, so that we do not speak only of a particular class.
- Recognition that women must fight not only for their future but for the future of the society of which they are a part, which means women must be involved in all political, social, economic processes and at all levels.
- Research and policy ought to have a pro-women ideological commitment to change the position of women for the better.

During this workshop, the participants prepared course outlines for different disciplines. Speakers, narrating their own experience, brought to bear upon the deliberations an Indian context to feminist ideas and ideology.

Another winter institute was held in 1988. This was organised as a purely participatory exercise. We met regularly twice a week, a few months in advance, to discuss and clarify for ourselves how we understood women's studies and what we were going to do with the participants. The format was to engage in a self-development process. The workshop aimed to

- review trends in women's studies
- examine the contribution of women's studies
- evolve new perspectives and methodologies
- prepare suitable course outlines
- evolve teaching methods

- prepare guidelines for research, and
- incorporate all the above in a teacher's manual.

A teacher's manual entitled *Getting Started* emerged, followed by others such as *Contributions to Women's Studies, Planning Women's Studies, Evolving New Methodologies* and *Oral History*.

Research

'Motherhood' as a powerful ideology has always been problematic for women. Our team research on this topic with scholars from different disciplines—history, literature, anthropology and sociology—was an exciting adventure.

We studied the bias in academic disciplines, an area in which not much work has been done in India. We started with psychology and economics. The latter was published as *Gender in Economic Theory and Practice*. This examined the study and teaching of economics over a 100 years.

In psychology, the concepts of masculinity and femininity and how they were used were examined by meticulous search through 25 years of psychology journals. A manuscript was ready but its publication got stalled, joining 'lost' causes in the attic.

Front-runners

The centre also initiated projects on newly emerging issues. One was an all-India study in 1987 on employment and training status, and the future needs of women in software. This was a period when software had just begun to emerge as a major professional sector, many M.C.A. courses in universities as well as private institutions were coming up and women were trying these out. We sought a grant from the Department of Science and Technology. The findings were communicated to software trainers, women software engineers and the media. Women w e mostly in programming and went into teaching, rarely were they innovators or system analysts or hardware engineers. CSIR wanted to publish this research but I had retired and was away. Very recently the Asian Institute of Technology at Bangkok asked for a copy of this report as the only study available in this area.

We had premonitions of what was in store for us with liberalisation and globalisation when we undertook a study of the entry of MNCs in the food processing industry and its impact on women. A slum study under ICSSR–IDPAD demonstrated that for poor women, proximity of jobs from their habitats was critical and clearing of encroachments by municipal authorities destroys their livelihood. There were many bits and pieces. Increasingly, one felt the need for a selected focus that could over a period of time build expertise in that area. Except for the planned conceptual series, research tended to be dispersed—a fate enforced by funding requirement. A possible solution is for women's studies centres to mark out specific themes for themselves.

Sisterhood

Many new UGC centres had come up and in 1989 a workshop was held to chalk out a Five-Year Plan for all the centres. It was during this workshop that it was decided to launch a collaborative project on the girl child, a unique experiment with the participation of 22 centres and it was hoped that a regional profile as well as a national picture would emerge. Three workshops were organised by the SNDT centre to design the project, to orient the others on method and on questionnaires.

It was a creative and constructive collaboration with persons from various disciplines like literature, history, philosophy, psychology, education, and the social sciences. However, when we reached the final stages, the earlier expectations of a substantive national report supplemented by state reports, were not met. Interdisciplinary collaboration was not as easy as we assumed it would be.

Another such collaborative research in which we took part was with CWDS on a UN university project where from conceptualisation to conclusion, the project was carried out through discussions between all participants, Indian and Asian. The centre had two projects on the 'Women's Work and Family Strategies theme'; one on cane bamboo workers and another on education and caste dynamics in Gujarat. We had other collaborations with CWDS, as for instance, a study on migration and another on childcare services. We also established links with ISST and its pioneering work under Devaki Jain with regard to measurement of women's work. Another small project with ISST on vocational institutes for women revealed that, predictably enough, the courses for women were stereotypical.

Thus, till 1991 SNDT made continuous efforts at outreach, at spreading interest and expertise in women's studies at other institutions, and at stimulating collaboration, if not always successfully.

Working with communities

Other major developments during this phase were the growth, as mentioned before, of the earlier Udwada project into a rural development section. A full-time coordinator was appointed, separate staff was recruited and grants obtained from different agencies. A production-cum-training centre emerged as a successful women's co-operative, 'Kalyani', which has diversified into many product lines. Science and technology inputs to reduce drudgery and improve productivity, legal counselling cells, promoting health awareness through health camps, integrated development for adolescent girls focusing on health, literacy and vocational skills etc., added other dimensions. A special audio-visual educational resource centre called 'Mahiti' to empower rural women through education on social issues, providing library services for local schools and training facilitators to create a resource bank for the future is a new venture. Rural transformation through such grassroots community action has generated considerable leadership among women and some have even graduated to political appointments. The close links between rural women and the university have continued to flourish in mutually enriching ways.

The second big action research project (mentioned earlier), aimed to develop women's inputs in the Kharland reclamation project funded by the European Commission and operated through their technical consultant called Euro Consult. This expanded into several villages and went on for many years.

To sum up this long narrative, the years 1982–90 were a period of expansion, consolidation, intensification and diversification. The successes were our teacher-orientation courses and our research methodology workshops. Our ideas and understanding grew to create a basis for conceptualisation as in questions of how gender works, the structure of family-household and its dynamics, the role of caste in gender and why women were poor despite their shouldering major economic responsibility. Our fieldwork gave us a better sense of rural women's lives. Each project taught us something about our country and society much better than books could.

> The centre's faculty had a firm commitment to women and the women's movement, which was stronger than vying for prestige and favours from national and international bodies. Its mission was more to serve as an inspiration to women and provide resources, both intellectual and financial. Women's studies has a heavy burden to carry, a mission to fulfill because improving the status of women is not a partisan demand but action for nation building.[22]

Rather a lofty statement and whether we actually lived up to it and to what extent, can only be judged by other impartial evaluators and by posterity, but it was a philosophy that one believed in.

In our own backyard

Throughout the years 1974 to 1988, we kept trying to stimulate interest in women's studies in other departments. Only after 1985 did many departments such as economics, psychology, politics, and literature, especially the English department, begin introducing papers in their courses. The first to show interest was unexpectedly the Home Science College which formulated a course for B.A. students as an optional course. In its first year, our centre taught the course. They have since expanded the course with our help. The PG department of sociology sought our help to revise their syllabus. We were invited as guest lecturers. However, the incorporation of women's studies across faculties was uneven and ad hoc, depending very much on the inclination of the head of the department. Only when women's studies achieved some credibility and visibility outside the university did other departments show some interest.

Kamalini Bhansali as VC asked us to organise a meeting with the heads of faculties and principals of affiliated colleges in September 1989. Thirty-five of them attended and reported on what they had done. Dr Sundaram of the Economics department confessed that it had been a one-way traffic—they took help from the centre but offered nothing in return. It was agreed that women's studies did not develop within the other university departments with a common thrust; individual departments went their own way. There was need for integration and restructuring the M.A. and M.Phil programmes in a systematic way such that women's studies would find a place in them. RCWS could help with material and guidance but the initiative had to come from other departments. A useful suggestion that Kamalini Bhansali made was that Ph.D guides in various disciplines should encourage students to take up research on some critical areas identified by the centre, so that over a period of time some good research would emerge giving theoretical insights or providing good empirical material. The centre helped the university bring out a small brochure on women's studies in the university called 'A new kind of academics, a new kind of action' which gave details of women's studies inputs in different departments. However, the process has been uneven and very fragmentary.

In retrospect

On the positive side, RUWS (and later the RCWS) was a place of growth for all of us, including the director, professionally both in terms of increased understanding of women's concerns and related theory, as well as in terms of more material rewards in the job hierarchy. There was visibility through conferences, seminars, consultations and appointments with important committees. In some ways this easy success also gave some members a false sense of accomplishment, not having faced the challenges of competition. Attempts to widen the discipline base of the staff of the centre did not succeed.

Our major failure lay in our inability, despite great efforts, to cement inter-institutional links that could have enriched women's studies in India. Ultimately, the fault lies perhaps in the circumstances that direct the way our institutions run, the training that academics are given and the notions of governance that form the background to institution-building.

The failure of our aspiration to evolve into an advanced centre of national standing was our second major failure. Though very serious thought had been given to the restructuring of faculties into separate schools in order to promote inter-disciplinary studies, it did not work because it would have necessitated drastic modifications in the university constitution.

We also failed in relation to staff-training. Not only were we unable to widen the discipline base of the staff, but we also mistakenly assumed that simply because they had been with us for long, they had all absorbed some of the ideals which guided the unit and had grasped the conceptual issues. In reality, not all of them lived up to these expectations. It appears on balance now that persons exposed exclusively to women's studies may develop sensitivity to issues, and pick up its language and rhetoric, but somehow lack the foundation of intellectual discipline that comes from grounding in a parent discipline and exposure to readings in other areas that are linked with mainstream developments. We find that the best research and contributions to women's studies have come from women scholars who work in their own discipline but bring to bear on women's issues the capacity for analysis. In future courses (diploma or graduate) on women's studies it may be made mandatory to take basic courses in social and political philosophies, basic economics and social science theories.

A new wind blows in

The closing years of the century

There is a predictable pattern in regime change and RCWS was no exception to the rule. A new vice-chancellor, a new director for the centre, a new advisory committee, and the experience of the period 1974–90, which benefited from the continuity of inception and initiators, brought in new winds of change.

The activist research mode, the partnership with the women's movement and the feminist underpinnings became muted. Earlier approaches such as student activities and the open house encouragement for students and faculty members from other departments and the Juhu campus to drop by for discussions or to invite us for lectures, including referencing in the library were discontinued after 1991. Other activities that were discontinued were an award for outstanding work done for the promotion of women's equality by any staff member or student *outside their line of duty*. During this phase, 1991–1999, work continued, but a broad-based strategic plan for the centre's development did not evolve. The scheme of visiting-fellows, under the Ford Foundation Grant was not taken up, rapport with women's organisations was not sustained and inter-departmental and inter-university cooperation suffered. The accent seems to have been on individual research, based on individual interest. The *effort to build on what existed* was missing.

On the other hand, more emphasis was placed on teaching, in the rest of the university. In the early years of RCWS, not much scope had existed for teaching; besides the founders had thought of RCWS more as a nodal point which would energise other faculties rather than as a teaching faculty. The emphasis on the teaching element seemed a timely move since the climate was right for it. A foundation course on women's studies was introduced for all undergraduates of the university. Hitherto, only some faculties had partial papers on women's issues in some disciplines and only sociology had a full paper. RCWS was invited to prepare the foundation course and we attempted an innovative course that would move away from didactic approaches. RCWS staff also prepared a Teachers' guide where a section brought together the history of women's struggle for rights by reproducing original texts like the Declaration of Women's Rights at Seneca Falls, the Charlotte Perkins Declaration of Women's Rights, and the Indian Women's Declaration of Women's Rights under Hansa Mehta. As part of orienting students to women's situation in India, the VC initiated a new kind of student's calendar with statistics and statements on women so that every student would be exposed to some basic facts. Lectures on Law were made available as booklets and brochures on themes related to two titles, *Gender Series* and *Women in the Public Gaze* and the Directory of Women's Organisations was updated.

A third Ford Foundation grant had been obtained in 1990. This particular grant envisaged building academic expertise and preparing teachers, in addition to continuing research thrusts and networking. The plan sought the improvement of women's studies as a discipline, to carry on gender critiques of other disciplines and to organise focused workshops for these.

The new director undertook *A Source Book on Women in Maharashtra*, to present analytical documentation from Censuses 1901–91 and other sources for all the districts, in collaboration with the national and regional census office. It was a very good idea but should have been organised as a team project involving other scholars from within the university and there could have been a special advisory committee to advise and monitor the progress. Periodic interim reports could have been brought out, with open discussions with experts. This would have reduced the burden on the director and the delay in the completion of the report might have been avoided.

There were some other research projects, commissioned by agencies, but no planned research programme to give a direction to the work of RCWS. A comparative chapter on Korea was added to the UNESCO country profile of violence (which was earlier completed as a collective project with activists). ESCAP commissioned a study on women executives but the report has not been publicised sufficiently.

Presently, RCWS has completed a very good study 'Responses to domestic violence in the states of Gujarat and Karnataka', sponsored by the International Centre for Research on Women, Washington DC.

Could the centre have run solely on its earlier momentum without reinvigoration? The problem of transition has to be faced by all women's studies centres. Some may be lucky in a smoother transition. Who is to succeed the first generation? How do we locate scholars who have not just their heads in women's studies, but also their hearts? Perhaps this is an unrealistic expectation. In any case, the climate has changed. The very success of the women's studies movement is also proving to be its bane. As long as it had no visibility or offered no perks, few established scholars bothered to enter it. Now we are going to face a situation where women's studies is seen as a career. This indicates the risks inherent in institutionalisation. Obtaining academic credibility sucks us into academic conventionality. Women's studies has as of now not been able to change academic culture in a manner radical enough to accommodate an alternate vision of knowledge. If women's studies remains small within universities it has the comfort of autonomy and the safety of a sheltered presence but also suffers from the penalty of being excluded from the mainstream, intrusion into which is the ultimate aim of women's studies.

The confusion and sudden changes of direction that appeared after the first generation of pioneers moved on, raises a number of larger issues, not restricted to either this one institution or set of people. The fruits of the bitter struggles waged by earlier feminists, when inherited by younger women, are not perceived as precious but taken for granted and the danger is that by default the opportunity to guard it is often lost. A second problem is that when new scholars, who have no links with the movement, enter the movement after it is established, there develops a disjuncture between women's studies and the women's movement. The danger of this is that women's studies becomes another 'area' of academic study, often esoteric, highly intellectualized and without a direct link to the burning issues of the day.

The above observations are meant to trigger reflection on the importance of wise leadership in the context of human institutions; how a departure from the basic direction in the absence of a clear alternative vision can erode the foundation of institutions. Building institutions demands other qualities in addition to scholarship. On the other hand, founding leaders are also required to recruit co-workers wisely. When we were growing, not enough attention was given to this and to a certain extent, the lack of a second line of leadership to guide new HoDs was an inhibitory factor. Which is also why, at a time of crisis, the staff expressed personal anguish at the change in management style rather than in RCWS' loss of direction.

There needs to be serious reflection on how, once an institution reaches maturity and the founders are gone, its ethos is to be sustained. The rigid rule of retirement, regardless of the needs of the time or prevailing conditions in particular cases, is a great drawback. In situations where continuity is deemed essential there should be provisions at least for a few temporary, honorary appointments. The variation between states is another hurdle. While central universities automatically grant extension till the age of sixty-five, states abide very strictly by the retirement-at-sixty rule and are unwilling to extend tenure even by a day. In those cases where the institutions' welfare is at stake, perhaps the UGC could make some provision for retaining seniors whose leadership is beyond doubt.

The future: A new perspective

The SNDT centre enjoyed the many advantages of being a pioneer; it also suffered from the corresponding disadvantages. Newcomers can avoid mistakes. Pioneers are often inhibited by old habits.

The third director having retired recently, the future of the centre is in the hands of new incumbents. The changed role of the centre in the new scenario with so many centres already functioning poses a big question. Perhaps a consultation like the one we held in 1988, including all UGC and non-UGC centres may be useful to chart out a future course. The centres must attract talent as well as retain it.

We can end this on a note of hope. The political situation in the country being as unstable as it is now, the centres may have to opt for more self-help, more cooperative work and more sharing.

Do I wish that things had been done differently? It is impossible to say. One now has a certain sense of humility that whatever success one achieved owed considerably to the times in which one lived and the location of the centre. Filled with enthusiasm for this new field, I was always on the move and had little time to consolidate my knowledge or synthesise my ideas. What was my own original and unique contribution to the knowledge base? Should there be regret? There will be others who will follow, others for whom the path has been made easier. That is reason enough to feel exhilarated.

I would like to end with what my friend C.S. Lakshmi has put in her inimitable and beautiful style:

> We have worked together and separately, disagreeing on many issues. We have felt victorious at times and at times utterly beaten. Often we felt estranged from one another, separating ourselves as academics and activists. The political atmosphere and the nature of women's participation in politics have also taught us that just because we have the same bodies we need not have the same thoughts. In this process of discovery some of us have become tired and disillusioned and some of us have opted out. Some of us have become lonely and have retreated into a shell of non-communication. Most of all we have realised that we have a lot to be humble about for we have recognized the demons within us— demons of jealousy, competition, arrogance, pride and hatred— just as we have learnt to celebrate our sisterhood and love.[23]

Appendix

It is not feasible to give a whole list of publications which the RCWS produced over 25 years. I give below only a few major works.

Neera Desai (1976), *Women in India: A Select Bibliography*, Delhi: Allied Publishers.

Malshe S.G. and N. Apte (1978), *Widow Remarriage Movement (1800–1900)*, Mumbai: RCWS.

Maithreyi Krishnaraj (ed.) (1986), *Women's Studies in India*, Bombay: Popular Prakashan.

Neera Desai and Maithreyi Krishnaraj (1987), *Women and Society in India*, Delhi: Ajanta.

Neera Desai (ed.) (1988), *A Decade of the Women's Movement in India*, Bombay: Himalaya.

Vimal Balasubramanium (1988), *In Search of Justice*, Pune: Shubda.

Malini Karkal and Divya Pandey (1989), *Studies on Women and Population: A Critique*, Bombay: Himalaya.

Divya Pandey and Meera Savara (eds.) (1990), *Between the Farm and Thali: Women and Food Processing*, Mumbai: RCWS.

Maithreyi Krishnaraj (1991), *Women and Science: Selected Essays*, Bombay: Himalaya.

Ramala Baxamusa (1992), *Assistance for Women's Development from National Agencies: A User's Guide* (3 vols), Bombay: Popular Prakashan.

S.P. Sathe (1993), *Towards Gender Justice*, Mumbai: RCWS.

Meera Kosambi (1997), *At the Intersection of Gender Reform and Religious Belief*, Mumbai: RCWS.

Veena Poonacha (1997), *Women's Rights as Human Rights*, Mumbai: RCWS.

Notes and References

1. I am grateful to the Director of the Research Centre for Women's Studies, SNDT, Meera Kosambi for giving me access to material and especially thankful to Jyotsna Sanjanwala who dug out papers from the attic. I thank Dr Veena Poonacha for material relating to the post-1991 years and Dr Harsha Parekh for giving me access to the archives section of the university library. I thank numerous others who shared their views, trepidations and hopes. Most of all, for whatever I have learnt, I owe a deep debt of gratitude to many mentors whose commitment to women's advancement was complete.

2. I am grateful to Dr Neera Desai for her valuable comments and corrections on the draft of this narrative.

3. While everyone spoke of how education was needed so that women could help others, no one spoke of how education should give women their rights as individuals.

4. A woman citizen's role was derivatory, as it was derived from being a good mother.

5. See Sulabha Panandikar, Neera Desai and Kamalini Bhansali (eds.) (1975), 'Report of the Round Table Discussion'.
6. Ibid., p. 34.
7. Golden Jubilee Commemoration Volume, (1966), p. 39.
8. Having done her M.A. thesis on the status of women in India, Dr Neera Desai was in a sense the first women's studies scholar.
9. While SNDT has won acclaim outside Bombay, within the city, the popular image of the women's university as 'for Manibens' meaning conservative, home-bound Gujarati women, is still prevalent. There is a general notion that it teaches cooking, washing and homekeeping and is unintellectual.
10. SNDT graduates have excelled in sports, National Cadet Corps activities and in many professional courses.
11. The university has a range of technical and professional courses, including pharmacy, analytical chemistry, computer science, management studies, human resource development, polytechnic, nursing, education and library science.
12. See Sulabha Panandikar, Neera Desai and Kamalini Bhansali (eds.) (1975), 'Report of the Round Table Discussion'.
13. Even after 25 years it is pertinent to note that Bombay University has not become hospitable to women's studies—it is left to their sociology department. Legitimacy is accorded, not in the form of acceptance of women's studies as a serious academic venture but in the form of the acceptance that women's issues exist and that a women's university could deal with it. Even today, students who are motivated to take up a serious examination of any women's issue are told to go to the women's university.
14. Recently, this was corroborated by Nirmala Banerjee.
15. It was a few years later that CWDS launched the first women's studies journal in India, *Samya Shakti*.
16. This was a style begun by Lady Thakersey who had a broad humanistic outlook, but who, lacking enough academic expertise, called upon her staff to help and treated their advice with respect.
17. It was in 1963 that I had read Simone de Beauvoir's *Second Sex* and Betty Friedan's *The Feminine Mystique* for the first time.
18. There are Hindi-medium colleges attached to the university but these are very few and were later additions.
19. Therefore it supposedly has nothing to do with the intellect or academics!
20. Padmavati University, Tirupati is currently compiling a similar directory.
21. However, this has become outdated and a revised, updated version is necessary.
22. Maithreyi Krishnaraj in an interview in 1991.
23. See C.S. Lakshmi (1999), 'An Awakening Song for Roshni' in BEAM, Vol. 18.

3

From cycle shed to powerhouse

Centre for Women's Studies and Development, Panjab University

Pam Rajput

To be a humanist one has to be a feminist.

Recalling the past and visualising the future is a Herculean task; it becomes even more formidable when one is attempting to retrace the path and envisage the future of an institution. An institution's genesis, its progression from a mere idea to a reality and then the establishment of its presence, the many ups and downs—all these depend upon a congruence of factors. These factors exist in symbiosis with internal and external pressures, of personalities and of ideology, which combine to make the task even more complex. In my attempt to recount the story of the Centre for Women's Studies and Development from its birth through maturity, the pleasures and pains of its being and becoming, I shall not merely enumerate the centre's activities, but carefully chart out its figurative and literal transformation from a 'cycle shed' to a 'powerhouse'.

The setting

It would be appropriate to articulate the locational and socio-cultural setting in order to get an idea of the context in which the centre had its genesis. Punjab, 'the land of five rivers,' is, due to its rich history, a culturally multi-nuanced society. What we see today is a veritable cocktail of tradition and modernity. One notes the ageless winding rivers and green fields, listens to the peals of temple bells, the *azaan* of mosques and *ardaas* from Gurudwaras, all reminders of at least six millennia of history. Industrial townships symbolise modernisation and the 21st century. Punjabi culture, economy and politics have been influenced by the legacy of the ancient Indus valley civilisation, the arrival of various tribal people from Eurasia and by the spiritually charged Sufi and Bhakti movements. Punjab has felt the deleterious effects of the British Raj; the hope inherent in the constitutional promises of independent India, and of late, the tension integral to the forces of globalisation. Punjab has attracted travellers, traders and invaders for millennia; some settled here to infuse their culture into Punjab's, while others pillaged it to leave it that much poorer. Through it all, Punjab retained the dynamism to respond to changing times. What has resulted is a hybridisation of its society and culture, making Punjab an inclusive society.

A watershed in Punjab's history was the advent of Sikhism in the 15th century. Primarily a socio-religious reform movement, Sikhism, the majority religion of the region, accords equality to women and men; approximately five centuries ago, it was a radical idea in the Indian cultural landscape.[1] However, it retained a contradiction in that it neither discarded nor challenged the patriarchal structure of values. Another powerful religio-intellectual movement was the Arya Samaj movement, the most profound effects of which were in the field of education for women. It questioned the premises of contemporary Brahminical Hinduism that denied women access to education. Additionally, from the mid-19th century onwards, Muslim women were also able to access education in institutions other than madrasas; obviously, this posed a direct challenge to the authority of the ulema.

Politically, after a successful rule by Maharaja Ranjit Singh, which gave the state its clear-cut geographical boundaries and a distinctive culture, Punjab was annexed in 1849 when it became a part of British India. Notably, it was Lahore, the capital of pre-Partition Punjab, that had the honour of being the city where the Complete Independence Resolution was passed. Ironically, Punjab and its people paid a heavy price for Partition in 1947. Its people were uprooted and its lands divided by the awkward Radcliffe line. Almost 10 million people lost their 'home and land'; a million lost their lives in the accompanying communal holocaust and women were unashamedly sacrificed at the male altar of family honour and revenge. After Independence, Punjab, which once extended from Delhi to Peshawar, was once again trimmed and divided to emerge in its present form in 1966. Given the complicated history of their land, Punjabis have had to be resilient and unconventional in their approach. An enterprising people, they have transformed arid wastelands into fertile fields. The Green Revolution of the 1960s made Punjab one of the most developed states in terms of agricultural development, with the highest per capita income and the lowest percentage of population living below the poverty line in the country. While the above may be seen as the common historical trajectory of the entire Punjabi populace, it is also true that the women in Punjab were affected by these events in ways that are singularly different from those of men.

It should come as no surprise that Punjabi women have distinguished themselves and contributed to Punjab's advancement in various fields, from the wheat fields to the dairy farms, from the artist's studio to the royal courts, from the halls of academia to the arena of decision-making. Mention ought to be made of Mata Sundari, Guru Gobind Singh's widow, who successfully guided the Sikhs for 40 years; of Rani Sada Kaur, Maharaja Ranjit Singh's mother-in-law; of Rani Jinda, and Rani Sahib Kaur and Rani Fateh Kaur, all of whom played important roles in Sikh history. The fearless Punjabi women were not lagging behind during the national movement. Some outstanding freedom fighters from Punjab are Rajkumari Amrit Kaur, Gulab Kaur, Adarsh Kumari, Kishan Kaur, Amar Kaur, Dalip Kaur, Sushila Devi, Har Devi, Purani and Pushpa Gujral.[2] Punjabi women have written beautiful poetry as evidenced by Amrita Pritam's moving lyrics[3], produced woman-centred art as in Amrita Sher-gil's paintings and radically altered the male-dominated bureaucratic services of India.[4]

Conversely, there is another side to this historically progressive social scenario—there co-exists a carefully fortressed patriarchal and feudal society where women are treated as inferior beings, where customs such as female infanticide, child marriage, purdah and the like were, and are, widely prevalent. Popular culture reflects as much as it reinforces unequal gender perceptions and realities. It encourages son-preference, diminishes the value of the girl child, objectifies women and celebrates women oppressing women. Keeping in mind their vast popularity and unquestioned acceptance, consider these examples: *Gudh khaain puni kattee/Aap jaayeen bhra nu ghallee* (Eat molasses, spin your skein/You depart, send a brother); *Jadh ghar jammaya put veh babula/ Hun daaru di rut veh babula/Jadh ghar jammee dhee veh babula/Sochi peh gayee jee veh babula* (It is time to celebrate when a son is born in the house/It is time to be concerned when a daughter is born); *Andhar bhethi lakh di/Bahar gayee kakh di* (A woman who stays indoors is worth lakhs/Who wanders about is worth a straw) and *Teri maa ne rinnian saag weh/Assa mangyan te ditta jawaab weh* (Your mother [the husband's mother] cooked spinach/When I asked for some, all I got was her caustic tongue).

Clearly, patriarchy is entrenched in the social set-up and is manifested in the current discriminatory pattern of gender relations. The very low sex ratio of 874 women to 1,000 men (it was 882 in the 1991 Census) and the lowest female workforce participation rate[5], underlines the heightened discrimination against women. Female foeticide (notwithstanding the legal ban on sex determination tests), neglect of the female child, violence against women, dowry deaths, a wide gap in literacy rates, low utilisation of health services, and restricted property rights are some of the major aspects of the prevailing gender inequities in Punjab. It is worth mentioning that seven out of the ten districts in India with the lowest child sex ratio are in Punjab.[6] Additionally, given the agricultural culture of Punjab, ownership of land plays an important role in discrimination against women. There is strong opposition to women's right to inherit land as stipulated in the Hindu Succession Act and there have been attempts to get the Act amended to curtail their property rights.

The most extreme expression of male chauvinism is evident in the violence directed against women. The first such occasion in the 20th century was during the Partition of British India. Patriarchy affirmed its existence during the accompanying holocaust. Women became the trope for nation—its defenders and its violators were hailed as heroes.[7] Thousands of women were raped, killed, mutilated, abducted and even traded in exchange for 'freedom'. Women were either killed, (not only by 'others' but also by their own kith and kin to save the family's honour), or they killed themselves. The name of the village Thao Khalsa where more than 80 women jumped into a well still sends shivers down one's spine.[8] The horrors of Partition were barely moving into the recesses of memory when Punjab was shaken by renewed bloodshed. A decade-long phase of militancy, yet another expression of male chauvinism and patriarchal control, commenced in the early 1980s. Militants ran a parallel government and felt powerful enough to dictate dress codes and social norms. Again, women became the worst victims of militancy. Punjabi women bore the double burden of being Punjabis and of being women. Violence against women was unleashed by curtailing their power to choose. It was reinforced when women were victimised by the militants *and* by the state. It was a time of fear, of subdued voices, and of silences that spoke volumes; fundamentalism and militancy were at their peak. Only recently has Punjab begun to emerge from the shadow of the gun. The environment of Punjab constituted a challenge to the women's movement. It was in these difficult times that we dared to host the Third National Conference of Indian Association of Women's Studies (IAWS). It was this event that marked the advent of the Centre for Women's Studies and Development (henceforth CWSD).

The genesis

It is an incontrovertible fact that prior to the formal establishment of any institution, there has to be a motivating philosophy or ideological persuasions. In the case of CWSD, it was a principled commitment to social justice, particularly for women, that started my professional journey towards the establishment of the centre. As a student, I was an activist, not a feminist, but as a young lecturer my political evolution towards feminism grew apace. Consciousness builds up slowly, even imperceptibly. My initiation into the women's movement was with the declaration of the International Women's Year, later Women's Decade. It grew with extensive reading, social activism and formal institutional alliances. Furthermore, as a member of the International Political Science Association (IPSA) and Chair of its Research Committee on Women, Politics and Developing Nations, a phase of internationalisation of the context of the women's movement/s was inaugurated in my journey. The correlation between gender and development repeatedly came home to me. For me, with this consciousness came the marriage of academia and activism. Academics has not accepted activists comfortably. This fact itself was a challenge to be overcome. To do so I had to begin somewhere—that somewhere was to begin an organised lobbying for the establishment of an unit for women's studies.[9] Impetus for this came from the Second National Conference on Women's Studies which I attended in Trivandrum in 1984. By a stroke of luck, the vice-chancellor at the time was gender-sensitive and he supported the idea.

The unit for women's studies was founded in 1986. It was imperative that the issues faced by women were made visible. Some of these issues were economic equity, domestic violence, state violence, the right to choose, the right to inherit, the right to education and the right to political participation, to name only a few. It was equally imperative that there be some systematic way of highlighting these issues because the ultimate goal was to conscientise the community so that there was some motivation to effect change. I was perfectly aware that there would be impediments to any attempts at institutionalising efforts at systemic change but I was also motivated by the belief that causes are bigger than people and bureaucracies, and that social justice is a cause that has its own strength and potency.

Almost immediately there was a debate over which department would house the unit. I strongly advocated for its autonomous status so that it could remain honest to its purpose and fulfil its mandate. My advocacy was successful and the unit began to operate as an independent entity in 1986. Official support from the university included one old typewriter, a fellowship of Rs 600 for six months and a Rs 5,000 contingency grant. We retain the old defunct typewriter as a symbol and reminder of our slender beginnings! Logistically, the unit may have been poor, but it was rich with hope, commitment and dedication. I moved ahead with vigour, believing in what I was doing and certain that opportunities would present themselves if I was patient. The first major task of this unit was to host and organise the Third National Conference of the Indian Association of Women's Studies (IAWS) in Chandigarh. Undeterred by the lack of infrastructural support and resources, we persisted in our task. I counted on the support of some of my colleagues and a few students. After that there was no looking back.

As mentioned earlier, at the time of the IAWS conference, the atmosphere in Punjab was one of militancy, fear, state repression, victimisation of women, participation of young men in this chauvinistic endeavour, acute unrest and unease. The theme of the conference, 'Women, Struggles and Movements', directly challenged the deplorable condition in which militancy had placed the daughters of Punjab. True to the spirit of womanhood, it was in the worst of times that we questioned the authority of the patriarchal expressions of control and hegemony. The courageous participation of 536 women made the conference a resounding success. For four days, the university reverberated with discussions on the various sub-themes of the conference. During the conference, an incident imprinted itself on my mind. The students, who ungrudgingly worked for the conference, however, demonstrated that their perceptions of feminism and feminists left much to be desired. The caricatures which they drew of some of the delegates were revealing—the frivolity reflected the assumptions and general unfamiliarity of the young generation about feminists and what they represented. My resolve to have a centre for women's studies was further strengthened.

Around the same time, the University Grants Commission (UGC) invited proposals from the universities to establish centres for women's studies.[10] Panjab University seized the opportunity and constituted a committee, of which I was a member, which was to make a proposal for the establishment of a women's studies centre. In retrospect, writing the proposal was not particularly difficult; what presented itself as hard work was pursuing that proposal so that it was not filed away on a shelf in some office. The doggedness paid off and when seven universities were selected to establish women's studies centres by the UGC, Panjab University's name was on that list. Furthermore, it was specially identified to play a leadership role in the region.

Now it was time to give the centre its physical and ideological contours. The ambition was to make it a model centre. The fledgling centre had no research staff and only one support staff, but work had to continue. I managed to rope in my research scholars whose personal loyalty to me was evinced in the work they did for the centre. Soon two Junior Research Fellows and eventually a Research Officer were employed, all of whom assisted me in putting the centre on its feet. Lack of a permanent and trained research staff was a major hitch in our journey. Many birth pangs and teething problems notwithstanding, the centre commenced its pioneering work from my room!

Next came the task of finding a physical space on the university campus that would house the centre and proclaim its presence amidst all other departments and faculties. We found ourselves being stymied at every step of the way. With a firm belief in self-reliance, we found a deserted bicycle shed—it would have to suffice. Years of goodwill and relationships came to the aid of the centre in making the space functional. We had to empty the shed of cycle support-stands and cleared the walls of vulgar graffiti before the place was usable. The walls still had *jharokas* or lattices that provided modern air-conditioning with hot air in the summers and cold air in the winters! However, we romanticised the not-so-perfect environment by quoting Gandhi, 'I do not want my house to be walled in on all sides and my windows to be closed. Instead, I want the cultures of all lands to be blown about my house as freely as possible. But I refuse to be blown off my feet by any.' While Gandhi gave us moral support, the inside of the cycle shed was furnished with furniture borrowed from other departments. We then had a proud sign painted outside that claimed that the erstwhile cycle shed was now the 'Centre for Women's Studies and Development.'

From visibility to acceptability

While the centre was now visible on the university campus, mere visibility was not enough. As its founder I could not be satisfied until there was wider acceptance of the centre, its efforts, and its foundational principles. The philosophical underpinnings of the centre were clearly stated as thus, to critique and question the existing social order through research and interrogation, to vocalise dedication to 'action' and to advocate for change. The prizes we were striving for were to change the way people in academia think, to equip young women and men with progressive ideas causing them to be sensitive to women's issues, to involve my colleagues in re-visioning their world-view, and to be a resource centre for women at the grass-roots level in the region. After all, as Michel Foucault said, 'Knowledge is power'.

None of this would be possible unless there was a self-conscious attempt to build an environment that was conducive to women's studies. There were expressed and unexpressed professional jealousies and academic conservatism. These explicit and implied challenges are not peculiar to Panjab University or the centre. There was incessant questioning, 'why women's studies?' 'why a separate centre for women's studies?' Someone quipped, 'Now we need a centre for men's studies.' Therefore, one of the conscious strategies was and has been to include male colleagues in the activities of the centre, such as seminars, training programmes, refresher courses or committees. They were made equal partners in all the work since we believed that it is by engagement in women's activities that men can be changed. From the earlier token involvement, several of them came to be actively interested in the work of the centre. There was an obvious shift from alienation to partnership to actual alliance with the centre. This alteration in attitude is a clear indication of the increasing acceptance of the centre and its agenda. The centre had established an identity.

Apart from its given mandate of research, training, extension and curricula development, the centre has also pursued a conscious and sustained effort to provide linkages between research, teaching and development activities. In order to provide the links, the centre is engaged in conducting action-oriented research which is socially relevant to the region, and in providing consultancy services. We were also organi-sing training and extension activities to empower women and to sensi-tise various strata of society as well as development functionaries to women's issues. Helping to develop close linkages between academics and activists is also one of our priorities.

Research

Research supports the claims for focusing on the special needs of women, illustrating as it does the reality of women's lives. Ergo, research is one of the core activities of the centre. It has conducted both theoretical and applied research and the scale of the research has been both major and minor. The first national study in which the centre took part was 'The Girl-Child and Family in Punjab and Chandigarh'. Keeping in mind the importance of direct political participation as essential in changing women's lives, the centre also participated in a national study on select constituencies from where women had contested for elections in 1996. We studied Ludhiana from where the wife of the assassinated Chief Minister of Punjab was contesting elections. The centre was also part of a committee constituted by the UGC–Commonwealth Project on Women in Higher Education Management. As part of the team, the centre collected data on women at management levels in institutions of higher learning. Some of the projects that have had an impact on policymaking are 'Credit Facility for Women: Availability,

Accessibility and Utilisation' and 'Situational Analysis of the Girl-Child in Punjab'. Two of the major evaluation studies that come to mind are 'Dairy Farming in Haryana under the STEP Programme' and 'A Study Of Awareness Generation Projects for Rural and Poor Women in the States of Punjab, Himachal Pradesh, and Jammu and Kashmir'.[11] Some of the other research projects that deserve a mention here include 'MNCs and Women: A Case-Study of PepsiCo', 'Women Milk Producers' Co-operative Societies', 'Women and Protest Movements' and 'Land Reforms and Their Impact on Women in Haryana'.

Once the centre initiated research on this scale, other departments followed suit. Now most of the social science and humanities departments are conducting research on gender-related topics. The centre has also initiated a Ph.D programme. In the absence of a Research Degree Committee, which precluded the registration of candidates in the discipline of women's studies, we resorted to an indirect methodology. An interdisciplinary approach is adopted and scholars from other disciplines interested in pursuing research in women's studies are encouraged to enrol in their parent discipline with co-supervision provided by the centre. The centre has a compilation of the research being done which demonstrates an increasing interest in feminist issues in Panjab University.

In the late 1980s and early 1990s, when some of the most significant research studies were carried out (for example, the situational analysis and the evaluation studies mentioned above), Punjab's atmosphere was not conducive to research of any sort. Conducting research was a daunting task. The challenges were enormous: militancy was at its peak, the roads were deserted after 5:30 p.m., public transportation vehicles were made special targets of militant attacks and travel was extremely dangerous. Our own limitations in transport and boarding arrangements compounded the external pressures. However, to the credit of our research team, they were fearless in their endeavours. Moreover, a prominent concern was about getting to the border and interior areas of Amritsar, Gurdaspur and Ferozepur that were the worst affected by militancy. Fortunately, the researchers missed the 'encounters' between the police and the militants by a hair's breadth. A third level of anxiety involved interaction with the villagers; before we knew it there was a bigger problem awaiting us. Finding admittance and acceptance in a Punjab village was at best difficult for a stranger. To get the villagers to accept you and respond adequately was even more challenging! Women were afraid to respond, as they feared repercussions at the hands of militants. For instance, the militants had forbidden intake of alcohol, so no woman was willing to admit that her husband consumed liquor. Again, in such complicated times, the content of the questionnaire could often lead to arguments and the respondents had to be pacified.

Pedagogy

The centre has had a great deal of success in first re-visioning and then facilitating the revision of the curricula in Panjab University to make it gender-sensitive. It sought to imbue feminist consciousness in various disciplines using the 'sprinkler approach'. The 'sprinkler approach' operates as a useful strategy for realising the aim and purpose of the centre's existence, which is to change those socio-cultural assumptions of our society that damage women. We believe that it is not sufficient to institute one course in departmental syllabi which exclusively address-es issues germane to women. It will have a limited impact; more than likely the professor will end up preaching to the converted. The centre strategised that while the converted ought to be encouraged there is no harm in recruiting more members into it. The 'sprinkler approach' makes inroads into already existing syllabi by insisting that every course have a component in it that addresses women's issues. The underlying hope is that as courses are being conceptualised and taught, there will be a conscious move to eliminate the invisibility of women from these courses (which is very different from providing visibility, which is a more passive act). Second, this approach encourages critiques of the established socio-economic normative; it happens as a consequence of inclusion of women's issues into the course work. Of course, the final outcome that the centre hopes for is to change the perceptions of women and men, students and colleagues. After all, the strategy's purpose is to conscientise the entire community in order to create a new culture of gender equity.

While the centre is on the threshold of teaching formally and granting degrees, its persistent advocacy for incorporation of women's issues in the existing curricula has paid dividends. Several departments such as history, sociology, political science, public administration, psychology, economics, Gandhian studies, and law have introduced changes in the syllabi at both the undergraduate and postgraduate levels.

We have attempted to be innovative in our pedagogical approach. The centre offers non-formal courses, like a 10-day certificate course on women and law and another on women and development. We also conduct weekend schools for housewives and rural women. We provide orientation for teachers through the programmes of the Academic Staff College in order to sensitise faculty members to women's studies. The centre has been assigned the position of academic nodal centre for the region.

Offering refresher courses is one of the most viable efforts, resulting in die-hard supporters for the centre. When the centre decided to offer refresher courses, we used the nomenclature 'gender studies'; the point was to not alienate those who form an automatic defensiveness to the word feminism but instead to bring them into the fold and then introduce them to women's studies in particular. The centre has held two such courses. These attracted a large number of applicants from various disciplines. We had to screen applicants in order to keep the numbers manageable. Significantly, a large number of the applicants were male.

Apart from the fact that the courses were widely appreciated, what is remarkable is that the participants wished to continue their association with the centre and so formed a group called Gender Watch. This group continues to meet periodically even now. A caveat necessary here is that there were a few people who had never heard of gender studies; they had come to attend a refresher course on general studies! By the end of three weeks most of them were converts. It is imperative that in order to provide acceptability and legitimacy to women's studies, people who are clueless about gender issues/women's issues ought to be strategically identified for re-education.[12]

Workshops and seminars

Strategically, in order to keep the centre in the news, to provide a forum for discussion and discourse on women's issues and to build a larger network of academics both from within and from outside, particularly from the universities of the region, a number of workshops and seminars have been organised by the centre.

The centre has held seminars on various topical themes, including policy, human rights issues, reproductive rights, globalisation and women and democratisation and women.[13] The centre organised a memorable National Convention of Women Freedom Fighters, the first of its kind. The enthusiasm of these frail old women, who came from the furthest corners of the country (one stated that she had to come without telling her family as they did not permit her to make such a long journey!) was incredibly moving and inspiring. It was for the first time that women freedom fighters from all nooks and corners of India gathered together and threw light on their contribution to the freedom struggle. They challenged the dichotomy between the private and public domain.[14]

Recollecting our most precious memories of seminars, we recall one of the liveliest—a seminar on 'Feminist Consciousness in Regional Literature'. Its premise was the re-interpretation of social givens. Regional and vernacular literature had, by and large, been overlooked by feminists. The key concern of this seminar was to examine how literature has handled and kindled feminist consciousness among its readership. It was the first time that such an angle was introduced in the region.

Workshops and seminars can be celebratory and instructional as much as they can be announcements of caution and care. Globalisation's effects on women in the developing world have been anything but beneficial. The centre took the initiative of looking at the entire issue of globalisation as far back as 1993. In an International Round Table, conducted in collaboration with International Political Science Association, several scholars from the various countries in North and South Americas, Africa and Asia participated. It led to the development of a network of scholars from the South on this critical issue. The papers presented at the Round Table were later published as *Women and Globalisation*.[15]

Beyond the four walls

It has been stated above that the centre is wedded to the task of academic change, but it does not eschew activism outside the university campus. As a strategy for provoking change in society and establishing the credibility of women's studies as a discipline from a womanist perspective, it is absolutely crucial that activism be an indispensable part of any centre for women's studies.

Outreach and extension programmes

The centre has been a pioneer in organising various training programmes. Some of these are geared towards those functionaries whose activities and actions have a direct bearing on the quality of life of women. Noteworthy among these are the training programmes for police personnel on crimes against women and gender sensitisation programmes for policy planners and development functionaries. The most exciting of all the outreach programmes are the ones in which the centre interacts with the grass-roots level.

As a result of the provision of 33 per cent reservation under the 73rd and 74th Constitutional Amendments, women have entered institutions of local governance in the rural and urban areas. The centre has been undertaking capacity-building programmes for these rural women since 1988, much before the reservation policy. The Department of Women and Child Development sent a team from New Delhi to document this event and a video film, *Mahila Panch Ka Ek Din*, was produced and telecast on Delhi Doordarshan. We continue to organise periodically, residential training programmes for women panchs.[16] The Panchayat Programme drew out several rural women from the seclusion of their homes for the first time. One of the members who received training attended the Beijing Conference as part of the Chandigarh team and is now a successful sarpanch.

In collaboration with the British Council, the centre has also conducted a series of orientation programmes for the newly elected women Municipal Councillors of Punjab.[17] Just electing women to posts of policy-making is not enough; centres such as ours need to ensure that the elected women are suitably equipped to be efficacious so that they are neither there by proxy nor are framed for their supposed incompetence. Contrary to the generally expressed apprehension that these women would be mere rubber-stamps for their menfolk, a large majority of them were inspired, motivated and eager to work independently for their areas.[18] The success of this programme has had wideranging effects. Besides making the immediate target audience more aware, it has intrigued the neighbouring states so much that they are seeking to emulate it in the training of their women personnel.

An innovative method in the centre's outreach activism is teaching responsible self- and civil government. To this end, the centre has taken the initiative along with an NGO, to organise a rural women's parliament—*Grameen Mahila Sansad*—in which the rural women have an open forum where issues are discussed and then resolved jointly. The point of the sansad exercise is to make it a model of political accountability and efficacy in order to make local governance true to the spirit of transparency and ethical governance. The elected women then convene at this sansad to listen to the voices of other women from their constituency. The elected women have begun to recognise the necessity of accountability to their constituents.

Networking

CWSD's credo has developed in such a way that it does not work in isolation, in a vacuum as it were, but in tandem with various governmental and non-governmental organisations. Thus, we have self-consciously created and respected relationships through an extensive network at the local, national and international levels. At the local level, the centre is a place where the NGOs feel comfortable to approach it for resources of various sorts. It provides leadership to the Joint Women's Front, which has done far-reaching work at the local level. The centre prepared local NGOs to participate in international meets such as the Beijing Conference. The sharing included lobbying techniques and issues most germane to women.[19] At the national level, we have attempted to build and sustain strong bonds with various movements and organisations. Representatives of the Chipko movement, *Women's Voice,* trade unionists and others have been our guests and have enriched the pursuits of the centre. The centre has been accredited by the UN Fourth World Conference of Women at Beijing (1995) as well as by the UN General Assembly Special Session for Beijing (2000). As one of the five speakers invited to address the General Assembly Session, the centre had clearly identified itself with the global women's movement.

The centre has been the site for national level policy advocacy and lobbying. It was part of the think tank supported by UNIFEM, which attempted to engender the Ninth Five-Year Plan. As a part of this exercise the centre organised a regional meeting where ordinary women and academics interfaced with the members of the Planning Commission. The recommendations resulting from this and other regional meetings substantially contributed to the formulation of the Ninth Five-Year Plan.

At the international level, the centre is associated with networks like South Asia Watch, Asia-Pacific Women's Watch, South Asian Association of Women's Studies, Association for Women's Rights in Development (AWID) and Women's International Coalition for Economic Justice (WICEJ). To learn of their world/s and to teach them about ours, the centre has worked hard to participate in conferences around the world. The centre was active in the whole Beijing Conference process and was instrumental in taking a number of women to Beijing. It is noteworthy that the entire research staff of the centre participated in the Beijing Meet. It actively participated in the NGO forum and organised workshops at Huairou on the Girl Child in difficult situations and on Transformative Politics. The centre was equally active in the Beijing process and the recent meeting of the Commission on the Status of Women.

The centre has played host to Fulbright Scholars, a Commonwealth Scholar and several Visiting Professors from the United States, Canada, South Africa, Bangladesh, Sri Lanka, and Malaysia. This has given the centre a boost to participate in the larger intellectual community of the world where we know that we are all learning from and teaching each other. To this end, the centre also hosted 20 students from the United States for a course on women and development; in fact it was one of their instructors who, after observing the functions and problems of the centre, renamed the cycle shed as the powerhouse!

Hurdles and pitfalls

The centre has gradually but surely built a space and identity for itself. However, it had to face and is still encountering a number of hurdles. Some of these impediments are unfortunately universal and afflict women's studies as a whole; there are others that are specific to the centre. This chapter has addressed several of the more obvious constraints and concerns in the earlier pages. Here it seeks to reiterate and highlight some of those that ought to be mentioned again.

Although women's studies has acquired the status of an academic discipline, it still has difficulty finding acceptability within the university system, a problem that the centre is attempting to rectify using strategy and goodwill. Furthermore, a teaching programme necessitates qualified teachers, at least postgraduates in the discipline, who are not easily available, at least in the northern states of India. A worrying aspect about women's studies is that it is still taught primarily through western literature. We have not written sufficient basic and standard introductory level textbooks, or perhaps there is not enough support for their publication. A final hurdle is that women's studies, in this day and age, cannot afford to remain limited to theoretical teaching alone. There is an urgent need to develop career-oriented courses in this discipline. Students need the assurance that they will get employment after they conclude their studies.

Regarding the specific obstacles before the centre, the system as such is not supportive and sensitive. For example, the UGC requirement of university takeover of the centre was couched in uncertainty for a long time; it was finally taken over in 2000 AD. Support may be forthcoming from individuals, but the system as a whole lacks sensitivity to our cause. The centre has made great strides when the persons at the helm of affairs were supportive and at other times had to struggle to keep its head above water.

Inadequacy of funds troubled us most. We had to look to other agencies like the Department of Women and Child Development, UNIFEM, UNICEF and the British Council to run our programmes. Even after the centre was placed in Phase III by the UGC and grants became available, the centre continues to be constrained in its functioning by the bureaucratic system which allows no room for autonomy. Systemic changes, therefore, are necessary. Accountability without autonomy can become a shackle and hence stressful.

Last, but not the least, is the hovering disquiet over the decision of the university to physically demolish the cycle shed, the 'birthplace' of the centre. We have been promised alternative accommodation in the new building, but for the time being we have been displaced from one cycle shed to another. For us in the centre, nothing can indicate the depth of the colossal emotional setback that this demolition and uprooting has caused. Our spirit will have to find buoyancy once again to recover from this; it remains to be seen whether we will adequately recover.

Re-visioning the future

We are at crossroads. Against odds, the centre, true to its pioneering spirit, looks to the future where the horizons are promising us limitless opportunities and daring us to 'overcome'. We continue our endeavours to create an equitable future even as we apprehensively await the demolition squad.

The (re)visions of our future are promising. The first aim is to consolidate the work of the centre. In terms of academic pursuits, the centre, after having indirectly initiated women's studies through other departments, now proposes to venture into formal teaching on its own with the introduction of a postgraduate diploma/M.Phil course. The challenge before us is to innovate a methodology of teaching women's studies that is different from mainstream teaching. Second, the centre will continue to be an outstanding resource centre for researchers and scholars. It has a substantial collection of books and journals, approximately 1,700, on makeshift shelves; what needs to be done is to professionally catalogue them. We are resource-rich in documents—be they local, national or international. These include news clippings on various issues pertaining to women, such as violence, poverty, politics and health. Another aim of the centre is to build and strengthen a second line of leadership for the centre. It is terribly important that the centre should not be fossilised nor lose its ability to constantly reinvent itself with the times. We have imagined our future while remaining grounded in our philosophical foundations.

A signature aspect of the Centre for Women's Studies and Development is that it is not merely a centre housed in an institution. It is a centre with a mission and a deep commitment to its basic belief in the equality of women and a desire for the upliftment of women. It might be a drop in the vast ocean of change but there is no denying the honesty of its efforts for understanding and changing the lives of women. Before we change the habits of a society we must change individual mindsets. The centre's academic effort is engaged in changing such mindsets; its activist visions and ambitions are engaged in changing society, one human at a time.

In conclusion, the journey from the cycle shed to the powerhouse has not been smooth. The road has been rough, full of potholes and obstacles—my spirit has agonised when the lurches were felt by the centre. The centre and my person have both paid heavy tolls in this journey. Yet our onward march has continued and today we stand as a trailblazing institution attempting not only to conduct research, collect data or effect curriculum development, but also to empower women through training and outreach and effective action. The various hitches and hiccups notwithstanding, the centre has come a long way since its inception. But we must not be complacent; a lot more needs to be done. As the plans for the new building grow apace, we at the centre weave a new dream for the powerhouse. We pull together various threads of support, colour them in the hues of the rainbow, charge them with the strength of our sisters, and call out, 'the cycle shed is demolished, long live the powerhouse.'

Notes

1. Ravinder Kaur and Amrit Srinivasan note, 'As far back as Guru Nanak women were already being encouraged to free themselves from the tyranny of caste ritualism and sexual practices. In fact, the third Guru Amar Das, explicitly forbade the practice of *sati* as an insult to human dignity. The Singh Sabha movement in the 19th and early 20th centuries harked back to these early reforms that had resulted in a higher age for marriage, encouragement of widow remarriage, bringing out women from ritual seclusion to education, albeit religious for its followers.' Many verses from Adi Granth prescribe equality between women and men; the most quoted of these is *So kyoon manda aakhiye jis janmiyen rajan* (Why call her evil, she who gives birth to kings). See Kaur and Srinivasan (1999).
2. See Harinder Kaur (1999) and Manmohan Kaur (1992).
3. A marvellous example from her poem *Waris Shah* is '*Aj aakhan Waris Shah noon kitton kabran vichon bol /Te aj kitab-e-ishq da koi agla warka phol/Ik roi si dhee Punjab di/Tu likh likh maare wain. Aj lakhan dheeyan rondhiyan/ tennu Waris Shah nu kahen "Kitton kabran vichon bol".*' (I ask you, Waris Shah, to speak from the grave/Start a new leaf in your Book of Love/You wrote sonnets to the tears of one daughter of Punjab. Today hundreds of thousands of Punjab's daughters weep as they call out to you, 'Speak of us from the grave').
4. Kiran Bedi is perhaps the best known of all as the first woman to join the Indian Police Service. Sarla Grewal is another example of a Punjabi woman who as an Indian Administrative Service officer became Cabinet Secretary.
5. It was 4.4 in the 1991 census.

6. These are Fatehgarh Sahib, Patiala, Gurdaspur, Kapurthala, Bhatinda, Mansa and Amritsar. Punjab has the lowest child sex ratio in the country (793), which has declined by as many as 82 points over the last census.

7. This is the general trend of the argument in Jyoti Grewal's 'Of Women, Home and Memories'.

8. For a detailed account of how women were affected by Partition, see Butalia (1998) and Menon and Bhasin (1997).

9. A note to my readers. The 'I' in this account indicates the involvement of my person in the centre's growth. It is not meant to indicate my centrality in the centre's development but to indicate the relationship between my philosophy and the institutional establishment of the centre. It was not merely an intellectual pursuit devoid of personal implications; my journey is closely linked with that of the centre's. We have both felt the sense of growth.

10. Dr Madhuri Shah was then the University Grants Commission Chairperson and the President of IAWS.

11. The findings and executive summaries of these research projects are available at the CWSD. These have not been included here for obvious reasons.

12. At this point it would be interesting to quote from Indubala Singh's musings on her experience at the course. (It made such an impression on her that she is now pursuing a Ph.D in women's studies). The actual atmosphere was described as 'a congenial atmosphere for future discourses, interactions, and heated debates which were rather the highlight of the course.' Her concluding comment was that her conversion had persuaded her to be 'active in Gender Watch as a platform to review gender discrimination and for sensitising young students in schools and colleges.' Quoted with her permission.

13. For a detailed list and methodology of these seminars, please feel free to contact the CWSD.

14. One of the freedom fighters bared her chest, which was burnt by her own family members because she had dared to participate in a procession.

15. See Rajput and Swarup, (eds.) (1994).

16. The funding for this particular programme came from USAID through the Department of Women and Child Development.

17. Nearly 60 per cent of the women councillors of Punjab have been covered already. We propose to reach out to all the women councillors of the state.

18. Some, such as the woman councillor from Phillaur, had very innovative ideas. She wanted to fight the use of plastic bags; she used her status as a schoolteacher to be effective. She asked her students to bring as many plastic bags as they could find in their homes and she filled an entire room with them. Then she disseminated information on the capability of these plastic bags to choke out the earth.

19. In the process of such interaction, it has been quite an exciting experience for CWSD to facilitate unlettered women like Kinkri Devi to present at a workshop in the Beijing Conference in 1995, her own struggle against quarrying as an environmental hazard.

References

Ravinder Kaur and Amrit Srinivasan (1999), 'The Better Half' in *Seminar* (476).

Harinder Kaur (1999), 'Women in Sikhism' in *Seminar* (476).

Manmohan Kaur (1992), *Women in India's Freedom Struggle*, New Delhi: Sterling.

Jyoti Grewal, 'Of Women, Home and Memories', unpublished monograph.

Urvashi Butalia (1998), *The Other Side of Silence: Voices from the Partition of India*, New Delhi: Kali for Women.

Ritu Menon and Kamla Bhasin (1997), *Borders and Boundaries*, New Delhi: Kali for Women.

Pam Rajput and Hemlata Swarup (eds.) (1994), *Women and Globalisation*, New Delhi: APH.

4

Integrating activism and academics

Unit for Women's Studies, Tata Institute of Social Sciences

Chaya Datar

Personal experience: The challenges of activism, social work and academics

When I joined the faculty of Tata Institute of Social Sciences (TISS), I was neither an academic with teaching and research experience in the social sciences, nor had I the qualifications of a professional social worker. I was a misfit of sorts; a housewife-turned-activist, working among Adivasis, textile workers and later devoting attention to the women's cause. I had revolted against my own experiences as a housewife, miserable doing the same monotonous work, day in and day out.

Upon joining a voluntary organisation established by radical youth, I found that although I was older than these young boys, all my experiences as a housewife and as a short story writer were trivialised in the face of what was regarded by them as 'high knowledge'—revolutionary theories and theoretical debates about strategies for revolution. My wisdom as a person who had managed a household for ten years, maintaining interpersonal relations with sensitivity, was simply rejected as having no value to any of life's 'real' action.

However, this organisation provided me the opportunity of close interaction with Adivasi women in Dhulia district and this became the turning point of my life. The interaction was mutually enriching.

We were still inspired by radical Marxism, and even narrated the experiences of Chinese and Vietnamese women revolutionaries to motivate Adivasi women to participate in various agitations and to boost
their morale. We also started group rap sessions where personal experiences from the workplace and family were narrated. Trainers like us
also shared the middle-class women's experiences of frustration.

My feminism was inspired by my familiarity with these Adivasi
women. At this point, I began to feel the need to sit down in a class, or
more importantly, in a library, to study feminist theories and crystallise
my ideas. The small component of fieldwork in my M.A. programme
which enabled me to interact with the feminist movement and its activities in the Netherlands was very useful in developing a critical understanding of women's issues. This also enabled a comparison between
issues emerging in different contexts—the First World and the Third
World.

With this background of rather sketchy knowledge and experiences,
in 1988, I entered an institution reputed to be the premier organisation
in producing professional social workers. I must say that in my case,
my participation in activism was given as much weightage as my modest research experience. It was Prof Suma Chitnis, the Head of the
Department (HoD) of the unit for women's studies, established in 1983,
who encouraged me to apply for a position in the unit, as if, despite
her reservations about my lack of academic background, she sensed
that I would fit in. It was a challenge for me to try and integrate the
three approaches to women's studies—professional social work approach, feminist activist approach and the approach of using the critical–theoretical base developed by feminists in all social sciences.

My friends were a little upset with me for leaving activism and going into academics. But, by that time I had become deeply convinced
that there were a number of contributions that research and theoretical work could make to the women's movement, and to furthering the
feminist cause. I also felt that, although a number of feminists were
giving these inputs as independent scholars and activists, it was important that these insights should be integrated into the academic curriculum, for only then could it reach out to other disciplines.

There have been certain objections to the institutionalisation of
women's studies by some activists. One of them is that attention is
diverted to the rules and regulations of the Board of Studies of the
University and curriculum development, and little scope remains then

for learning through action. The eventual result is that insights and ideas generated by the women's movement are lost. A counter-argument points out that these insights, strategies and case studies of struggles can be systematically documented through the university system and thus, dissemination of knowledge can take place at a wider level, even reaching out to future generations. Institutionalisation is useful in anchoring any movement till it becomes a mass movement, so that both women and men internalise the principles and ethics for which they are fighting. However, the fear of misappropriation of the activists' experiences is valid and all strategies should be considered before envisaging any partnership between academic institutions and NGO groups or activist groups.

Movements tend to behave in the manner of tides—rising and receding. The difference is that there is no regularity to the waves of the movement, and academic anchoring would serve the purpose of recording the memory of these tides, passing it on to following generations and helping to build on past experiences. Each has much to offer the other and this mutual interaction is important in furthering the cause of women's studies.

The unit for women's studies at the Tata Institute of Social Sciences was established in 1983, with an initial grant from the Ford Foundation. Dr Suma Chitnis was then heading the unit. Three major activities were undertaken immediately. Of these, the most important was the setting up of the library and documentation centre, as it was a time when very little material from India was available in book form. The second major activity undertaken by the unit was the introduction of a women's studies component in the curriculum for M.A. in Social Work. The third was the launch of a major research project on the history of the reform movement in Maharashtra.

In the beginning, first year students were required to do a foundation course, which was later truncated into a number of different courses, focusing on various aspects of women's studies in the context of the status of women in India. Four courses are offered as optional subjects in the second year; these are, 'Women and work', 'Women and health', 'Women and law', and 'Child rearing: socialisation and gender identity'.

The Tata Institute of Social Sciences has been assigned the position of an academic nodal centre for Colleges of Social Work by the UGC and to date, the Unit has organised three refresher courses on women's studies themes—'Integrating women's studies perspective in social sciences' (1993); 'Gender and development' (1996) and 'Gender issues in development: perspective and methodologies in research and training' (1999). TISS aims to conduct these courses every year, and since they are over-subscribed, we find that we have to narrow down the number of admissions to each course through stringent selection.

We feel that the unit for women's studies at TISS is equipped to start its own M.A. courses in women's studies or women and development. Being a small university, which is administered by Section 3 of the UGC Act, it has considerable autonomy, thus enjoying flexibility in designing courses and updating these as the need arises. Since the faculty members of TISS are from diverse disciplines, and its students are from all over India, this will enable wider dissemination of the women's studies approach. Likewise, the advantage of having a large social work faculty will benefit us in fieldwork. However, what holds us back is the uncertainty of how many students would like to sign on for such a specialised course, since we have designed the courses with less of the applied component than is generally regarded by students as necessary for a professional course.

Research and action projects

Academicians at TISS fall into two separate streams—research and teaching. All the social sciences are part of the research stream and are called units. The unit for women's studies has been part of the research stream, having had only the posts of one reader and one lecturer from 1983 to 1994, but by transfer of posts as and when needed, there are now two Readers and two lecturers. Quite a few of us teach not only women's studies, but other courses as well, though by being part of the research stream, we are expected to engage in activity related to research, extension, outreach, action research, workshops, training programmes and seminars. All of us are occupied in some research or other, and are also involved in organising seminars and workshops which usually lead to publications useful in teaching, and to policy revisions for women's organisations to adopt in their practices, etc. The choice of topic is usually the researcher's prerogative, though occasionally the unit has been commissioned to research and document specific areas of interest. In course of time, individual faculty members have developed special interest areas within women's studies. Today we can claim that our faculty members have been active participants in developing a theoretical perspective on women's studies.

Funding has come to us from several sources, such as the Ford Foundation, the Indian Council for Social Science Research, the International Centre for Research on Women (ICRW), the British Council, the Department for International Development (DFID) and the Indian Association of Women's Studies (IAWS). A few events have been sponsored by internal funds of the Board of Research Studies (BRS) of the Institute. Many papers, books, monographs and other reading material have resulted from the research carried out by the Unit.

Diverse areas of interest

During her tenure as head of department, Prof Suma Chitnis, the well-known sociologist, had sponsored research on the history of changing concepts of women's liberation in Maharashtra from the period of the saint poets of the 11th century to the close of the reform period in the 19th century. This research was initiated in the context of the realisation that the status of women in India was drastically declining, a fact highlighted for the first time in the report of the Committee on the Status of Women (1974). It was felt that policy research was the need of the hour and that the historical roots of feminism in India needed to be analysed. The research findings were later published in Marathi as *Liberation of Indian Women: Footprints from Maharashtra*. However, since the book was never translated, its appeal was limited.

Another important study guided by Dr Chitnis was that of the Shraddananda Mahilashrama, the longest surviving shelter for women, which provided data of casework spanning 60 years. This study also included a glimpse of contemporary shelter homes and their style of functioning. A book resulted from this, and has been published by Rawat Publications.

When I, with a background of experience in the textile union, of organising rural labour and of being deeply interested in rural development, took over as HoD, it was natural that research–action would proceed in this general direction. I had done two major studies—one of beedi workers in Nepani and women's employment under the

Maharashtra Employment Guarantee Scheme, and a small study on *Devadasis* in the border regions of Karnataka and Maharashtra.

A small project funded by the JRD and Thelma Tata Trust was begun, which aimed to train women in using a small plot (1.4 acre) of land, with assured water supply and innovative techniques of cultivation. This was done as a response to the question of why women working in the water harvesting projects of the Employment Guarantee Scheme could not themselves benefit from the water they harvested; if the necessary water was allotted to them, they could lease land and undertake cultivation on their own.

The Tata-funded project was based on the idea that by using neighbourhood resources of biomass and scraped wasteland dust, a small plot of land could be turned into an asset with the help of the EGS scheme. The project is nearing completion and has provided some useful lessons, which are to be collected into a monograph soon. A paper based on these experiences called 'Nurturing Nature' has already appeared as part of a book.

The findings from this project were later linked up with our participation in the debates on 'development', which was at that time undergoing serious re-examination and reformulation from an altogether different view—that of women. To start with, the present path of development seemed inadequate, having emerged against the backdrop of the policies of globalisation, liberalisation and privatisation, dictated by the World Bank. Foreign governments and donor agencies likewise facilitate a number of our infrastructure development projects. Although such projects are said to be informed by the component of participatory methodology, ultimately they are part and parcel of the mainstream economy, which is ruled by market and technology forces. There was then, the need to define an alternative path, and this challenge was taken up by the women's movement, because of its concern that any new model should be built from the vantage point of women, particularly poor women, whose needs of livelihood security and mechanisms for coping with the dual burden of production and reproduction should rightly be at the centre of any development model. This became a sub-theme at the Conference of the Indian Association of Women's Studies (1995, Jaipur), coordinated by me. The commissioned papers were later put together into a book, *Nurturing Nature: Women and Nature at the Centre of Regeneration of Society.*

Another important field action/research project implemented by us, brought us face to face with the second level of realities connected to the process of development, that is, its operationalisation, or the *how* of development. Equality between men and women as well as between landowners and resource poor are important aspects of whether any developmental project has been equitable in design and implementation, just as the redistribution of resources by consensus and gender equity are important criteria for evaluating a project design. The project undertaken by our unit was a Community Development Consultation in Drinking Water and Sanitation, which continued for seven years in two districts of Maharashtra. Three regional piped water schemes, covering 189 villages, with engineering by the Government of Maharashtra and funded by the British Government were set in motion. The project followed a two-pronged approach—on the one hand, it aimed at sensitising the bureaucracy in the philosophy of community participation and building motivation and communication skills, particularly at the block level. On the other hand, it aimed to help field officials conduct night meetings in villages with the aim of empowering the people and building their capacities towards managing the scheme within their own villages. Women were to be the main beneficiaries and managers; 50 per cent of the membership of the village water committees was reserved for women by a government resolution.

This field action project was also guided by the awareness that communities have been disintegrating under the pressure of market forces and the politics of favour. We realised that 'participation from above' was necessary, because as a result of the populist measures of the last three decades, the self-identity of village people as a community acting to plan for its future course of development had been eroded. This had affected the potential for self-initiated programmes and the process of self-activation.

The project needed us to prepare a specific strategy of participatory methodology with focus on women and the scheduled castes and scheduled tribes. Training, including gender sensitivity training, was an important activity at various levels. Although the thrust of the project was on action, we had to be part of the main decision-making and designing process where we were acting as conduits for direct feedback from the people. The project was a learning process; it helped us to critically review the overall drinking water and sanitation project of the Government of Maharashtra, and to understand what alternative strategy might work. Eventually, I was included in a panel that designed an alternative strategy for four districts. The contribution of our team did not remain at the level of action, but reached policy-making levels.

Insights from this process led to a number of other developments. Marathi training manuals have been prepared for various levels, a gender training module for this sector, that is, government officials, and modules of two-day workshops for block and district level government officials are also ready. The team also produced several assessment reports and documented case studies. A video film of 35 minutes was made for the Government of Maharashtra depicting the positive effects of commitment to participatory methodology among government officials. We were also able to develop a variety of innovative formats for presenting the information and ideas of this project.

As far as the women's studies perspectives goes, one particularly important revelation of the project was that special efforts are required to integrate women into and to make them vocal in mixed groups like the village water committee. While engaged in activities such as social mapping, women were seen in the forefront, but when it came to making decisions regarding the management of any scheme, women did not take initiative or responsibility, and neither did men encourage them to do so. Other experiences of women in groups have shown this truth—that only in women's groups, such as SEWA and Mahila Samakhya, do women assume capabilities and take on responsibilities unhesitatingly.

However, the one thing we did help bring about, even if only minimally, was the participation of women in an area where their presence had always been negligible, that is, in the role of village water persons (VWP). Women were barred from this as it was considered that they could not possibly be capable of doing such a 'technically skilled job'! Out of 189 villages, in 20 villages, women became VWPs!

As a result of this project, the Government of Maharashtra has requested the women's studies unit of TISS to set up a resource centre for training in participatory methodology for the Department of Drinking Water and Sanitation. The unit is considering the viability of such a project.

Gender and health issues

On par with the achievements, knowledge, expertise and proficiency in training in the context of rural development and environmental degradation, the unit now also has a high degree of expertise regarding women and health. The focus has been on the issue of reproductive rights and new reproductive technologies, because of the interest of Dr Lakshmi Lingam, who is also the coordinator of the Centre for Health Studies (CHS). The activities of the Centre are carried out by faculty of different departments, such as those of hospital management, health administration, medical psychiatry and social work. Dr Lingam had organised a workshop on 'Women's Occupational Health Hazards and Reproductive Health', funded by the CHS and supported by the ILO. In 1995, the Tata Institute of Social Sciences was invited to contribute a chapter on 'Women and Health', by the Ministry of Human Resource Development, for the state report to be presented at the Fourth World Conference on Women, Peace and Development in Beijing. It was Dr Lingam who coordinated the work of the faculty members of different departments and put together this chapter.

Recently a reader, *Understanding Women's Health Issues* was compiled, introduced and edited by Dr Lingam and was published by Kali for Women. Among Dr Lingam's significant works are the four sections she contributed to the WHO/WHD Country Profile on 'Women's Health Status in India'. She was also invited to cull out women's issues from the National Family Health Survey conducted by the International Institute of Population Studies (IIPS). She coordinated the report on the Status of Women in Maharashtra.

Women's rights at the workplace and violence against women

With Asha Bajpai joining the department in 1995, we now have an expert in law. Since social work education requires a basic grounding in law, Ms Bajpai has had to take on the responsibility of teaching a major course with a large number of students. Her interest in child rights makes her expertise valuable to the government, and recently she was invited by the high court to investigate children's homes in Maharashtra. Asha is also a legal expert on violence against women, child exploitation and abuse. She was invited by the British Council to visit Newcastle University and Liverpool John Moore's University to speak on comparative aspects of the justice systems. She has also conducted workshops on women's rights at the workplace in which the rights of coloured women were also explored.

Nishi Mitra is an anthropologist who did an interesting project on 'Best practices among responses to domestic violence', for which she extensively contacted women's organisations in Maharashtra and Madhya Pradesh that have been providing support to women victims of domestic violence. She has also documented the efforts of the police department to enforce legal rights secured through the women's movement. The project was a part of a larger investigation in which other organisations too had taken part. In her conclusion she states that the physical and mental abuse faced by women at home is still not recognised as a violation of human rights, and that the state still tries to maintain the dichotomy between 'public' and 'private', relegating the issue of domestic violence to the private domain, and so enforcement remains half-hearted and lacks political will.

Challenges faced by the unit in the premier institute for social work

Though we have been granted the status of a separate unit and have taken off well, after the initial momentum garnered by the efforts of Suma Chitnis, and the director, Armaity Desai, we have not yet succeeded in meeting the challenge of becoming so significant a part of the Institute as to influence the discipline itself. In interviews conducted with the social work faculty, to understand how they perceive the influence and relevance of women's studies, a number of them spoke of having been profoundly influenced by the women's movement, but an equal number were found to be downright negative and disinterested. What was particularly disheartening was the trend noticeable among members of the faculty; some, even women faculty members, trivialised and downplayed the need to introduce women's issues in the course curriculum.

To understand the reality of how little the women's studies perspective has influenced social work or other disciplines at the institute, one just needs to take a look at the courses being taught. The most telling instance of omission is that the personnel management and industrial relations (PMIR) course offers no option for electing any course taught by the unit for women's studies. In spite of the fact that more than 50 per cent of the students are women, not a single dissertation from this course has focussed on gender issues. When the HoD was asked to explain, his answer was that they treated men and women personnel equally and hence, felt no need to formulate or understand separate rules for women, as part of personnel management and human resource development.

In the social work departments, there is no paper at the foundation level dealing with gender issues; four papers on women's issues are taught, but only in the fourth year. Some of the social work teachers strongly feel that there should be one first paper in the first year dealing with areas of women's studies such as discrimination against women, which could help to remove the gender biases inherent in our socialisation process. However, the faculty at the unit for women's studies feels that if these issues were introduced in the first year itself, there would be pressure to abolish the four specialised papers. One often hears remarks from the social work faculty that there is too much focus on gender and that, this tilt may eventually upset the balanced attitude which the social worker is supposed to cultivate. In the first year of sociology the course includes a small module on women's issues, but since sociology itself is only one of the four optional social science courses, all students do not choose it.

Uneasy relationship

The few examples cited above are meant to show that, till quite recently, the social work faculty had not accepted the feminist analysis of unequal power relations between men and women, and its manifestation in everyday life. In a special workshop (1992) to review the curriculum of social work education, there was vehement opposition to the term 'patriarchy' from one of their faculty members. Similarly, during a workshop organised for students on the issue of violence against women, the analysis that this violence was structural and had historical roots, which explained how and why women came under the control of men in all activities—labour, procreation and sexuality—was considered an extremist view.

Responses like this give rise to the feeling that the association between feminism and social work is an uneasy one. It is a well-known fact that relations between feminist activists and professional social workers have always been more than a little strained. Feminist activists are viewed by social workers as being self-made and self-trained, making their strategies lopsided and short-term. The strategy of feminist activists, based on the feminist principle of 'personal is political', is not necessarily supported by social work education. Social workers seem to feel that feminist activists are prone to using particular cases of atrocities to politicise issues. It is a pity that stray incidents, cases of certain approaches being adopted by some feminist activists, have led to the perpetuation of a bias against feminism and in turn against women's studies.

It is in feedback from students that we get positive responses—they feel that these courses have explanatory power and can expose the discriminatory processes prevalent in diverse fields of reality. Only very rarely do we get complaints that the course is too theoretical.

Positive effects of cross-fertilisation between women's studies and social work

Kalindi Mazumdar wrote in 1998 in the *Indian Journal of Social Work*, about the significance of field instruction, which is the distinctive feature of social work, as a catchment area where students re-examine old values and, through introspection, formulate a new value framework. She feels that in the context of revaluation and creation of a new value base, gender awareness can be nurtured in students through field instruction.

This method-based approach of professional social work, which enables the student to develop new and more equitable value bases with close supervision and interpretations offered by the teacher, projects an important lesson for feminist activists as well as women's studies scholars. Feminist activists have often not ventured beyond emulating a political party approach of maximising the opportunity to politicise events and issues. The slow and steady approach, methodical documentation of case histories in personal counselling and keeping records of community activities, is a vital contribution of professional social work. This rigour helps analyse behaviour patterns as well as mobilisation patterns of the community. Another striking feature I have noticed in social work practice is that though there is a use of the hierarchical terminology of 'expert client', there is a lot of sensitivity exercised in enabling the 'client' to make choices or take decisions. Although the relationship between the two is based on power, the professional social worker is constantly made aware that she or he cannot represent the 'other' and cannot impose views. This approach is a result of the liberal ethos within which professional social work operates while the feminist approach, in contrast, appears aggressive at times. There have been reactions to the above-mentioned feminist approach within postmodern feminist theory, which believes in multiple viewpoints based on the specific location and site of the person involved as a client, thus refusing to acknowledge that any help/support is really possible in the long term. This may be an extreme position but it is based on the rationale that feminist action should not emanate from a positivist point of view. The social worker being located constantly with the 'other' or the community, he or she can escape positivism because of continued and first-hand exposure to the tremendous diversity in the life of these people. Feminist activists and women's studies scholars should be able to consciously adopt this approach so as to escape the rigidity of ideological positioning. The new term, 'facilitator', rather than 'social worker' or 'fieldworker', best describes this new approach.

Bringing about a changed and gender-sensitive value system is also one of the primary concerns of women's studies and feminism, and it is here that a common wavelength can be found with social work. Women's studies also, at the same time, believes in building up new knowledge bases and new epistemologies. Therefore, it becomes necessary to capture the specificities of women—their oppression as well as their agency and capabilities. Women need to be studied while they are in action, through a variety of methods such as participant observation and through partial identification with the group being researched. Thus action, extension, outreach, networking and advocacy are all integral parts of women's studies. Data so collected has to be analysed and theorised, for which a theoretical base is necessary. And this is the singular contribution that women's studies can make to the women's cause and feminism at large.

In fact, as Lena Dominelli points out, social work would benefit from becoming oriented with the 'feminist social work' approach, which is more enriching and appropriate in the post women's movement era. She enumerates some of the general principles of this kind of practice—integrating theory and practice; listening to women and providing women the space to articulate their own voices; examining the connection between their private lives and their involvement in the public sphere; responding to women's needs as women, without ignoring the needs of those to whom women relate in their roles as nurturers; valuing women's personal knowledge and skills; etc. The stress in feminist social work is about the integration of theory and practice and about the linking of personal and public knowledge, skills and roles. Making this a basis for work is something that social work and social workers could benefit immensely from.

Building bridges

It is encouraging to think that a bridging of the traditional chasm between two schools of thought so central to the whole endeavour to better women's lives, is at hand.

As more and more people and more academic departments begin to adopt a gender-sensitive perspective in their teaching and practice, the women's studies department feels a sense of pride and accomplishment. As I look back on this paper and all that it has sought to describe, a rather funny thought strikes me, that is, if all the disciplines within the education system became gender-aware and gender-sensitive, would the significance of women's studies be negated? One would like to end just by saying that, in fact the ultimate aim of women's studies is the formation of a society where 'women's problems' and 'women's issues' need not be a separate and segregated category, different and more horrifying than the problems of society at large, needing a separate discipline to study and theorise it. Women's studies works towards the annihilation of those discriminatory forms of oppression, cruelty and torture that create the need for women to be viewed as a special category, needing special theories, special action and special forms of redressal.

5

Catalysts and deterrents

Women's Studies and Development Centre University of Delhi

Susheela Kaushik

I guess there are many routes by which people enter into and journey in women's studies. Of course, one will always find some personal motivation, for it is only when objective factors focus on and are conjoined by subjective experiences, that any serious concern or deep commitment takes birth. My own induction into women's studies was accidental, sparked off by a chance meeting with a charismatic person, whose power to inspire was irresistible.

Some of us (particularly Prof Aparna Basu, of the department of history), believing that nothing more than one's interest and the inspiration and support of other academicians is needed for initiating an activity, ventured to start the Research Group on Women's Studies in the University of Delhi. Limited in ambition and activities, the group met every Tuesday afternoon to hear research presentations by colleagues and research scholars. When, in December 1984, it came to be recognised by stalwarts in the women's studies movement that we could now draw out the resources to organise a day-long workshop, encouragement and physical support was easily and readily forthcoming. We were put in touch with an excellent speaker in Ms Louise Myer. Support came in many forms—the UN Information Centre offered us their prestigious hall, the FICCI Ladies' Organisation and Vikas Publishers provided the required material support and a number of well-known women's studies scholars agreed to be resource persons. It was through this event that the Delhi University Research Group in Women's Studies launched itself.

The Research Group owes much to Dr Madhuri Shah, who as the President of the Indian Association of Women's Studies (IAWS), selected our group to host this workshop being held to discuss the organisation and perspectives of women's studies in Indian universities. She had also, as the chairperson of the UGC, sanctioned the necessary grant. As the first of its kind sponsored by the UGC, this workshop, held in 1985, received much attention and cooperation, with experts from universities and research institutions far and wide responding to our invitation. The comprehensive report of the workshop, later recommended by the UGC for all new centres, formed the basis of the UGC Guidelines for Women's Studies Centres (1987). Even though the subsequent guidelines of the UGC (1997) reflect a different type of thinking on the subject, the 1987 guidelines still stand as a valid document on the approach and structural issues of women's studies in the university system.

The women's studies centre in the University of Delhi was founded in 1987, and followed those guidelines closely, structuring itself as an independent unit directly under the leadership of the vice-chancellor. Till date, the vice-chancellor has been the chairperson of the advisory committee, and all but one vice-chancellor have chaired meetings. I consider this to be of singular importance to the functioning and prestige of the Centre.

The nomenclature of the centre was deliberately chosen to be 'Women's Studies and Development Centre' (WSDC) so as to include academicians as well as community action and interaction. Started in a single cubicle with individual donations of books and papers, today the centre has five such cubicles and more than a 1,000 valuable books and reports. Started along with six other universities, today the Women's Studies and Development Centre of the University of Delhi has been recognised as one of the better performing centres and placed under 'phase III' by the UGC.

Location

The choice of its location as an independent unit, and its equidistance from other departments in the university has been a major factor in the success of the centre. Other departments have found it easy to relate to the centre, and students from different departments have continuously been motivated to associate with its activities and access its resources. Various committees of the centre, including the Advisory Committee and Expert Committee on Counselling, have been drawn from the faculties of different departments, the principals of various colleges and a number of university authorities. This has not only helped greatly to broaden the base of the centre, making it seem to belong to the university as a whole, but also brought in the specialised expertise of different disciplines and facilitated association with the extra-curricular and community action-oriented activities of the university. The centre has been called upon to participate in the planning schedules of the university—in working out international exchange programmes, promoting and designing future research and teaching etc., thereby giving scope, in the national arena, to the innovative alternative methods of pedagogy and research that women's studies has been associated with.

The objectives and interdisciplinary nature of women's studies as well as the guidelines of the UGC suggested specific methods of locating and organising the centre. Clearly it was necessary to avoid the features of a department, existing separately from other disciplines, involving a hierarchy of authority, with specific loads of work and limited types of activity geared more towards examinations and degrees rather than community action. Putting women's studies in a department or incorporating it into specific existing departments, was considered nonproductive. The experience of those centres that are part of departments has, by and large, confirmed this. A few have managed to change location and become independent bodies, working directly under a faculty and the vice-chancellor.

Simultaneous to our beginning the Women's Studies and Development Centre (WSDC), the University of Delhi also started quite a few interdisciplinary courses with a little seed money. To coordinate and monitor these, the university passed an ordinance to constitute the Board of Interdisciplinary Studies, which would meet at least once in six months to monitor the activities and give additional grants, when available. The WSDC was also brought under this board, which gave us the first statutory recognition and brought us into a section of the mainstream. However, this still did not mean equality with other departments or the status of being part of a faculty. All these moves remained at the level of a half-hearted experiment with subsequent vice-chancellors being none too interested in the venture.

So far my own university has not shown itself to believe in either a Department of Women's Studies or the rotation principle for its Heads of Departments (HoD). Perhaps the underlying assumption may have some truth—the departmental status and a rotation of directors would rob the venture of meaning and commitment, making it routinised and subject to petty politics and personality clashes. Also, a degree in women's studies (BA, MA, M.Phil or Ph.D) still has little value in the job market and this marginalises women's studies and robs it of its balanced and critical outlook. The consequence of all this is that, by and large, women's studies has come to rely on individuals, the most central being the director herself. Of course, many have sought to reduce this role by decentralising power, forming committees and the like. However, as far as the reality goes, decentralisation simply does not seem to work in India. The director still ends up doing much of the work and taking on most of the responsibilities.

The functioning of women's studies centres is often seen to become the overriding responsibility of the director, who, limited by paucities of time, funds and support structure, and her own increased responsibility in addition to duties in the parent department, is not able to enlist much cooperation or coordination with other university bodies. Mobilising the support and voluntary contributions of students and faculty of the university and colleges, keeping their enthusiasm going and drawing up a participatory agenda—all require much organisation, time and attention.

Role and status of the director

One of the issues that makes many think twice about the post of director is the fact that it is honorary, the reason behind this is that under these circumstances, only those really committed to women's issues and women's studies would accept the post. Another aspect is that since those who do accept the post would do so irrespective of their chances of promotion, or because they have already reached eminence in their fields, it would be possible to keep out the element of rabid competition. Earlier, women's studies scholars and the UGC had also felt that the direct appointment of directors to women's studies centres would isolate and marginalise the programme as directors thus appointed may not be from the field of women's studies at all.

Drawing the director from another department also helps in keeping the director in touch with developments in the main discipline and also prevents her/him from losing chances of promotion and other involvements in the main discipline, thereby enriching the women's studies centre with cross-disciplinary interactions. Over the period, this has perhaps been responsible for many early (in many cases the very first) directors continuing to head the centre for a considerable number of years, in some cases up to retirement.

At the same time, this also leads to over/burdening the director who is not exempted from duties in the parent department such as participation in research and seminars, visiting lectures, foreign tours, international conferences, etc. (Women's studies expands one's horizons intellectually, geographically and physically). Overwork may make it difficult for the director to be imaginative and innovative. Many directors have been on absentee status at the university, leaving departmental colleagues and students unhappy. Hence, it has led to the demand to make the post of director a paid position, even if the incumbent is on a deputation from one of the departments. There are also some who would like it to be rotated.

The present directors themselves have been complaining of the dual load and overwork, while at the same time not wanting a change. Given this situation, they would rather continue to be a part of the main department, for though women's studies may provide an entry to many areas—national and international—it is not yet a substitute or even equal to the traditional disciplines. The position of HoD is more influential and prestigious than that of director of women's studies.

Incidentally, it can be pointed out that the so-called 'better functioning' centres are those which are being headed by the original director for a considerable period of time (till retirement). What will happen when they leave? In more than a few cases, this has led to their decline. This is an issue that needs to be squarely faced if women's studies has to survive. Unlike NGOs or research organisations, universities should be able to develop a reserve of scholars and activists who, despite their specialisations and enormous commitments would be able to come forward to shoulder the responsibilities and support the special nature, role and objectives of women's studies. How many are willing at present?

Response of university authorities

Women's studies has emerged as a prestigious showpiece in quite a few universities, but its influence is not proportionate. More and more vice-chancellors have expressed the noble intention of opening a women's studies centre, but once these are sanctioned, how many display any active interest in endowing it with commitment, hard work and time? How many take the trouble to identify 'appropriate' support persons, and to ask for or follow suggestions. Proposals to start child care centres, counselling centres, to introduce foundation courses and syllabi changes or to offer courses by women's studies centres have been received with benign indifference. Even the issue of granting of permanent status— merging with the main university and creating permanent positions— has received scant attention, despite repeated communications from the University Grants Commission since 1996, leading one to conclude that possibly this is due to the fact that women's studies and women themselves do not have the necessary money and muscle power behind them. Women feel embarrassed at having to repeatedly pester the authorities and give up at a certain point, preferring to find other ways of worthwhile functioning than chasing files or persuading authorities. Many women are also led to conclude that this is a patriarchal game which they will lose anyway, unless they can follow the market system of raising resources, particularly of foreign origin. Perhaps more women, especially the younger ones, should seek to do so, for after all, it is crucial for women to become free of economic (and political) dependence and stop being merely convenient beasts of burden.

In a way, the experience of WSDC has been similar. Though finally the university has taken over the four positions, it had to be preceded by considerable pressure, innumerable communications and visits, a veritable football match between the UGC and the university and the wearing down of the director and the staff. It is rather disheartening to know that even now seniority, personal prestige, credibility, hard work and the goodwill of people are not adequate as forms of pressure.

Women's studies and its centres have, of course, their allies. Any scholar/teacher/visitor to the centre is an ally because he/she recognises its existence, believes in its usefulness and capacity to serve and encourages it to work better. Our library and documentation collection have been the most central and sustained of our activities. That we have a lot of readers, male and female, is very satisfying. Over a period of time, there has been an increase in the number of workshops and seminars conducted by various departments, colleges and university teachers. Many university teachers have also formed NGOs which have become the 'arms and legs' of the centre. The centre has been helping them with information, materials and other resources. Our tasks have been considerably reduced by the fact that the WSDC has made its presence widely accepted, and its activities are being recognised and accepted as valuable to other institutions and to society at large, with the result that others have taken on activities which the centre was, in its beginning stage, left to handle all alone.

Activities

It is now 10 years or more since a few women's studies centres started functioning. Apart from promoting research in women's studies, documentation, etc., these centres were also entrusted with the responsibility of lobbying, advocating, initiating and backing up the teaching of women's studies, as a part of curriculum development. Over time, these centres have come into their own. Academically though, this is a time when seminars and discussions are at a low ebb, women's studies still claims attention, thanks to its practical social implications as well as the expanding nature of its enquiry. This is most evident in the fact that various departments have now begun to include a women's studies component in their syllabus, without the prodding and persuading, the unhappy encounters and unsuccessful canvassing of the past.

The centre at the University of Delhi has been trying to work practically on all aspects of the women's question—developmental issues, rights issues, violence and atrocity issues, etc. The centre has undertaken much lobbying and advocacy from its very inception. More than anything else, we have focused our attention on aspects such as the promotion of women's studies in higher and school education, in the

NCERT and the UGC, in the university system all over India; and alternate teaching and research methodologies for women's studies.

Involving ourselves closely with governmental agencies, research institutions as well as discipline-oriented bodies like the Indian Association of Women's Studies (IAWS), the Indian Council of Historical Studies (ICHS), the National Commission for Women (NCW), the World University Service, etc., we have been able to espouse the relevance and cause of women's studies in a wide variety of fora. The coincidence of the director having been a member of the Executive Committee of the IAWS, and, later on, its Joint Secretary and Secretary, helped in this. The director could also take the message of the Indian experience and innovations in women's studies, its concepts and methodologies, to nations across the globe, with her participation in international seminars, cross-country research projects and visiting lecturer assignments. Thereby the Third World point of view in women's studies could be disseminated.

The WSDC, in later years, has moved to organising policy debates, lobbying for science and technology education for women, focusing on girl children, and rights of children, particularly those of child labourers, and of the children of sex-workers. It undertook campaigns against sexual harassment in universities and violence against women. One of its lobbying activities was for the formulation and implementation of a National Policy for Women. Through its series of student-led symposia on the Beijing Conference (sponsored by NCW) and on violence against women (sponsored by UNIFEM), it advocated the cause of women's rights among the youth in this country.

However, over a period of time certain issues have come to the forefront. Among these, the most significant is the whole new area of women in politics and decision-making, particularly in the context of Panchayati Raj and the reservation issue. Other issues, which have now come to the forefront are globalisation, structural adjustment policies and the rights of girl children. At the same time, documentation has continued to take place on all other issues and the WSDC has been able to compile bibliographies on a number of topics.

With the WSDC undertaking the facilitation of curriculum development as a major aspect of its activities, the incorporation of women's themes in the syllabi motivated and challenged the documentation section of the centre. The centre has been helping students and teachers with identification and dissemination of relevant materials and by providing xeroxing services and production of dossiers.

Curriculum development

In the initial years, curriculum redesigning to incorporate women's issues was not easy and for years it remained all but impossible to reflect, in the teaching of other departments, the vast material that came out of seminars, paper presentations or research. The autonomy of other departments needed to be respected, even while the significance of women's studies was to be disseminated. While some departments like those of education, law and political science were relatively receptive, history questioned our motives and economics remained obdurate. In most departments, any element of women's studies could only be included in the M.A. or M. Phil optional papers, while in some, such as law, applied psychology and education, there could also be components in under-graduate programmes. In political science, it was possible to include an optional paper both at M.A. as well as at B.A. (Honours) levels. With the passing of time, many departments introduced women's studies themes—mostly as optional papers at the postgraduate level. Initial resistance and feelings of insecurity had given place to condescending tolerance and finally acceptance, if not positive enthusiasm and at the moment, all social sciences with the exception of economics, have introduced women's studies into their syllabus. In a similar unobtrusive manner, more and more term and research papers have begun to appear recently on women's issues, in addition to an increasing number of seminars and talks on such issues. The examination system also now gives space to women's issues.

Women in the university system, in general, have been involved in women's studies and a number of activities for women—counselling, legal aid awareness activities and celebration of women's day—which has led to the emergence of gender studies groups and activities. These activities have helped to bring together teachers and students on various issues, cutting across colleges and disciplines, drawing the attention of the university and other authorities to the issues under consideration. The result of all this is evident in a number of instances. Committees now have more women; women principals now manage coeducational colleges; university bodies take up women's causes and the university has finally taken the initiative to frame guidelines against sexual harassment on the campus and even formed a committee for the same.

However, there is a not-too-rosy side to this picture of positive changes—the enthusiasm, commitment and the eagerness to know more and further clarify oneself, which characterised the early years, is declining. Possibly this is due to a widespread recognition of women's studies as having progressed into a well-accepted, regular field of study, increasing familiarity with women's studies or simply the fatigue being experienced by women's studies scholars after long years of struggle for recognition.

Collaboration with other centres and departments

WSDC has collaborated in a number of interesting projects. Most recently, it worked closely with the data archives of ICSSR and the Department of Science and Technology, to produce software for a catalogue of available material as well as a directory of resourcepersons.

The centre also successfully participated in what has become a unique experiment in India—networking among women's studies centres. We had co-coordinated a research project on 'Child labour in beedi making', in which five women's studies centres had participated. We were also part of the co-ordinating group for the research-cum-action project, 'Girl Child and the Family', in which 22 centres took part. These studies provided valuable lessons in networking and the limitations and immense possibilities of such collective studies, as well as training in the leadership role. This model of shared research should be sustained not only because it helps to build a collectivity among the centres, producing data of a national nature which reflects the multifaceted nature of India's culture and society, but also because it furnishes an agenda for and empowers the new centres.

Some of our most memorable and significant moments have been our interaction with women and girls in the form of field research and data collection. These have been important encounters, providing significant data and a singular kind of learning process. Personally speaking, women's studies has taken me to remote places and unknown corners that political science never could have. From the remote heights of Tawang and Dimapur to the rugged terrain of Garhwal to the windy coasts of Trivandrum and Madras, various research projects have taken my colleagues and me to what seems to be the 'real' India and its women.

From 1986 onwards, the University of Delhi began an experiment in 20 colleges (of which 17 were girls' colleges) to fund Women's Development Centres (WDCs) with money from the Department of Women and Child Development. Even though the venture collapsed, all too soon in some cases, by and large, it worked rather well. A few more have now joined the ranks, including two coeducational colleges. The opening of these centres has made the colleges the scene of vibrant activities—street plays, debates, quizzes, seminars, counselling of students and community, and networking with other colleges, university centres, NGOs and resource persons. These centres have been a great help for the Women's Studies and Development Centre in organising our activities and reaching out to the university community, which is spread across the whole of Delhi. The coordination of the WDC's activities and networking with them has been one of the main areas of activity for the university centre.

At times, however, collaboration with other departments has not been too satisfactory. While it has been easy to organise special functions like legal literacy campaigns, awareness raising or even seminars, it has been a lot more difficult to enthuse them on a day-to-day basis.

The Women's Studies and Development Centre of the University of Delhi also has the advantage of being located in the national capital. It has not only brought to us many national and international scholars and visiting faculty but has also helped in networking with many women's studies research institutions, NGOs, government departments and the National Commission for Women. This networking has enabled us to organise seminars and conduct and publish research. This exposed our students, staff and teachers to the action component of women's studies and NGO activities, thereby considerably boosting morale, prestige, visibility and information within and outside the university. We owe to these outside agencies and their leaders immense gratitude for our growth.

Equally important was our accessibility to women's studies scholars and those interested in women's issues, already motivated and exposed to the women's movement, which made it possible to put the UGC grant and support into prompt and effective use. The understanding and support of the vice-chancellors, since 1985, cannot be undervalued; their benign leadership and support, readily forthcoming whenever needed, has indeed been one of the basic reasons for our success. We also owe the centre's growth, design and successful image, particularly in the earlier years, to a very dedicated team of workers, each of whom (project officers, Junior Research Fellows, counsellors, office staff) came with previous experience in women's studies and action, and so had considerable empathy. It was thus simple for all of us to learn and apply the women's studies perspectives.

Looking back, many are happier and wiser for having been associated with the Women's Studies Centre and sensitisation has spread wide and deep so that we can say with pride that women's studies, particularly within the university, has been responsible for removing at least a small part of the gender biases that had free rein. It would seem that many of our teachers, both female and male, are not satisfied with merely becoming aware of women's issues, but would like to learn more, considering the rush for the four refresher courses in women's studies which the university has been conducting. The keenness with which students and teachers, particularly from the coeducational colleges, participate in the various events organised by us, may be considered an indication that women's issues are finally being treated with the attention that they deserve.

One wishes to end on a note of hope, and I can think of nothing better than to say that the brief interlude when we struggled to get recognition and space, permanence and political support is over and now, the atmosphere is reminiscent of the older days of excitement and innovation. The centre has matured, having been able to influence at least certain levels of the policy and administrative machinery. One is no longer surprised to see that the authorities (in the University of Delhi) are appointing more women in enquiry committees, academic panels, structural committees, etc., besides of course, in committees dealing with women's issues and concerns. However, women are yet to emerge in decision-making positions or as part of the all powerful university team. As in politics, it is still a patriarchal game played in the 'mal(e)ish' way, demanding from women, qualities and modes that not every woman may opt to imitate.

At the end, one would like to sound a note of warning, that women's studies is as much vulnerable to the kind of backlash that the feminist movement had to face in the not-too-distant past. The lessons we learnt may yet stand us in good stead, holding us back from spreading ourselves too thin, of jumping onto too many bandwagons in the name of women's issues and women's rights, and allowing the actual issues to get out of sight.

6

Being a woman is not enough

Centre for Women's Studies and Development, Banaras Hindu University

Surinder Jetley

Writing in retrospect is not always an objective exercise, and in fact, this account of the Centre for Women's Studies and Development (CWSD) at the Banaras Hindu University, as well as of my own journey in teaching women's studies is mingled with nostalgia and fantasy on the one hand, and shadowed with memories of failures and obstacles on the other. However, it is the obligation of pioneers to leave behind a record of the initial terrain, with the hope that it will possibly provide guidelines for future generations of scholars taking up the calling to promote and strengthen women's studies in the higher education system. This is an effort to present both a narrative account and a critical analysis of the first decade of the CWSD at the Banaras Hindu University.

As the founding director of the CWSD at the Banaras Hindu University, I cannot but simultaneously recall my own journey into women's studies, so closely linked to events of the late 1970s and 1980s—an exciting and vibrant period which gave wide currency to women's studies in academia. I feel privileged to have been part of many of these events; it was during this period that my orientation 'changed tracks'. It was not so much a change of tracks as an 'enlargement of vision' which the microscopic lens of women's studies provided, enabling me to see the finer details and hitherto dark areas within my own field of observation. What I saw was both disturbing and challenging.

As a rural sociologist, I had just published my doctoral thesis, *Modernizing Indian Peasants*, which dealt with the adoption of technological innovations by peasants, breaking many traditional beliefs and practices in their agricultural calendar, yet retaining their social attitudes towards hierarchical social arrangements sanctioned by religion and ritual. At a chance encounter, the then director of the Women's Studies Programme at ICSSR, Dr Vina Mazumdar, the living legend, disturbed the apple cart of my intellectual smugness with her question, ' What about the women in your study?'

What about them, I too wondered, for my study was of the principal actor—the male—who decided on all the major changes. I set out to find out how the Green Revolution had affected women working in agriculture. Funded by the ICSSR, I spent a year studying the impact of the development that had brought phenomenal prosperity to the peasants in Western Uttar Pradesh (UP), on the women in the fields, and learnt from their own narratives that development had actually increased the burden on 'women and beasts'.

Thus it was, that after 25 years of work as a rural sociologist, I started to focus on the situation of rural women from a totally new viewpoint. Research opportunities came my way, to undertake studies of other situations in which women live and work—a study of women in the food processing industry under the Indo-Dutch Programme of Alternative Development, followed by a UNESCO project for a cross-cultural study on the impact of male migration on rural women, and so on.

Around this time, a premier institute of women's studies was set up with Vina Mazumdar as its director. She invited me to organise their first action-cum-research programme on income generation through women's organisations. On deputation from my university for two years (1980–82), I had a most fulfilling time working with women in Punjab while in touch with the UP and West Bengal situation. There were endless informal sessions in which much introspection and discussion on the relationship between the women's movement and women's studies took place. Many a cobweb was cleared away on both sides when activists and academics approached common concerns. I owe my own personal transformation to this background which gave birth to a new awareness and an awakening of conscience. It was no longer sufficient to observe, to record and to publish. My concerns went beyond—there was a new sense of empathy with the people one worked with. A new ethno-sociological methodology which perceived the world through their eyes, deepened one's vision. It is this in-built activism that seems to run through all enquiry into women's situations, which dissolves the boundaries between activist and academic.

The early 1980s was a period of great happenings and the CWSD at the Banaras Hindu University was the hub of national and international dialogue on gender issues. The emergence of networking between women's organisations of varied political hues was beginning to strongly and positively influence several state policies that adversely affected women. The landmark of the period was the formation of the Indian Association of Women's Studies. I was a founding member and was privileged to assist it as vice-president in one term and general secretary in another. I also edited the newsletter of the Indian Association for Women's Studies for some time.

My stint at CWSD was so fulfilling that I almost quit the university; but my professional mentor, Professor A.R. Desai, advised me to go back. I could do all that I had the opportunity to do at the centre; in addition, there was the tremendous potential to work towards changing the thought processes of young men and women through the propagation of women's studies at the university. I remain grateful for that advice.

The rather long narrative of my personal journey into women's studies is not as personal as it might at first seem, for it is really the same process through which most of us come into women's studies, that is, through our own empirical research and personal involvement in women's issues. Back at the university, the fire of enquiry in women's studies was kept burning through continuous teaching and research, even though one had to constantly face charges from colleagues that women's studies was little more than the effort to feminise sociology. However, this early scepticism was replaced by curiosity and later with active interest, when the UGC approached us to frame the curriculum for women's studies through revision, reappraisal and review of the syllabi of social science disciplines such as sociology, political science, history, economics and psychology. Later law and education were also added. These exercises were undertaken in vigorous interaction with similar activities in the University of Delhi, SNDT University etc.

When Dr Madhuri Shah wrote to the university asking us to submit proposals for setting up centres for women's studies, it was not by accident, but by choice that I was asked to submit a proposal, and later, when the centre was set up in 1988, to be its founding director.

The announcement came from the then vice-chancellor, during an ICSSR-sponsored workshop on women's studies for northern India organised at Banaras Hindu University. Thus, there was already familiarity and a certain amount of acceptance of women's studies at Banaras Hindu University when the centre was set up.

Location and autonomy

The Centre for Women's Studies and Development of the Banaras Hindu University is located in Uttar Pradesh, one of the largest and most backward states of India. It has undergone considerable social degeneration since the beginning of the century as a result of poor development, for which some blame the British practice of deliberate neglect of the region because of its intensive political participation in the freedom struggle. The eastern part of the state in which Banaras Hindu University is located is even more backward than the rest of the state. However, the city of Varanasi, besides being a great pilgrimage centre for the Hindus, is a major centre of commerce and three universities are located here. Even in ancient times, every new idea of philosophy had to be tested against the might of the pundits of Kashi— the indigenous name of the city. The Banaras Hindu University is a premier national institute founded by Pandit Madan Mohan Malviya, who sought to combine the best of East and West within its portals. Today there are 105 departments ranging from astrology to astrophysics. It has a women's undergraduate college with celebrated alumni like Madhuri Shah, Kamaladevi Chattopadhyaya and Vina Mazumdar, among others.

There was a time when the university had a truly national character. Today, thanks to the Hindi agitation of the 1970s, the over-riding influence of caste and flexing of local muscles, there is an increasing number of both students and faculty from the immediate hinterland, especially in the faculties of arts, social sciences and humanities, while technology and the sciences still retain their all-India character.

Varanasi is a mini India; different provincial and linguistic groups keep their sub-cultural identities intact and live in identifiable neighbourhoods. There is also a sizeable Muslim population in Varanasi. Much continuity is to be seen in the value system of Varanasi, for which its rural hinterland may in large part be responsible, and because of this, caste and communal boundaries are maintained and respected. After the Mandal Commission, however, there has been an increasingly sharp divide between castes, with new power equations deriving from numerical strength and political weightage, which, in turn, have had reverberations within the ranks of the intelligentsia. Though UP may rank low on all indices of economic and social development, it is a highly politicised society, and both the faculty and the students of the Banaras Hindu University are politically alert. The university is a fertile ground for the preparation of state and national-level leadership.

As far as woman-relevant indicators are concerned, UP has marked social inequalities including gender inequality, a highly hierarchical and strongly patriarchal society with low age of marriage, high infant (higher for the female) mortality rates, high birth rate, high level of son-preference and low female work participation. In such a social milieu, prioritising areas of concern is indeed difficult.

Autonomy and placement

As already stated, the Banaras Hindu University had been, with the help of experts, engaged in exercises on curriculum development for women's studies and it was during one such workshop that Dr Vina Mazumdar had a meeting with the then vice-chancellor, Dr Iqbal Narain regarding the modalities of the proposed centre. I was invited to the meeting. It was debated whether the location of the centre should be under the umbrella of one department or if being an autonomous unit would be more fruitful. Dr Mazumdar and I strongly advocated an independent unit, if its role as a catalyst for interdisciplinary focus was to be realised. This was accepted. Thus, an autonomous unit with an honorary director was set up under the faculty of social sciences. The faculty of social sciences had acquired a new building and its dean and the founding director, i.e., myself, belonged to the same department. This facilitated the allotment of space and basic materials such as furniture, etc. The central registry too was very supportive and the centre was given secretarial staff—a clerk, a typist and a library assistant.

The first obstacle was the appointment of a research officer and research assistants, for although the funding for CWSD was like that of a project—a specific sum for a time-bound period—it was treated like a department in the matter of appointments. Advertisements and interviews took a long time, in addition to which there was pressure from those who glimpsed an opportunity for employment, were armed with a degree and grade, but utterly lacked qualifications for women's studies. During the interviews, even the members of the interviewing committee emphasised 'proper qualifications' and experience rather than the sensitivity of the candidates to women's concerns or a basic familiarity with the concepts or theories of women's studies. It is heartening to remember that I was given sufficient freedom in selecting research staff. It is another matter that, except one, none of them could be retained, for when they found permanent positions in other institutes or organisations they left without a qualm, though their work at the CWSD was in no small measure responsible for this upward mobility.

We had a handsome grant from the Ford Foundation in addition to a UGC grant for books and journals. Efforts were made from the beginning to turn CWSD into a focal point for researchers in need of source material and consultation. For the faculty, the adoption of the changes in curriculum also required ready referencing which the centre tried to provide.

The table at the end of this paper gives an inventory of the centre's activities but let me briefly discuss our mandate, performance and the degree of success in each of the objectives commonly accepted for the centre.

In this book, many case studies will repeat the four-pronged approach of programmes and activities of centres for women's studies, namely, teaching, research, action and extension. It must be stated here that a centre for women's studies was not intended to undertake research by itself, in fact it was not designed as a teaching department, for the honorary director and research staff are drawn from varied disciplines and subjects. Centres for women's studies are really meant to play the role of catalysts in assisting revision of teaching curricula to include the gender dimension, contributing to preparation of teaching/learning material, identifying resource material, and building a data base as well as making inventory of concepts, theories and knowledge emerging from feminist writings/women's studies. In these areas the Centre for Women's Studies and Development of Banaras Hindu University has achieved a considerable degree of success.

One looks back with satisfaction on faculty participation in the revision of curricula, which is reflected in the teaching programmes of sociology, law, political science, education and, to a smaller proportion, in history. These changes depend a great deal on the heads of particular departments and the willingness of the faculty to pursue revisions in the curriculum, and above all this, to be willing to exert themselves in inculcating these changes within their teaching. Wherever such transformation has made headway it has been made successful by a labour of love. Centres for women's studies at some institutions have not only themselves been involved in teaching but are now also conducting certificate and degree courses. This is easier in women's universities. Yet, a feeling is now generally gaining ground, which is also reflected in the new guidelines of the UGC for the Ninth Plan, that teaching should be a part of the programme of centres for women's studies. The new nomenclature of staff is also at par with designations in the university. I am sure with the strengthened infrastructure, women's studies centres will succeed in promoting conceptual, theoretical, methodological and pedagogical aspects with interdisciplinary inputs from other faculties.

A word of caution is necessary here. A teaching programme in women's studies must be adequately linked to the examination system as well as employment opportunities. Already existing fellowships instituted by the ICSSR, the UGC and various development agencies have been acting as incentives to scholars to opt for women's studies. At Banaras Hindu University, the CWSD has been organising lectures for students in different departments and helping teachers to use emerging knowledge in women's studies. As a professor of sociology, I worked with the department to include optional courses in women's studies at the M.Phil and M.A. levels. Several topics in women's studies were incorporated in courses taught at the undergraduate level. We also contributed to the undergraduate textbook on women's studies prepared by SNDT University with UNESCO support. The department of sociology at Banaras Hindu University has a professorship in women's studies, which is now lying vacant subsequent to the retirement of the founding director of the centre.

At the CWSD, besides the work of the research staff engaged in their own fields of enquiry (all related to women's studies), we began by taking stock of existing dissertations/theses on various aspects of women's lives and all not could be classified under women's studies, it gave us a general idea about the type of research being undertaken in the university. As noted earlier, the CWSD is a researcher-friendly place and many scholars from different disciplines have interacted with us and a number of colleagues have been inspired to embark on work in gender issues. One from the law school acknowledges the influence of the centre and its library resources on his interest in feminist jurisprudence; another from political science began work on women as riot victims; and the economics department has for the first time showed interest in the segmented gender market. The real spurt took place in doctoral research on women. Earlier, women students were given research problems relating to women to make things easier for them and for their families to allow fieldwork, but now scholars undertaking research into women's lives and work are not only women, but to a large extent also include men.

The Centre for Women's Studies and Development at Banaras Hindu University has assisted scholars from various departments within the university as well as from other universities in the region. Scholars from USA, Canada, the Netherlands, Iran, etc., have also profited from their association with the centre. Since all research scholars of the centre were also engaged in their own research work, it has not been possible to launch a sustained long-term project.

The opportunity to be part of the multi-centre study, 'The Girl Child and the Family', was instrumental not only in providing an extensive data base but also in strengthening the networking between the women's studies centres involved in the study. Many gaps in the methodological skills of smaller units and cells from non-empirical disciplines were bridged in the workshops for this study.

As part of its training activities, CWSD held a workshop for college teachers in the northern region and a smaller one for those from UP and Bihar. These proved to be very educative as did the incorporation of women's studies in the refresher courses for different subjects. Students at the Institute of Technology, Banaras Hindu University initiated debates on women-related issues in their forum.

Women's studies has often effected personal transformations, many times in the value systems and lifestyles of those we worked with, of which the most lasting would, I hope, be in the minds of the young. Men who at one time would jeer and heckle during seminars later sobered up as the gravity of the situation of women became clearer through statistics, case studies and research. When Seema Sakhare graphically described the physical and mental mutilation of a rape victim, or Sudesh Vaid unravelled the nexus between big businesses and sati worship, there was shock and disbelief, leaving the assembly speechless. Women students spoke of feeling a new sense of dignity, drawing strength from the awareness that there really is nothing to be ashamed of in being a woman. Many found the courage to speak to parents or elders about letting them choose their careers or marriage partners. These gains cannot be overlooked for finally it is the sense of dignity and self-respect that women get from here which keeps them going in the search for a space in society.

The citizens of Varanasi and the vernacular media took keen interest in the activities of the CWSD but it was generally believed to be a structure for women's upliftment, an institute undertaking social work and was expected to carry out the role of policing society! Research reports and seminars were widely discussed and the centre's staff was invited to speak to the 'Rotarians', 'Lions' and 'Lionesses' and other outfits, evidence of the considerable interest that was being generated in the community.

Extension work, considered to be a significant component of the women's studies programme, and its distinctive approach within the system of higher education, was problematic for us due to lack of personnel and resources. An opportunity, though time-bound, came our way through the UP government (supported by Dutch funds) proposal for social motivation of rural population towards acceptance of safe drinking water and household sanitation. We accepted the project eagerly as it was the ideal chance for an entry into rural areas (27 villages around the Banaras Hindu University with 9,000 families). We organised the women's groups in each *mohalla*, apparently to discuss the client's objectives of constructing household latrines and persuading people to use tap water supply, but with the implicit goal of providing a forum for the women, which would break their isolation and bring awareness about their common social problems and the mechanisms to deal with these through joint action. The extension work for this project was a great learning experience for the researchers.

Another major extension effort was possible through a project from State Innovations in Family Planning Agency (a World Bank and UP government collaboration), which the CWSD took up. It was a challenge to work with the women pradhans, newly elected under the Panchayati Raj. Earlier, in an advisory capacity, I had sought to direct public focus on women's reproductive rights and the need to respect their decisions concerning the same. Thus, women leaders were at the heart of our extension work. They, on the one hand, talked to the women in the villages about their needs, aspirations and options for family size, and on the other, were themselves motivated to discuss their newly acquired political strength and how to use it for development. This was a unique experience for the pradhans, many of whom bloomed before our very eyes, from shy, veiled and silent observers to very vocal and impressive participants.

It is sad that the work undertaken under these two projects with in-built extension prospects had to be discontinued with the completion of the project. It may be noted here that not every one has the training or inclination for extension work. Thus, it would be preferable to identify persons with research aptitude or extension work, each of which would supplement the other.

Lastly, it may be confessed that the centre was weakest in the sphere of action. While action was evidently present as participation in campaigns against sati, population policy, economic reforms, etc., only a few incidents can be recounted where action led to redress. In the case of rape in a boy's hostel, the chief proctor said that since the victim had not made any complaint, they could take no action. In the case of forced entry by police into the homes of some sex workers, CWSD took up the issue with the district administration leading to quick action, restoring the dignity of sex workers. When we were approached for assistance by a young person working among the children of sex workers through his organisation, 'Guria', we were able to take up the matter with the chair-person of the National Commission when she came to the *Mahila Adalat* organised by the CWSD. She met with the sex workers and held a dis-cussion regarding their rights as citizens.

Looking back at the first 10 years of women's studies at Banaras Hindu University, one is struck by the multifarious activities taken up during the initial period, with such little resources. I remember how a senior women's studies colleague was astonished at the high activity maintained by the centre, including 29 seminars and workshops organis-ed from 1988–96. These kept women's issues alive and visible.

The sudden brake

Months before my retirement, I had requested the vice-chancellor to put in some careful consideration in choosing the new director for the centre, to which he agreed. He also asked me to help in orienting the new person. But when the time did come, not much thought was given to the suitability of the candidate for the post of director. Being a woman was enough and this became the only centre in the country where a medical doctor was appointed as its co-ordinator. A decade of sweat and blood on the nurturing of a fledging was abandoned to routine and remote control.

However, with the revised guidelines of the UGC for the Ninth Plan having directed that the position of coordinator/director of a women's studies centre be a full-time position, to be filled by a selection committee having a member of the Advisory Committee of the UGC, it is hoped that right direction will be provided to the centres, including the Centre at Banaras Hindu University. Now with the prospect of full-fledged department status, it is expected that women's studies will finally come of age.

One can only hope that all is not lost yet.

Activities at a glance: 1987–96

Teaching

- Curriculum development at undergraduate level (report).
- Introduction of optional papers on women's studies at the M.A. and M.Phil levels, as well as incorporation of several topics in different courses taught at undergraduate level in sociology.
- Preparation of teaching/learning material. Classification of material in 15 dossiers.
- Contribution to a textbook on women's studies.

Research and action–research

- Documentation for research consultation.
- Research work on women and dowry, women in coal mines and stone quarries, women and law, women and media etc.
- Research projects on girls' science education, rural sanitation and health education, the girl child and family and women pradhans

under Panchayati Raj (The Centre took up a survey-cum-action project for the Rashtriya Mahila Kosh in 1997–98).

Workshops, seminars and camps

- Women's studies for college teachers of northern India
- Women's political participation in India
- Rural sanitation and health education
- Teaching women's studies
- Rape and rape laws
- Women and religion
- Women and peace
- Women and media
- Women and communalism
- Women and health
- Gender and history
- Women and law
- New economic reforms and women
- A refresher course for faculty (1998)

Networking

- VHAI
- CHETNA
- CWDS
- RUWS/SNDT
- IAWS
- Mahila Samakhya
- Mahila Mukti Morcha
- Jagori

Extension and action

- Social motivation for sanitation and health education.
- Training of women pradhans and motivation for reproductive control and decision-making.

7

A challenging and inspiring journey

School of Women's Studies, Jadavpur University

Jasodhara Bagchi

The genesis

I find it difficult to write an 'analytical case study', having been the Founder-Director of the Women's Studies Centre in Jadavpur University. The richness, in terms of interpersonal warmth and interactive self-discoveries that the experience involved, often made me want to reverse the famous opening lines of Dante's *Inferno*. Instead of 'In the middle of my life I lost my way', I have wanted to say, 'In the middle of my life I found my way'. Endorsing the repudiation of the private/public dichotomy in the early feminist slogan 'personal is political', I would like to begin with the personal.

I begin by confessing a major slip-up—my relative gender blindness in defining my own involvement in the Left democratic movement, which comes home to me again and again as I look back at my (mis)reading of the Status Committee Report in the *Economic and Political Weekly*. It took me quite a few years to fathom what a major text it was, as this unprepossessing-looking government document became the 'founding text' of our movement. I have used every conceivable opportunity later to make amends, once I acquired the skills of reading *Towards Equality*.

However, as contrasted with that early faux pas, there were several positive contributing factors. Getting to know, through Maithreyi Krishnaraj, Neeraben (Prof Neera Desai) and the rich library of the

Research Centre for Women's Studies at SNDT University, the enthralling world of women's studies was an unforgettable experience. The constitutive factor, however, was the feminist collective some of us founded in Calcutta in 1982, named *Sachetana* by Sukumari Bhattacharji, with a consciously gendered political thrust. We were committed to consciousness—not as an essentialist category but as a major component in the material existence of women. Some of the insights I gained from working in this group helped me to conceptualise as well as operationalise the School of Women's Studies, when I was entrusted with the task of starting it.

An interesting aspect of the School of Women's Studies in Jadavpur University was that it was germinated with seed money from the university as one of 11 interdisciplinary schools that were going to push the boundaries of existing disciplines, on major issues of social concern, such as environment, energy, water resource and management, and media communication and culture, to name a few. This was the time when the UGC Guidelines on Women's Studies Centres arrived in the University.

Teaching/research/extension was the mandate of the first UGC guidelines. It was like having to start a garden in the middle of a desert. What follows is not an exhaustive account of our activities—there is a report that gives a fuller account. What I shall try to describe is the nature of the opportunities that came our way, and the ways in which these opened up human resources within the university, and the outreach we were able to achieve. We took on the challenge of the UGC's mandate in a spirit of rare collaboration. From the Dean, Prof Amiya Dev, to Karuna Chakraborty who ran our office, we braved the world and won significant victories.

Early support

Feminist scholars lent friendly support to get us started. In early 1988, an Interdisciplinary School of Women's Studies was on the anvil and as head of the English department, I had invited Susie Tharu to spend two weeks as Visiting Fellow. To raise the consciousness of the university community, I arranged a talk by her on 'Women Writing in India'—a project that was to launch women's studies with a splash. The topic was of special significance to me as it was an area I had demarcated in my mind as one that we would take up in a big way as a possible part of our course. In December 1988 my friend and former pupil, Dr Himani Banerjee, gave a series of five lectures on 'Feminism and method'. All this was before any grant from the UGC had come through. We opened a tiny office in the central library and charged a small fee for the xeroxed material we circulated. The response was overwhelming. Not only colleagues from all the departments, but teachers from other institutions, and activists from women's groups and NGOs, began to attend in larger numbers as the days went on. This crossing of barriers stayed with us as a source of strength and support. We got started in this small way despite certain initial skepticism.

The School of Women's Studies had no room of its own, but it had a major ally in Krishna Datta, the librarian, who gave us not only un-stinted support but also the use of her room on the ground floor of the central library from where we operated in the first few months. The incipient School of Women's Studies was given an initial blessing by the UGC in the form of a Ford Foundation book grant of Rs 1 lakh. Krishna Datta and I had a gala time going through catalogues and plac-ing orders with our local booksellers. As the books started coming in, Krishna rummaged through the assets of the central library and iden-tified three or four almirahs to house the books. This was the nucleus of the School of Women's Studies in a corner on the top floor of the central library and which still continues to cater to many readers.

The beginning

Academic networking

The first budgetary sanction came practically at the end of the aca-demic year of 1989. Our first venture was a national seminar entitled 'Indian women: myth and reality'. The collective spirit, with which the School has always operated, was easily visible in the organisation of this challenging seminar. For instance, it was here that I learnt to rely on Dr Anuradha Chanda, beginning the mutual trust and confidence that has continued to this day.

Support from outsiders was also overwhelming. Ashapurna Debi, the famous writer, agreed to inaugurate the seminar, despite her physical disability. We gauged the warmth and fellow feeling of women's studies activists. Neeraben and Maithreyi Krishnaraj came from the oldest of women's studies centres. Susie Tharu, Leela Gulati and our fiery journalist, Manimala, came to lend support. Nirmala and Ratnabala, two comrades-in-arms, were present. Manabendra Bandyopadhyay and younger scholars like Sibaji Bandyopadhyay and Mainak Biswas spoke and have continued to provide unfailing support. Tapati Guha Thakurta's collaborative presentation with Ratnabala on gender representation in art remains memorable. Sukumari Bhattacharji and Tanika Sarkar, the mother-daughter scholar-activist duo, who have continued to expose gender inequality in ancient and modern India, were both present. Kalpana Das Gupta, opened the book exhibition we had mounted in the central library; her salutary warning on the arduousness of the search for material on women's studies, remained with us and helped us out in several ways. The intimate bonding that the School had felt with the library and information in general, owes not a little to this early association with the library. With this seminar began the dialogue with our redoubtable colleagues.

Curriculum development and teaching

It is in the library that we organised, in 1990, the next big workshop, this time a far more participatory one—on 'Curriculum development in women's studies', inaugurated by Prof Vina Mazumdar. We were divided into three sub-groups to explore concepts and ideas relating to culture, social sciences and technology and each sub-group made its presentation. Only the technology group decided to have a brainstorming session. From this point we began our decade-long effort to dialogue with the mainstream departments within the university, bringing out the commonality of gender boundaries. Once we started bringing out our newsletter, we regularly reported on the ways in which women's studies was making its presence felt in research and teaching in other departments.

Quite a number of us believed that women's studies should play an interventionist and catalytic role, rather than get absorbed in mainstream teaching. Happily, we have on the whole, succeeded in keeping to this. To mention a few prominent instances, Prof Jaba Guha, who has worked with us closely, has strengthened the gender and development component in the M. Phil course in economics. Dr Anuradha Chanda, during her tenure as head of the department of history, organised a very interesting three-day seminar on 'Women and history', which is being put together by her as a book.

The J.D. Birla College of Home Science, our only affiliated college, sought our help in framing a women's studies syllabus and in helping them to get started in teaching the course. We worked out a course curriculum and took turns teaching it for two years. Afterwards one of their faculty took it up, having gone through intensive sessions with us. Similarly, we have helped out a leading NGO, the Jayaprakash Institute of Social Change, to handle the MSW course on behalf of Vidyasagar University. Sarbani Goswami has continued to teach the 'Gender and development' course for them and I have been setting questions and examining answer scripts.

Our greatest challenge in putting to use our experience in curriculum development has been in running two refresher courses in women's studies. We had the good fortune of collaborating with the Centre for Women's Development Studies, who shared their resources, human and material, with great generosity. I think the School of Women's Studies lived up to the challenging task that the UGC assigned it, particularly in catering to the north-eastern region. Once again, commitment to women's studies and cooperation has been the mainstay of this fine teamwork.

Information and advocacy

The first recruitment of the UGC-sanctioned centre was that of Sarbani Goswami as the Research Officer. A feminist activist with a background in information science, she shared our conviction that 'right information to the right person', played a crucial role in promoting gender awareness in society. We learnt by experience that a women's studies centre could become a major resource centre for the community at large. Arun Ghosh, the then librarian of the Centre for Studies in Social Sciences, Calcutta, was our great ally in this venture. I learned from him the important lesson that in women's studies, the so-called 'ephemera', i.e., leaflets, posters, slogans, broadsheets and reports, were to be considered on par with books and journals. We have taken this advice to heart and the sense of vocation with which our little office has catered to the needs of the community at large, both academic and extra-academic, owes not a little to this orientation.

In this also, we have had considerable assistance from the stalwarts; Harsha Parekh of SNDT University library and Anju Vyas of CWDS, have indulged many of my harebrained ideas. The volume called *Information on Religion and Culture* that was released during the IAWS National Conference held in Jadavpur University in 1991 was the product of one such idea. Conceding to my request, the collaborative information workshop on 'gender and development' was turned, happily, into one on 'Gender, Culture and Development', without a murmur. Harsha's presence in our refresher courses has been a cause for celebration.

A room of one's own

For the first few months of the School's existence, Sarbani and I operated from my tiny cubbyhole in the English department to which I had moved once my headship was over. We had brought out a mimeographed list of the books we had acquired with the UGC–Ford Foundation grant and moved from place to place in the university. However, our great ally and fellow feminist, Prof Amiya Dev, then the dean of the Faculty of Arts, managed to find us a room on the ground floor of the older Arts building. After a trip to Paris and New York in the summer of 1990, I came back and moved into the room, having bought minimal furniture out of the UGC grant. The school began to acquire an identity of its own.

Projects: major and minor

Apart from individual research, the School opened up possibilities of collective research based on fieldwork and archival work. It helped to broaden vistas and to bridge the gap between the university and the world outside. I learnt as much about women's studies from these projects as from the books I read or the seminars and workshops I attended.

Local

Calcutta for women   One of the earliest projects we undertook was a mapping of the terrain. At the very start, we had decided to network with the local organisations that were working for women's interest. Our modest project began with the municipality of Calcutta and this was the start of our decade-long association with women's organisations. The booklet we brought out was our tribute to Calcutta on the occasion of the tercentenary of the city.

National

As a UGC-funded centre, we were involved in a number of collaborative projects in which several women's studies centres participated.

Girl child and the family   'Girl child and the family' was a nationwide project sponsored by the Department of Women and Child Development, under the Ministry of Human Resource Development. Twenty-two centres took part in the project which was based on a common questionnaire translated into the languages of the different states where it was administered. As a venture in joint collaborative research, this was a unique experience for women's studies centres under the UGC.

The survey was conducted among 600 households and I have no hesitation in claiming that the massive data that was unearthed must be quite unique anywhere in the world, both in quantity as well as quality. The book that we brought out of the project report, which we have called *Loved and Unloved,* has received overwhelming response from readers at the national and international levels, notably from activists of human rights, UNICEF, the District Primary Education Programme and so on.

All these studies, looked at in tandem, are an indication of the collective strength of women's studies within the university structure.

Women and child labour in the *beedi* industry   A number of women's studies centres were brought together once again, this time by the initiative of Prof Susheela Kaushik, in a project sponsored by the Ministry of Labour, to study the plight of *beedi* workers. We took up Murshidabad district, in North Bengal. Among the aspects we studied were: the revival of the 'putting-out' system, the suppression of information in denying women workers their proper identity cards, and the double exploitation of children, who are denied the opportunity of schooling, and are harassed as virtually unpaid labour.

Impact study of Rashtriya Mahila Kosh   It has by now become a homily to assert that micro-credit made easily available to women, is the primary panacea for the troubles of third world women. At the instance of the dynamic leader of Rashtriya Mahila Kosh, Indira Mishra, a number of women's studies centres came together on yet another occasion to do impact studies of the micro-credit programme run by Rashtriya Mahila Kosh in different states in India. We studied two NGOs, a very large one called Mass Education, in the adjacent district of South 24-Parganas and a rather smaller one in Howrah district. The entire sample came from families that lived below the poverty line.

International

Shastri–CIDA collaborative project with York University, Toronto, Canada   For this collaborative project on the dynamics of women's empowerment within the limited resource base of an urban slum, we chose to study a very well-known and established slum in Khidirpur, one of the oldest parts of Calcutta, through a variety of methods such as household survey, focus group interviews, workshops with NGOs and surveys of clubs and NGOs. The focus of the study turned out to be woman's body—related to her fertility as the terrain of her agency. The entire team of researchers travelled to Canada and the dissemination of the reports drew a great deal of interest, both nationally and internationally. A manual in Bengali on women's health, prepared by Krishna Banerjee, has reached many rural areas and has been translated into Hindi by an NGO.

Our very own

Women writers of Bengal: A reprint series   One of the most cherished and representative projects of the School of Women's Studies, the Women Writers of Bengal series, was partly inspired by the Anveshi project on women's writing and partly by a galling awareness of the socially-induced amnesia with which the many-splendoured percept-ions, insights and creativity of these writers had been neglected, side-lined or co-opted, leaving only very faint traces, if at all. Prof Subir Roychoudhury, a man of immense scholarship on the 19th and early 20th century, responded to my call for help with much warmth, and became the editor of the series of reprints of the writing of Bengali women. Most of these writers were born within a span of 15 years, from the last decade of the 19th century to the first decade of the present. Prof Roychoudhury lived to edit two books, but left his legacy in Abhijit Sen, who has continued to edit the relevant texts, often digging them up from the old and brittle pages of periodicals, some of which will perish soon. This has been a prolific series. Many of the older writers had not had formal schooling worth mentioning, but the level of understanding of what in current terminology would pass as 'Gender and development' is often mind-boggling. It helped to cement the alignment our School had made from the start, of 'development' with 'culture'. Another offshoot was the massive work undertaken by Dr Shivani Banerjee Chakravorty on stories about the girl child by women writers. She compiled and translated a series of stories that are awaiting publication. Three of her translated stories were included in *Childhood That Never Was,* edited by Veena Poonacha, which was the outcome of the joint work of many women's studies centres on the 'Girl child and the family'.

Research associates

Apart from Dr Shivani Banerjee Chakravorty, we have had two other research associates in succession—Dr Indrani Basu Roy, whose work on the women artisans of Kalighat, was published in a volume on the gender aspects of artisan culture in the Asia-Pacific region, which was released at the Beijing Conference; and Dr Ashim Mukhopadhyay whose work captured the early years of the large-scale participation by women in Panchayati Raj in West Bengal. Dr Mukhopadhyay has also helped me in coordinating the project on 'Women and child labour in the *beedi* industry'.

Notable collaboration

Indian Association of Women's Studies

We are proud to have collaborated with the Indian Association of Women's Studies which has played a central role in the spread of women's studies in the country, the most important instance of which was the hosting of the Fifth National Conference of Women's Studies in Jadavpur. On this occasion, it was our privilege to bring out a collaborative bibliography of regional holdings related to religion and culture. Subsequently, we have collaborated in the organising of three regional seminars. The last one saw a collaboration of both the Women's Studies Centres in Calcutta. Organised at our end by my successor, Dr Anuradha Chanda, it was by all accounts the liveliest of all the three events. It fills me with special pride to think of the splendid teamwork on which the functioning of the School of Women's Studies has rested.

Indian Science Congress

In 1995, Jadavpur University hosted the Indian Science Congress. We were asked to host a forum on 'Women and science'. For three days we organised discussions on different aspects of the ways in which science impacts on gender issues. It certainly gave an added fillip to the continuous dialogue we have tried to keep open, with our colleagues, male and female, in the science and engineering faculties. A breakthrough appears to be in sight—Dr Anuradha Chanda has succeeded in forming an active committee on 'Women and science and technology'.

Indo–French–Russian colloquium

It was during a visit to the Maison de Science de l'Homme in 1990, that Prof Svetlana Anivasova of the Science Academy, USSR, and I, got together with feminist activist groups in Paris and decided to organise a colloquium entitled 'Feminisms: France, India and Russia'. In 1992, a group of feminist activist scholars went to Paris and a team from Russia was organised by Svetlana. Between the planning and the execution of the colloquium, USSR had become plain Russia and the colloquium became a very important dialogue between women from three different societies, between whom there were major interconnections of commonalities as well as differences. The second colloquium was held in Calcutta. This time, Prof Bharati Ray who headed the Women's Studies Centre at the University of Calcutta, joined me and the two Centres collaborated on the venture. I appreciatively look back on the verve with which Prof Ray conducted the concluding panel discussion on the political activism of women from each of the three countries. Prof Ray was chosen to edit the volume which resulted from the colloquium and it is now awaiting publication.

Visitors and affiliates

Prof Himani Banerjee, our first affiliate, has continued to participate in our academic activities in each of her visits to Calcutta. She has also completed her gender research from our school and is all set to publish a book called *Reform and Hegemony: Bodies and Power*. Another book based on our collaborative work in Khidirpur is in the process of completion.

Suzanne Benton, the noted metal sculptor, spent a few delightful months here. We had given her an open space in the electrical engineering department where she could be seen wearing her gas mask and welding her pieces of sculpture.

At the end of her stay, Dr Shefali Moitra hosted a seminar on 'Women, heritage and violence', where many activists from different fields discussed the latent violence that women are forced to face in the name of heritage. Rachel Weber, the urban geographer, used our contact with a former refugee resettled area, and completed a piece of work on reorganisation of space by refugee women in Calcutta. Reba Som is expected to write up her field-based study of middle-class South Asian immigrant women in Ontario.

We celebrated Helen Cixous' visit to the Calcutta Book Fair in 1997, with a distinguished panel of speakers who sat face to face with Cixous addressing different aspects of her colourful feminist thought. Dr Shefali Moitra interrogated her on the epistemological foundation of her work,

Prof Supriya Chaudhuri looked at her theory of *écriture feminine* and Dr Rustam Bharucha explored her play on India. Cixous's responses were warm and rich.

'Ay, there's the rub'

If my case study has taken on a carnivalesque edge, it is because we have been in a continuous state of marvelling at the ways in which the university could be made to open up to such a wide social spectrum of common pursuit. Did it mean, however, that it was all smooth sailing with no rough weather? This would hardly be possible, seeing as how we began from scratch; gathering substance along the way, battling storms and vanquishing monsters. Here I describe some patches of the rough weather we had to negotiate, sometimes failing in our attempts. In spite of the failures, the journey has been momentous and continually inspiring.

Artasangee: A failed experiment

The gender dimension to our entire venture is as evident in the failures and difficulties as in the successes. One training-cum-extension activity we planned was taking up a para-nursing training programme on home care of the young and the aged, which had been drawn up by Vivek Chetana, a local NGO with whom we had been working in close collaboration. We organised this training in collaboration with the Adult and Continuing Education and Extension Centre, Jadavpur University, the famous Cancer Hospital in Thakurpukur, and Nabaneer, a home for the aged. Some of the best doctors and teachers of nursing were involved. We arranged for a stipend and uniform for the trainees. At the end of two years, we found that it was next to impossible to find proper placements for them. In theoretical terms, families and homes proved to be unsuitable places for recognition of 'skilled persons' and the nurses tended to be treated as domestic servants. Also, the girls, mostly from nearby rural areas, once trained, were more eager to go in for further training, rather than use the skill they had acquired. After two years we simply decided to discontinue the training programme.

Sexual trade unionism

A few students from the Department of Bengali appealed to us for redressal against sexual harassment by a male professor. In the absence of any existing machinery to handle this, we tried to urge the university authorities to take up the matter. We even managed to move the administration to institute inquiry committees. Though we did succeed in generating some sense of confidence among the students concerned, and possibly among others too, we realised in very concrete terms how important it was to have a cell with well worked-out modalities of complaint and appropriate action. As a result of our persistent tenacity in this particular case, the university did form a grievance cell with Dr Shefali Moitra as a permanent invitee from the School of Women's Studies. While we could consider this a partial success, it was a revelation to see the kind of gender-based hostility we faced not only from our male colleagues but also from some women colleagues who clearly felt more comfortable cooperating with patriarchal hierarchies than with challenging them. The biggest eye-opener was that our own Teachers' Association decided to back their male colleagues in a spirit of trade unionism. This confirms the oft-cited gender hostility of trade unions in many different aspects.

Administration

This brings me to another curious observation. My retirement from the professorship and the honorary directorship of the school at the age of 60 was according to my personal wish. Yet, I cannot help but observe the curious fact that while I was told that re-employed teachers could not remain directors of interdisciplinary schools and centres and, therefore, was not asked to continue by the university administration, most male colleagues have continued as directors of the schools they founded. It was Dr Chanda's personal effort that made the authorities appoint me in the position of adviser to the School for Women's Studies at Jadavpur University. While I am happy that I could move on to another phase of my work of research and advocacy after retirement, the whole thing leaves me a little worried about the existence of gender discrimination in the administrative setup of the university.

The worst eye-opener was what I experienced as a member of the Standing Committee on Women's Studies, before Prof Armaity S. Desai came to be the Chairperson. Meetings were not held because the Convener could not face demanding and aggressive women! The difference was especially visible after Prof Desai joined. The personal warmth and efficiency of the Chairperson and the Convener, Professor Kamalini Bhansali, has generated a momentum which has brought us this far.

The last word

Constantly rocked by oscillating encouragement and obstruction, the School of Women's Studies now has a presence locally, nationally and internationally. Dealing with socially-induced violence, in theory, documentation and action, has emerged as one of our focal points of interest. Collaborative work with the Counselling Cell started on the campus is increasingly bringing this about. We have also made a campus-wide survey and have recommended the opening of a crèche—not an easy job once you get down to it. Our emphasis on women's active political participation has found a major focal point in the oral history project that Kavita Panjabi and Shivani Banerjee Chakravorty have just completed on the Tebhaga Movement that rocked Bengal before and after Independence. The revision of unyielding canons, and the crossing of disciplinary boundaries have made the School of Women's Studies at Jadavpur University a major presence in academia and in the 'concerned' sections of our society. We have adopted a motto from Kant, which I think sums up the challenging experience of these years: 'dare to know'.

8

Towards justice

Centre for Women's Studies, Calcutta University

Bharati Ray

It was the early 1980s. Initially a historian of colonialism, I had been increasingly drawn to women's studies and was engaged in research on women in India. As I proceeded, I realised that we needed a team of researchers to survey and study the status and condition of women in India in the context of the women's movement worldwide. It also became increasingly clear that if the ultimate aim of women's studies was to eliminate the gender-related inequities in what we call 'development', so as to improve the quality of women's lives, academic research must go hand-in-hand with activism. I felt frustrated about not being able to communicate or collaborate with scholars and activists who I knew were working in the field. I too wanted to contribute to the movement towards justice for women; I wanted to organise, to interact, and to collaborate.

An opportunity presented itself when I became the pro vice-chancellor of the University of Calcutta in 1988. I set women's studies as the priority area in my agenda of academic programmes and immediately applied for a UGC financial grant to establish a women's studies centre. It was approved in 1989. Work started modestly. The centre was inaugurated by the then Chief Minister of West Bengal, Shri Jyoti Basu, in April 1989. The celebrated Darbhanga Building was full; students, male and female, exhibited genuine enthusiasm; a two-day seminar followed. But, functions and ceremonies hardly make a centre. There was need for hard work and planning. This short piece aims to describe three things. First, the plans we made and the actions we took to implement these; second, the support we enjoyed; and third, the obstacles we faced.

Resolute first steps

Involving the university community

We decided at the beginning that we would act as a catalytic agent in drawing involvement from various departments of the university, into women's studies. When we conveyed this mission to the staff and students of other departments, most were keen to pool resources, and so we organised seminars, workshops and discussion meetings with their collaboration and often in their halls. The departments of biochemistry, botany, chemistry, history, sociology, political science, education, journalism and economics, frequently provided us venues and other required infrastructure. On such occasions, the teachers of these departments took over the entire charge, the core members of the centre assisted, and the director presided. We invited interested teachers to be 'associate members' of the centre—a designation created by us to give these teachers a formal/official connection with us, mostly in order to represent the centre when necessary and to guide young scholars in research and extension work. Here our success was phenomenal. Teachers worked and undertook research in cooperation with the centre; a good number arranged meetings in their faculty; many introduced a women's studies component in their syllabi at the M.A. and M.Phil level. The fact that more than 50 doctoral theses in women's issues were undertaken after the creation of the centre, is indicative of the appeal of women's studies, and the involvement of the university community in women's studies.

Mobilising the young

The major thrust of our activities was to involve the undergraduate colleges under Calcutta University (there were 204 of them). We organised more than 30 seminars in undergraduate colleges outside the university campus, the purpose of which was to attract the young—both male and female students—and enthuse them about women's studies. We strongly felt that merely pointing out the gender blindness of our social structure, whether traditional or modern, was not enough; it was necessary, at the same time, to build a new, younger generation that would start with a gender-aware, gender-sensitive and gender-equitable base. Here our strategy was novel and our success unexpected. We organised a students' forum consisting of undergraduate students, who became the core group of the centre, participating in discussions and facilitating the participation of many other students and teachers. Our seminars were widely attended—sometimes overcrowded for an academic venture, which served our purpose of sensitising and involving as many as possible and spreading the message of women's studies. The students often took centrestage, frequently conducting discussion meetings in other colleges as well. I had planned to form a group that could go to schools and colleges in the district towns with the same agenda of activity; however, before the plan could be put into action, it was time for me to leave.

Participation from schools

We went to several schools in Calcutta and its suburbs, held talks with secondary and higher secondary students in girls' schools, to make them aware of the gender biases in society, and about the discriminations that they would be or were already facing, simply for being the 'wrong' gender. These talks were intended to raise the level of awareness of the girls about their own status in society, about their right to just and equitable social responses, to raise their level of self-confidence by bringing to them knowledge of the changes that were taking place all over the world and in India particularly, in the status of women, and to show them how the fight for justice was continuously being carried forward by strong and courageous women. It was great to hear the girls respond with slogans and shouts, and request for further talks.

Collaboration—A crucial key

We interacted with several NGOs and associated with the National Service Schemes of different colleges and even persuaded a few colleges to allocate their financial and human resources for the promotion of health awareness and the creation of facilities for new mothers and their children such as the 'Safe Motherhood Programme'. We also joined hands with the literacy mission activities in the state, and encouraged the participation of women in these activities. There was an opportunity for one of us to serve in the *Lok Adalat*, where a number of cases relating to the wilful desertion of wives by their husbands and a few cases regarding maintenance came up. Our member tried her best to see that justice was done to the complainants, who were mostly women.

Networking is crucial

We also attempted to network with scholars and activists in the field and participated in state, national and international seminars. Young scholars like Supriya Guha, Nandini Chatterjee and Paula Banerjee attended seminars in India and abroad on behalf of the centre, and benefited vastly from the exposure. It became very clear to us that networking was a crucial element in carrying forward the torch of women's studies.

Research is fundamental

We conducted investigations in various fields, for instance, among scheduled caste, rural as well as urban women. We concentrated on original research in three areas: history, science and local language writings on women and by women. Of our significant publications, mention may be made of *Sekaler Narisiksha: Bamabodhini Patrika (1863–1920)* (Women's education of yesteryears: *Bamabodhini Patrika*), a collection of articles on education hand-copied from the outstanding journal *Bamabodhini Patrika; Women and Science,* a volume of articles on the contributions of women scientists; *Persisting Disadvantages: Women Engineers,* a study of women engineers vis-à-vis male engineers; *Detecting Disadvantages: A Study of Scheduled Caste Women in Three*

Villages of Bengal, based on empirical field study; *From the Seams of History: Essays on Indian Women,* a collection of essays on Indian women, written especially for this volume by distinguished scholars on women and gender; *French and Indian Women,* a comparative study of the political participation of Indian and French women; an unpublished thesis, 'Medicalisation of child-birth in Bengal'; and about 20 other articles published by scholars of the centre. Ten small booklets on women and law, commissioned by the Department of Social Welfare, were translated from English into simple Bengali for easy comprehension by rural women.

Becoming a part of the women's movement

Our objective was to become a component of the women's movement, for though we were technically part of the university system, we saw ourselves as a part, however tiny, of the larger movement for gender justice. While carrying out our own research and field surveys, we also participated in women's collective meetings and activist programmes, to the extent possible and joined in *jathas,* processions and demonstrations to object to atrocities against women and to demand equal civil, economic and human rights for women. In collaboration with the State Commission on Women (the Director was a member of the Commission), we became involved in dialogues with and training programmes for newly elected women panchayat leaders. It is our hope that from their midst will emerge the new generation of women leaders. We also made our modest contribution in the movement for 33 per cent reservation of seats for women in the state legislatures and the national Parliament.

How did we achieve what we did?

Team spirit

The most important factor that ensured our success, however modest, was the dedication of the research staff. We had three of them—a research officer and two research associates, apart from an office assistant and support staff (Class IV staff). Each did his/her job exceedingly well. Supriya Guha, our first research officer, also managed to start and complete her doctoral dissertation during her term. When she left, Nandini Chatterjee joined us, conducted research on women engineers, and subsequently got a lecturership in Calcutta University. In her place came Sarbani Gooptoo, who also carried on research and got a lecturership in a Calcutta college. Of our research associates, Anjali Ghosh got a readership at Jadavpur University, much to our delight. Dr Paula Banerjee was instrumental in forming the Students' Forum. We were also fortunate to get unalloyed loyalty and dedicated service from our office assistant, Sukumar Jana, and from our support staff, Sudhangshu.

The point I want to make is that I believe that the members of an organisation will nurture it with pride and labour, provided they are given adequate power, responsibility and freedom. They must grow with the centre. It is the responsibility of the director of the centre to promote junior scholars, and give them as much exposure as possible. For instance, the junior scholars from our centre participated in national and international seminars on behalf of the centre. The office assistant and the bearer were made to feel that the centre really belonged to them, and that the centre was looking after their needs.

Students' enthusiasm

Students, rather than established scholars, formed the target group of the centre, and their interest was manifest in the programmes and activities of the school. At both undergraduate and postgraduate levels, they came in as individuals as well as in groups, making meetings and activities worthwhile.

Teachers' co-operation

Teachers from the various departments were always ready to come forward in support of the centre; we only had to approach them with our agenda. One very important contribution made by the teachers was to allow us to use the Academic Staff College for disseminating our knowledge. Every single refresher course had a women's studies component.

Support of agencies outside the university

We were able to secure the help of many institutions outside the perimeter of the university, as for instance the Department of Small Scale Industries, Government of India, which gave entrepreneurship training to 40 women sent by us, and helped 12 of them to set up their own business.

Assistance from pro vice-chancellor's office

The Director being the pro vice-chancellor in charge of Academic Affairs and the Chair of the Council that approved the decisions of the Boards of Studies helped to facilitate the work, although in a minor way.
Did we face problems?
Yes, indeed, we did.

Red-tapism of accountancy

The first of our problems and the most annoying was the red-tapism, the illogically complicated rules of the accounts department. This, in spite of the fact that the Accounts Chief was sympathetic. Giving them the benefit of doubt, I try to convince myself it was not non-cooperation, merely procedural complications. Getting money from the UGC in due time was impossible. I tackled the problem by spending my own money and then getting it reimbursed when it pleased the Accounts Department to do so. But this can hardly be described as a healthy procedure. I had to go to the UGC many times just to get the money released, and to get my reimbursement. A terrible expense.

Lukewarm attitude of university authorities

Nor did we find the university authorities enthusiastic. If there is no willingness to help, or sympathy for the cause (as there was among the core staff of the centre), it is very difficult to get assistance from people.

I could not help wondering whether our male-dominated university administration truly desired women's initiatives.

Communication with the UGC

A third problem was negotiating with the UGC. The contact person for the UGC was the university UGC officer, and not the director. The women's studies centre was just one of his several responsibilities. Certificates were slow to come in from the university accounts section, submission of reports to the UGC took time, and the whole experience was frustrating.

Learning from experience

From the experiences gathered during nine years of directing a women's studies centre, I have come to feel that women's studies, if it is to be pursued, has to be treated in the manner of a cause. In its pursuit, we have to face opposition from various quarters, even from those who verbally profess support. I have often noticed a half-hidden smile of patronage or condescension where I least expected it. The danger of ghettoisation of women's studies is grave. The risk to scholars, who give up established disciplines for women's studies, is not negligible. The discipline is yet to gain recognition as a serious scholarly branch of academics. We have to deal with all these issues. Our strategy must comprise continuous research within a theoretical framework, collaboration with activists, advocacy of the mission and providing evidence of our impact on society.

As immediate administrative reforms, I suggest three methods: first, more dialogue between the university authorities and the UGC, to simplify rules and procedures; second, more freedom for the director to dialogue directly with the UGC; and third, giving younger scholars as much exposure as possible, to represent the centre, participate in national seminars, etc. I do hope that the new generation of directors in the different UGC centres and in centres outside the universities will be able to do much more than we were able to do, and give new meaning and effectiveness to women's studies in India, where it can and does make an impact in the fight for justice for women.

References

Bharati Ray (ed.) (1990), *Women and Science* (mimeograph), Calcutta: Women's Studies Research Centre.

———— (ed.) (1994a), *Sekaler Narisiksha: Bamabodhini Patrika*, Calcutta: Calcutta University Press.

———— (1994b), *Detecting Disadvantages: A Study of Scheduled Caste Women in Three Villages of West Bengal*, Calcutta: Women's Studies Research Centre.

———— (ed.) (1995), *From the Seams of History: Essays on Indian Women*, New Delhi: Oxford University Press.

9
Crossing boundary politics

Centre for Women's Studies, Alagappa University

Regina Papa

Introduction

The Alagappa University merits a space in this volume, being the first general university to introduce women's studies as a separate discipline and to have the only UGC-approved Centre for Women's Studies (AU-CWS) in the state. Placed alongside the other 22 centres in the country, relativism and stark distinction are the hallmarks of women's studies in Alagappa University, where the term 'women's studies' encompasses multi-pronged activities and skills. This paper situates women's studies in an institution of higher learning and explores its relationship to the institute and the community. The stage is not a metropolitan city but a remote, backward rural town called Karaikudi, in Tamil Nadu.

Cultural and historical identity of Tamil women

Tamil Nadu is the southernmost part of peninsular India, with a 1000 mile-long coastline on its east and the states of Andhra Pradesh, Karnataka and Kerala towards its north and west respectively. It is the seventh largest state in India and its population of 62.11 million (2001 Census) is equivalent to that of Italy or France.

The diversity of India is obviously tremendous. As Nehru observed, at one end of the socio-cultural spectrum are the Tamils and at the other

end are the Pathans of the north-west; all others lie somewhere in between. This statement underscores the distinctively unique culture of
Tamils. Generally, to the West, Indian identity is presented as that which
is seen in metropolitan cities, such as Bombay, Delhi and Calcutta. Even
those historical texts that profess to recount the history of India or
Indian women, allot only a few sentences or at most, a few paragraphs,
to Tamil history and Tamil women. This is because Tamils have a separate cultural and historical identity of their own, which is as distinct as
the Indianness into which they merge easily. This makes an understanding of the ideologies and institutions of the Tamil culture essential. If
planting women's studies in Indian universities is a national exercise,
the firmness of its roots, the rate of its sprouting and growth, and the
colour and ripeness of its fruits depend on the unique socio-cultural
ethos of the region.

Tamil society is Dravidian in origin; its hoary tradition and literary
history spans not less than 20 centuries. Tamils have never been over-
whelmed by the Mughal invasions from the north and hence retain their
peculiar Dravidian traits. Women's studies in Tamil Nadu cannot dis-
pense with those traits that inform prevailing institutions and political
ideologies in the state.

Pre-historic Tamil society was woman-centred and matri-pedestal;
at its heart was the cult of the mother-goddess conceived of as a virgin,
with women priests and women enjoying an enhanced social position.
Early Tamils did not follow the caste hierarchy of *varnashrama*; rather,
they were divided according to the kinds of land they habituated—
hilly tracts, pastureland, cultivable land, littoral and desert land.

The recorded history of the Tamils starts with the Sangam age (BC
300 to AD 100). It was a war-ravaged period and great stress was placed
on valour. Even in marriage, the determining factor, apart from the mutual
consent of the couple, was the heroic valour of the prospective groom.
The social and religious practices of early Tamil society were sidelined
to the status of a 'little tradition' by the Brahminical hegemony that
gradually crept in (200–100 BC). A hierarchical relationship between social groups was established through rigid norms and rites built on narrow notions of 'purity' and religious exclusivism. Chastity was imposed
on women, with chaste women supposed to have miraculous command
over the forces of nature, such as rain, space, time and death. Caste
and religion became the governing principles of life and one so reinforced the other that it created inequalities in every section of society;

alongside this, the cult of renunciation also spread due to Buddhist and Jain influences. In combination, these led to the emergence of the 'evil feminine' concept. The transition from female as symbolic of positive fertility to female as temptation to evil saw the arts and rituals performed by women being restricted to the 'little tradition'. Consequently, the principles that were to govern women's life became ambivalent, cast in terms of opposites and dichotomies. The belief that a woman is auspicious as a mother and goddess but polluted as a wife and a woman is still prevalent.

The colonial period was a period of awakening for some sections of Tamil women. The Church Missionaries Society opened the first girls' school, in 1821. Women were allowed to sit for examinations for a degree only from 1887, though the Madras University was established in 1857; and the entry of women into public life was made easier by Gandhi's call to women to participate in resisting the British. However, these privileges—education and social mobility—became the prerogatives of women of upper castes and the educated Christian women only.

The Dravidian movement

The fight for freedom from British imperialism developed a strange offshoot, in the form of the Dravidian movement, in the erstwhile Madras Presidency. Started in the 1920s, the movement aimed to revive the self-respect of Dravidians, which had been corroded through years of Brahmin hegemony.

The movement was founded and propagated by E.V. Ramasamy (1879–1973) who was popularly known as Periyar (the 'great'). The Dravidian movement was a liberation ideology, of revolt against the so-called 'Aryanisation' of Dravidian culture. Periyar went to the roots of the various forms of social oppression; he derided the caste system and religious myths, as mechanisms that bred inequalities. He invited all non-Brahmins to unite and fight against the supremacy of Brahmin oppressive institutions.

Periyar's feminism was part of his crusade against all forms of slavery and includes the cardinal concepts of feminist theory from liberalism to post-modernism! He spoke of equality, urging women to become educated, and gain entry into all non-traditional careers (police, army, political leadership, business, etc.); he foretold the breaking free of women from reproductive compulsions; he pointed out how language is symbolic of gender discrimination; he viewed sexuality as a site of male power and advised women to free themselves from all religious and cultural falsities that use sexuality to oppress women and establish male domination. Periyar brought into practice the 'self-respect marriage', later legalised by C.N. Annadurai, his follower and Chief Minister of Tamil Nadu. This form of marriage does away with rituals, the role of the priest, compulsions of dowry, discrimination through language and is formalised on the basis of mutual agreement between the bride and the groom on equal basis.

Periyar's view of self-respect was a powerful influence on both the intellectuals and masses of Tamil Nadu, so much so that the Dravidian parties, which started as the political propaganda machinery of Periyarism, have been winning elections and ruling the state, since 1967. Despite their factions and divisions, they all hold Periyar as their unquestionable leader.

Of late, the Brahmin–non-Brahmin dichotomy has lost its keenness. Instead, communal clashes are witnessed among non-Brahmin communities. Every caste has started its association; political parties have forsaken ideology and lean towards these associations for electoral success. Caste groups demand special favours for their community in lieu of votes. In these socially pernicious and disruptive conditions, the worst sufferers have continuously been women.

The two major Dravidian parties, Dravida Munnetra Kazhagam (DMK), and All India Anna Dravida Munnetra Kazhagam (AIADMK), vie with each other to rule the state and it has become customary for whichever party comes to power, to announce a number of women development programmes, to lure women voters.

Language is an emotive issue for Tamils and struggles are on to 'safeguard Tamil from Hindi domination'. Recently, the state government issued an order to use Tamil in Matriculation schools as the medium of instruction, up to the fifth standard and extend this to the higher classes in phases. This order has raised a furore among advocates of English medium schools.

The hold of the silver screen on Tamils is by now legendary, with cine-heroes and heroines being deified, each with a *rasigar mandram* (cine fans' association). Those at the zenith of this popularity even determine the political direction of the state and mention should be made of Mr M.G. Ramachandran—'MGR'—the matinee-idol and populist hero, who later became the Chief Minister of Tamil Nadu. This charismatic leader always addressed women as 'mothers' and was adored by them. He broke away from the Dravida Munnetra Kazhagam (DMK) to start the All India Anna Dravida Munnetra Kazhagam (AIADMK) and ruled continuously as the undefeated Chief Minister of the state from 1976, till his death on 24 December 1988.

Entry of women's studies in Tamil Nadu

It was MGR who paved the way for the entry of women's studies in Tamil Nadu. He planned to start a women's university in the name of Mother Teresa, in the hills of Kodaikanal, a beautiful summer resort. He set up a Preliminary Committee to formulate the objectives of the proposed university. This committee proposed that the new university should focus on promoting women's studies through various academic subjects with a focus on women's studies. By then, thanks to the UGC and its first woman chairperson, Madhuriben Shah, the term 'women's studies' was gaining currency among academics. The committee members included Dr Malcolm Adiseshaiah, the vice-chancellor of SNDT Women's University, Dr Radha Thiagarajan, the vice-chancellor of Alagappa University, Karaikudi, et al.

The Mother Teresa Women's University (MTWU) was established in 1987. It started with a skeleton structure of administrative staff and had no teaching faculty or students. Hence, the university conducted summer courses in various subjects for teachers drawn from all over Tamil Nadu and neighbouring states. Women professors with experience in teaching and research guidance were invited as resource persons in their respective disciplines. As a professor of English, I was invited to teach and guide research scholars in English Literature. But none of us were oriented in women's studies, its concepts, theories and methods. We were only particular about having components relevant to women in the course. We were dealing with women or women's issues, without a gender perspective or application of feminist tools. Most academicians who are recognised today as women's studies scholars or teachers in Tamil Nadu, have at some time, been on the resource team of the Mother Teresa Women's University's summer course.

Women's studies in Alagappa university

Prime facilitator: A sensitised vice-chancellor

What is significant about the women's studies programme in Alagappa University is that it functions through both a department and a UGC-approved centre. Such a situation has a parallel only in Padmavathi Mahila Vishwa Vidyalaya, Tirupati, in Andhra Pradesh. Padmavathi Mahila Vishwa Vidyalaya is a women's university whereas Alagappa University is a general institution. Hence, it devolves on me to deal with both the units in Alagappa University, their differing activities that are interwoven and mutually reinforcing. The UGC Review Committee which visited the centre on 8 April 1994, commenting on the enrichment deriving from the interdependence of the centre and department, said:

> A unique feature of the centre is that it has a symbiotic relationship with the Department of Women's Studies in the University. The staff of both the centre and the department have close interaction and actively participate in all their functions.

Indeed, this case study presents the two-way experience of women's studies—academic thought and social activism—as interrelated and mutually buttressing. Thought and action are held together in women's studies—the former by the department and the latter by the centre.

That the Alagappa University gave an academic stance and maturity to women's studies in Tamil Nadu is indisputable. The university is situated in the small, quiet town of Karaikudi, and was founded by the Tamil Nadu Act 51 of 1985. It is named after Dr Alagappa Chettiar whose munificence and love for education are legendary. Women's studies would have been unthinkable in such a remote semi-urban place had it not been for Dr Radha Thiagarajan, the first vice-chancellor of the university. The prime facilitating agent for introducing women's studies in most universities has been a sensitive head who is vibrant and dynamic. An influential head can make or mar things. Dr Radha Thiagarajan, known for her dynamism and forceful vision was in her second term as vice-chancellor when she thought of establishing a department of women's studies in the university and used her influence on academic bodies like the Syndicate and Senate of the university, to gain approval. This was quite daring on her part because Alagappa University is a general university, with male professors heading all departments, and not a women's university. The main focus of Alagappa University was on Science and Commerce courses. There were also colleges of education and physical education of long standing. Women's studies was quite an alien in such a milieu. In 1989, the department of women's studies was established with a postgraduate course, and I was invited to head the department.

Director's profile

Speaking of myself, I realise that I have been always sensitive to women's issues in society. When I was doing a comparative study of D.H. Lawrence and Jayakanthan, the Tamil progressive novelist, for a Ph.D in Comparative Literature, I did not have a theory or methodology to interpret the anger I felt against Lawrence's misogynist aversion to women. This was in the 1970s, yet I did not know the term 'women's studies'. My arguments and views on women's issues were unsubstantiated by a theoretical and ideological framework.

I have always tended towards an interdisciplinary approach. My graduation was in chemistry, my postgraduation in English literature and doctorate in comparative literature. I studied economics and politics as minors and physics as an ancillary for the degree course. The three years of research I spent on my doctoral thesis was the most intellectually enriching period of my life. It was then that I read all I could lay my hands on, be it philosophy, History or Sociology. My sentiments and convictions find a most suitable voice in Gloria Bowles, who like me, has been in comparative literature and moved to women's studies. I find my own experience mirrored in her observation quoted here.

In my own case, the choice of Comparative Literature was a way to study not a single literary culture but to find relationships between traditions. After the Ph.D, I became a student again, much of my reading in the last four years has been in the social sciences and History, I have learned just how much I can learn if my reading is selective, if I look to colleagues in other fields for guidance. This exchange of articles sometimes even results in collaborative pieces. The experience taught me again how many forms of knowledge, how many ways of looking at the world are accessible to us: we must work hard not to cut ourselves off from these multiple perceptions—or to feel too over-whelmed by all there is to know.

Bowles's feeling echoes mine almost word for word.

Although I had field experience in women's development, it was only when I was invited as a resource person to the summer courses in Mother Teresa Women's University, that I became familiar with the term 'women's studies'. The breakthrough came when I joined Mother Teresa Women's University as registrar, fortuitously under a vice-chancellor who evinced real interest in women's studies—Dr Jaya Kothai Pillai, who had previously been a resource person in the summer course. By this time, the university library had a good stock of materials on the subject and I read avidly and even prepared a handbook for students on the basic theories of women's studies. Dr Pillai had been building plans of starting a full-fledged postgraduate course in women's studies and after a visit to universities in the USA and UK, she commandeered all resources to realise this. Both Dr Pillai and I began working on the syllabi for the proposed course. The course began in MTWU in 1989. The same year the course was also started in Alagappa University, Karaikudi. When I took over as the Head of Department, uppermost in my mind was the thought of how to make women's studies an academically strong discipline which could achieve individual and social transformation. I was already in the cadre of a university professor and the new position was in no way a professional advancement for me, either in terms of rank or emoluments. At the end of almost 11 years in this most exciting and painful field, I can say that the initial commitment I felt has been all the more strengthened.

Major thrusts

Though women's studies was started as a major discipline simultaneously in Mother Teresa University and Alagappa University, there is a marked difference in the courses offered by the two universities. MTWU did not have a separate department for women's studies, but the course was offered as a collective exercise of various departments. Each department in MTWU offered a paper under the rubric of M.A., women's studies. It was a grouping of disparate papers such as 'Feminist theories and movement'; 'Women in Tamil literature'; 'Women and law'; 'Women and work'; Women and education'; 'Women and economics'; 'Women in history', etc. Just this year (1999–2000), a separate Department of Women's Studies has been started in MTWU at the initiative of Dr Yasodha Shanmugasundaram, the present vice-chancellor of the Women's University.

When Alagappa University started women's studies as a postgraduate course, clear thrust areas were identified and course papers were structured appropriately. The constraints and limitations of offering MA in women's studies were debated. We were apprehensive of the absence of feeder courses in the subject at the BA level in any college or university in the state. Every other postgraduate course drew its students' strength from the corresponding bachelor degree courses in colleges. After successful completion of the postgraduation, more women students were absorbed as teachers or lecturers in the same subject in schools and colleges. We were sure this could not be our case. In addition, the course has also to confront the chronic unemployment and underemployment situation in the country. Finally, we fixed on self-employment and social action as the major thrust areas. As management was essential in entrepreneurship as well as social action, administration/management was added as another thrust area of the course.

Curriculum building

The curriculum for women's studies had to be formulated keeping in mind the special nature of this subject, taking into consideration both 'intrinsic' and 'extrinsic' demands made on the course, giving equal weightage to both theoretical and practical inputs including fieldwork, internship and project assignment according to the career choice of the student.

In our case too, the syllabus was framed so as to instil in students a feminist consciousness and enhance the specific skills needed to enlarge their career choices. To help us in framing syllabi, we sought the guidance of Dr Kamalini Bhansali, herself a women's studies expert and the then vice-chancellor of SNDT Women's University, Bombay. On our request, she sent Dr Maithreyi Krishnaraj to Karaikudi, who stayed with us for three days, working to integrate feminist thought and action in the curriculum being framed. Working with Maithreyi's committed scholarship, has taught us more about the subject than an acquaintance with texts. 'Feminist theories and movements', 'Women and law', and 'Women and development' were offered as common papers. Specialisations were in the thrust areas of 'Women and entrepreneurship', 'Women and management' and 'Women and technology'.

The syllabus, originally framed in 1989, was overhauled five times after feedback from the staff and students. The government of Tamil Nadu examined our course syllabus and expressed its appreciation of the meaning and relevance of the course:

We have carefully examined the contents of the Master's Degree Course being offered by Alagappa University. We are of the opinion that the course is designed in such a way that the students get a very comprehensive understanding of women and their lives in India and of the programmes required to improve their socio-economic status in society.

The Tamil Nadu government has issued an order recognising the course as being 'on par with relevant postgraduate courses for purpose of scholarship, employment and higher studies'.[1]

The Board of Studies later approved the renaming of the course as 'Master of women's studies and computer applications'. Computer applications was added as the required skill component in consultation with our present vice-chancellor Dr K. Rukmani, who too has been a resource person for the summer course of Mother Teresa University! The revamped syllabus makes room for students to advance on the information highway. Videography and photography are also part of the syllabus. Technological applications related to women's development with a feminist perception are taken up as field projects.

Fieldwork is a special feature of the curriculum. The students are oriented in the adoption of villages and organising rural camps and are taught to identify the level of women's status and needs through participatory methods. They are trained to form self-help groups of rural women, interact with officials on women's issues, create awareness among women about their rights and development programmes and help NGOs to implement and evaluate these programmes.

Moreover, the potential of any academic subject is correlated to the pulse of the job market. The students are guided to make career choices and select projects appropriately. They are helped to undergo hands-on training in the related concerns, industries, administrative centres, and NGOs. Projects are closely related to career choices in order to make entry into the job market easy after the completion of the course.

Social action is perhaps the most sought-after field. Almost 70 per cent of the students choose projects with NGOs and join organisations that work with the disabled, child labour, women's thrift-and-credit groups, health, etc. Some of our students have taken up government jobs after writing Public Service Commission examinations. We feel confident that the self-confidence, positive self-image and skills learnt during the course are sure to sustain students throughout life whatever may be their vocation.

Staffing

Women's studies is a humanities discipline and its survival and sustain-ability in a highly competitive university set-up depends on the strength of scholarship and the commitment of its faculty members. When it comes to the selection of teaching staff, women's studies confronts a great challenge. As it is a new entrant in academia, it is a futile exercise to search for candidates with Ph.Ds in women's studies and considerable teaching experience. Since the course has to be run by any means, we are required to make some compromises. It is taken for granted that a candidate who fulfils the stipulated qualification and exhibits commit-ment to women's issues can be groomed to become an expert in women's studies once she has displayed initiative. Commitment is a value-laden quality, which cannot easily be measured through an interview.

To start with, women's studies in Alagappa University was established with only one staff member, i.e., the director, who was asked to avail the services of staff from other departments. The misconception behind this temporary arrangement is obvious. Women's studies was wrongly conceived of as a subject that anyone could teach, merely with an emphasis on 'women', as an add-on component to other disciplines. The difficulty was that most of the professors with long-standing experience in their own disciplines were male and there was some resistance on their part to understand women's studies, its theories and methodology. Tactically, the director would repeat the units taught in earlier classes to train students to identify gender issues using the women's studies perspective. In the second year, two more staff members were appointed. In addition, provision was made for the department to invite experts as guest lecturers. This eased the staff problem to a great extent. The staff appointed was from different academic backgrounds related to the thrust areas. The pertinent question here is their conversion to women's studies. As Sandra Coyner asks, 'are we sociologists, historians, and artists who happen to be interested in women—or women's studies people who happen to be particularly interested in social roles, history and art?'[2] Coyner contends that we must think of ourselves as women's studies persons and must accept women's studies as a framework for organising knowledge, a framework with its own internal structure and approaches.

Enrolling students

Enrolment has been a haunting problem; the intake has been uncertain and fluctuating. Whenever any batch had a good number of students, we felt renewed and rejoiced. On occasions when admissions were at a low point, we were in the same state as Patricia King when she describes the newly opened women's studies library in Radcliffe, 'In those days, if any one walked through the door, we had a celebration'.

Six years after the starting of the women's studies course, the Board of Studies insisted on admitting male students also. Though advertisements were made to this effect, there were no male takers for the regular course. However, with distance education, it was a different picture altogether, the strength here gradually increased year by year and now the course has a larger number of men enrolling.

Involvement of other departments

Till the founder–vice-chancellor, Dr Radha Thiagarajan retired, there was an ebullient climate, supportive of women's studies activities. Frequent workshops and seminars were organised by the department so that people started calling us the 'Seminar department'. In every meeting, a good number of staff and students from each department were enlisted as participants. The vice-chancellor's presence, particularly at the plenary sessions, ensured the attendance of senior professors in the seminars. Themes ranged from science and technology to human rights. Whenever international seminars were organised by the department, the steering committees included representatives from all departments. Thus, academic and non-academic sections in Alagappa University, alongwith outside participants became oriented to women's issues and aware of the existence of a different perspective. Gradually, the number of research studies on women in other departments also started increasing. People started accepting women's studies as an inevitable part of the academic system.

As the people became familiar with the department, we were able to win the support of a few donors. A businessperson instituted a gold medal for the best student in women's studies in the name of Periyar. Another organisation came forward to institute a scholarship for meritorious and economically backward students in the name of Thillaiyadi Valliammai, a young Tamil woman freedom fighter who, at the age of 18, worked with Gandhi in South Africa and died in prison.

Expansion

After the university started the Distance Education Programme in 1992, the department started receiving requests for part-time courses. We came forward to offer a postgraduate course through distance education. The course included a week of contact classes. We were, in the beginning, uncertain about the motive of male students who enrolled in these classes, but found, to our surprise, that most had joined out of sheer interest and ideological commitment. Some of the students were even senior and retired officers. They were candidly critical about the structure of masculinity in society and joined freely in discussions with other students. Distance education has widened the academic recognition of the course and has increased our space of operation even though the nature of distance education does not permit field programmes at this juncture.

Research

As women's studies matured at the postgraduate level, research programmes leading to M.Phil and Ph.D degrees were started. On the research front, the arduous task is in integrating feminist theory, methods, and analysis. There is burgeoning interest among both staff and students to do 'real' feminist research. Postgraduate students, as well as M.Phil and Ph.D scholars are carrying out research work. The staff of both the department and the centre also do their individual or collective research. The themes vary from AIDS and tribal women to political participation and technology. The thrust areas—entrepreneurship, social action and management—are covered widely, besides evaluation of development programmes. Workshops on feminist research methodology are organised.

Centre for women's studies

Need for a centre

Offering women's studies as an academic course benefits only a very limited number of students every year. Moreover, a formalised academic system limits the space and extent of its operation. The very purpose of women's studies being the 'transformation' of society through empowerment of women, it is imperative to reach out to a large number of various categories of women outside the academic system.

Alagappa University is situated in Karaikudi, a suburban town, amidst thickly populated rural habitations. The district (Sivaganga) has a high sex-ratio (1024:1000) of women. The majority of rural women are agricultural and construction labourers. Women in large numbers are found working in brick-making, petty trades, brewing illicit arrack, etc. Girl children from impoverished families are absorbed as semi-bonded domestic labourers. The district has no strong NGOs working on women's issues. Reaching women at the grassroots, beyond the boundaries of the university requires a functioning unit that can overcome the limitations and constraints imposed on scholarship.

A proposal was submitted to the UGC explaining the need for a centre for women's studies and the UGC's approval was obtained in 1990. The inspiration behind this venture was once again gender-sensitive leadership. Even before the UGC's approval was received, Dr Radha Thiagarajan was encouraging some professors to run activities under the banner of 'Centre for Women's Studies and Rural Technology'. Sporadic science exhibitions and competitions were being conducted for rural schoolgirls. The UGC's approval was immensely helpful in widening the scope, space and dimension of activities. It was easy to institutionalise the Centre, as there was a department of women's studies already in existence. The department had set the stage for the centre's activities to get academic recognition.

To start with, the department spared two rooms for the centre, which was provided with a skeleton staff. The staff of the department shared the burden of strengthening the centre and was involved in planning all its activities.

Objectives and activities of the centre

The objectives of the centre cover dissemination and outreach. They are detailed below along with relevant strategies.

Table 9.1

Objectives	Strategies
To examine the diverse aspects of the lives of women and develop a critical and balanced understanding of their position and potentials in society.	Research. Awareness programmes. Interaction and dialogue with concerned women's groups. Seminar/workshops/symposia. Fieldwork.
To empower women with self-employment possibilities, inculcate in them entrepreneurial concepts and skills, and open avenues for economic independence. To promote development of women in terms of career goals, decision-making and effective life options.	Self-employment training. Science and technology workshops and training. Entrepreneurship development programmes. Training in leadership and career choices; training in decision-making and political participation. Village camps with people's participation; formation of self-help women's groups in villages.
To incorporate knowledge about the relevance of women's studies in the established disciplines of the university.	Curriculum-designing and counselling for universities and colleges in starting courses in women's studies. Producing relevant teaching/learning materials. Seminars/workshops/symposia.
To encourage research that will generate knowledge of women's studies, role and contributions of women in family and society, and programmes on women.	Action-oriented research. Field projects. Evaluation studies.
To introduce new perspectives, framework and tools of analysis for inter-disciplinary work.	Guest lectures/seminars/workshops on inter-disciplinary basis.
To reach out to rural women in order to enhance their status through productive employment and ensure their participation in an integrated development process with greater awareness of their roles, rights and potentials.	Adoption of villages. Camps/workshops/training courses for village girls and women. Networking with women's groups and establishing linkages with government and non-governmental agencies.

Thus, the agenda of the centre presents a spectrum of activities: framing curriculum and helping start courses in women's studies, research, conducting awareness and training programmes, facilitating income-generating programmes, field work, formation of women's groups, documentation, publication, free legal aid and counselling and networking. They can be broadly classified under two major heads: dissemination of feminist knowledge and outreach.

Dissemination, one of the two major objectives of the centre is mostly a joint effort of the department and the centre. Dissemination implies not only the mainstreaming of women's studies inside the university but also making it accessible to the academic communities in colleges and other universities outside. A number of autonomous colleges and universities have invited the Director and staff to help them in introducing women's studies as a foundation course or as an add-on subject and in two cases, as a major discipline. A textbook is also under preparation.

Translating research into action

The centre is particular that the results of micro-level research should be translated into action in collaboration with the constituencies involved—women, government and non-government agencies. Special attention is paid to villages of SC/ST women. The very first activity of the centre sprang from a survey-cum-camp conducted in nearby villages. The survey revealed that a large number of girl dropouts were idling at home with no alternatives or purposeful direction, just waiting to get married. Based on these findings, the centre plunged into action. The situation was explained to the District Collector and was discussed with the rural development officials. Their approval was received to start skill-training programmes for these dropouts. The centre managed to get an old tiled building, which was cleaned, renovated and put to use by the trainees themselves. Initially, training in non-traditional skills—motor rewinding, maintenance and repairing of domestic electrical appliances and screen-printing—was imparted. Later, a training course in bakery technology was offered. The centre invited the department staff and students to hold regular dialogue with the rural population to gender sensitise them on every possible issue. The training was rigorous, using a high level syllabus structured by experts. Marketing survey and in-service training, examination and viva-voce were the other components of this programme.

Our first experiment was a grand success and received wide media coverage. We included all possible agencies—Small Industries Service Centre (SISI), District Rural Development Agency (DRDA), nationalised banks, service clubs and the District Industries Centre. The liaison with external agencies brought social recognition and respectability to the centre.

The centre's research work is sustained by grants received from external agencies other than the UGC. The main donors have been the Department of Science and Technology, the Central/State Social Welfare Boards, Department of Women and Child Development, the National Commission for Women, Rashtriya Mahila Kosh, and the Tamil Nadu Corporation for Women Development Limited, Agricultural and Finance Corporation etc. The findings are forwarded to the government and relevant bodies for appropriate action. Thus, the Centre maintains a balance between research and action. The most educative, experience for us has been the collective research on 'Girl Child and Family' in which other UGC Centres were involved.

Considering the outreach focus, the centre's activities are structured and extended with a twin purpose: first, to create awareness among women about their potential, entitlements and rightful place in society, second, to help them attain economic independence from where they move on to a status of empowerment. The situation of women here lends itself to varied activities from awareness to attainment level. International seminars organised in collaboration with the British Council have been immensely contributive to the emergence of concepts and theories from a women's perspective in different areas.

Training programmes have become a permanent structure of the centre's activities. They include upgrading the traditional skills of women and introducing new skills which are in demand. The major target groups have been girls and women in rural areas. In recognition of the centre's meritorious work in promoting entrepreneurship among youth and women's groups, the government of Tamil Nadu has recognised the centre as the designated agency to run EDP training in the district. The Centre has been training both men and women in entrepreneurship under the Prime Minister's Rozgar Yojana (PMRY), ever since it was first started.

The adoption of villages based on the survey is taken up as a continuous exercise and the women of these villages are helped to form self-help groups and are trained in health and nutrition, income-generation,

accessing resources, linkage with officials and cluster group formation; programmes for gender sensitisation and adult literacy are also
conducted.

The research carried out by the centre is of three kinds: researches
sponsored by external agencies, evaluation studies, and action-oriented
micro-level projects. The research findings of our micro researches on
issues such as female infanticide, women self-help groups, female illicit
arrack distillers, status of girl child in the family, women entrepreneurs
in the district, have been promptly transmitted to relevant government
bodies. Now and then, we were assured of remedial measures through
policies and programmes. Among our evaluation studies special mention may be made of International Funding for Agricultural Development (IFAD), Women Development Programme of the State, the Girl
Child Project of the UNICEF to eradicate female infanticide in the
Salem District of Tamil Nadu and the Rashtriya Mahila Kosh Scheme
in Tamil Nadu. The evaluation results have helped in pruning and strengthening the existing schemes, especially the thrift-and-credit programme
of the government for women's groups in the state.

The advocacy researches and activities of the centre gain their meaning, relevance, credibility and support through strongly forged linkages
with the government's policies and programmes of the time. From our
experience, we find that the government functionaries are also looking
out for gender-sensitised and committed institutions of higher learning
to implement their programmes effectively and successfully.

Free legal aid centre

No university in Tamil Nadu other than the Alagappa University,
through its centre for women's studies, runs a 'Free Legal Aid and
Counseling Centre' (in collaboration with the Tamil Nadu Legal
Advisory Board). Since its inception in 1995, the Legal Aid Centre
has successfully attended to 274 cases. The Centre has also brought
out monographs on women's legal rights in simple Tamil and conducts
legal camps in collaboration with the District Legal Board and voluntary agencies. Slides and posters are prepared to be used for legal awareness. The Legal Aid Centre has close linkage with human rights agencies

such as SOCO Trust and People's Watch and the Indian Social Institute (Bangalore). The Centre has adopted 18 schools in the district and has mobilised official agencies to introduce human rights in the curriculum for eighth or ninth standard students.

Networking

The greatest strength of the centre is its wide network of linkages with varied agencies; local service clubs, voluntary agencies, government officials, village heads and women's groups have tied up with the centre in one way or another. These linkages have been strengthened through research projects, seminars, workshops, and collaborative field and research activities. Outside the district, the centre has spread its networking not only with women's studies centres in other universities and government agencies but also with universities abroad. More importantly, mention should be made of the agreement with the centre for women's studies of York University, Canada. I had a chance of giving lectures in different universities in Canada while on the CIDA–Shastri WID Fellowship. Through the programme for exchange of students, we had two York University students from Environmental Studies who offered directed courses as part of their degree programme.

Our most convincing and visible face is the centre. Women from villages have been contacting the centre for different purposes—to get legal counselling, to know about government policies, as trainees in the various training programmes, for group formation, for bank assistance, for awareness camps, etc. We were elated when SUN TV interviewed these rural women, who openly declared, 'Our mother-house is the women's studies centre of Alagappa University'. Every year, International Women's Day is celebrated as Rural Women's Day and the attendance has been increasing in number.

The hard way up

Starting women's studies, and that too in a general university, entails excruciating experiences and specific problems. The initial challenge comes from academic circles, because it is a difficult task for women's studies to gain academic acceptance as a credible discourse. As the only woman Head of Department, I could sense an uneasy silence descending on my colleagues in meetings on academic affairs whenever 'women's studies' was mentioned. There was no open derision or acceptance; it was a sort of indifference, implying that women-related studies do not merit attention. I had to be plucky, pushy and at times aggressive in order to win an equal footing for women's studies. Whenever gender discriminatory language or issues were pointed out, sniggering smiles were the response. In course of time, at the sight of discriminatory terms or issues, the very same colleagues reacted instantaneously with the comment, 'let us change these or else women's studies will make mincemeat of us'.

The situation changed once we started fanning out our activities and began to win strong social respectability and heightened visibility. As a result, what had been mute tolerance turned into disgruntlement. Every initiative of the department and the centre faced grumpy remarks such as, 'we have not done this before in this university'; or 'how can one department be allowed to be different from others?' We had to confront unexpected comments at the most inappropriate moments.

Whenever leadership changed in the university, the director had to go back to square one and start all over again to explain where and how our course differed from other traditional disciplines. It so happened that one unfavourable administrator, a misogynist to the core, wanted to cut the strength of the course. When a candidate with a postgraduate degree in another discipline wanted to join women's studies, she was told that no double graduation could be permitted and was denied admission. In the face of such trials and tribulations, the director has had to combat to consolidate and stabilise the department. Our basic strength was the multi-pronged dimension structured into the course in our attempt to judiciously combine theory and praxis. The linkages established and the social support won, stood us in good stead as shock absorbers. In the course of time, we took the confrontations as part of the game and could foresee and adopt pro-active strategies.

The occasional decline in enrolments is another problem we face. Tension mounts at the beginning of every academic year. An unfriendly administration may use this occasion to raise unwelcome questions.

The problem still continues. The main reason besides the lack of awareness among the general student population about women's studies as a
discipline lies in the way the course is advertised. An advertisement
goes from the university including women's studies as one among the
many disciplines offered, which makes it indistinct and nondescript.
When separate advertisements are given and visits to colleges are made
at the fag end of the previous academic year to explain the objectives
and practical benefits of the course to prospective students, we find
there is a marked increase in the enrolment. This substantiates my statement that women's studies needs a godfather or a godmother in a university structure, in matters which are not in our hands but relate to
extraneous situations.

However, the most scarring experience for us was one generated
from within—a member of our own staff did things to sabotage the
very foundation of the course. In the Indian university setting, once a
teacher is appointed and regularised, he or she cannot be removed from
service easily. Moreover, many colleagues will lie in wait for chances to
unsettle a non-conformist subject like women's studies, whose frame
of action does not match with their orientation, and is therefore, easily liable to misinterpretation.

What sustained us in these bleak moments was the multi-dimensional
strength we had built up, extending our impact beyond the Alagappa
University campus. It took sometime for others to understand how strong
women could be when they commit themselves to a cause. As one male
professor commented, 'suppress them [women's studies] and they will
take *vishvarupa*' (the archetypal incarnation of Vishnu, encompassing
the whole universe as he stood with his head beyond the heavens and
feet in the entrails of the earth).

Doing feminist research is still a messy and complex proposition;
the queries we ask, the theoretical perspective and methods we use,
and more importantly the purpose of our work, if not sourced and
directed by unambiguous non-sexism, will tilt the research to contrary
ends. Cases of research guides carrying out nominal research just to increase the number of doctorates guided by them are not unknown. They
utilise the gaps in the university research rules (framed for general application) and escape scrutiny.

Unsavoury situations arise when research guides exhibit ambivalence
in their guidance. The papers they present change colours according

to the discipline of the organising group. Once a staff member, who was teaching non-sexist research methods was found criticising the experiential component of feminist research in a seminar under her parental discipline, which surprised even the traditionalists, who reminded her that they too were veering toward intra-subjective methods.

Another problem is in framing a theory, which will rightly interpret the experiences of Tamil women. Caste, religion and customs form the ideology that governs their life. It is a mix of the Dravidian and Brahminical, of the 'great' and 'little' traditions, as I have explained earlier. Building up a Tamil feminism is an imperative task. It will serve both epistemological and methodological ends. In workshops on feminist research methodology, it is often found that resource persons, except a few, exhibit poor understanding of feminist research, resulting in perplexing the participants as to the nature and validity of feminist research.

The UGC grant to our centre has been both a stimulus and a spoke. Had it not been for the motivation and backing of the UGC, starting women's studies in institutions like Alagappa University would have been unthinkable. But our zest and spirit are dampened when grants are delayed and the university does not lend a supportive hand. A crucial period was during 1992–93 just as the Seventh Plan ended. We were asked to wait for the UGC Review Committee's visit and assessment. The university administration had ousted all the staff of the centre except the clerk, leaving undisturbed only the honorary director. The director was forced to take on the burden of continuing the Centre's research and field activities. Projects left unfinished by the staff were completed with the help of postgraduate students. The Director conducted awareness camps, workshops, counselled and sent projects to funding agencies as usual. The ground won was retained with redoubled tenacity. When the UGC Review Committee visited, they were astonished at the strength of the Centre even though there was practically no staff in the centre. They observed,

In brief, it may be pointed out that due to the dynamic leadership of the honorary Director and the various programmes and activities initiated by her, the presence of the centre is felt both inside and outside the campus. This has been achieved in spite of the lack of full complement of staff. There is increasing demand for the expertise and support from the centre in promoting various developmental activities related to women.

As I write this case study, the university awaits the second instalment of the grant to be released by the UGC and two of the centre's staff members have been asked to leave.

Administrative rigidity

Some administrators demand that everything should be microscopically scrutinised by them and approved. The activities of the centre shrivel under the heat of the bureaucratic gaze. Women's studies, by nature, can bloom only in a liberating climate and resists like a recalcitrant horse, the dictates of a whipping authority. There is a wide gap between autonomy and decentralisation as advocated by the UGC and the reality in our universities. Women's studies suffers by virtue of its being suffused with the intrinsic spirit of freedom.

Geopolitics

In a vast country like India, geopolitics cannot be ignored. Karaikudi is 3,000 kilometres away from New Delhi, the capital of India, and the seat of the UGC. The centre at Alagappa University has suffered due to its geographical position 'down south'. Being nearer to the powers that be, or at least nearer to the power centre has its own privileges and advantages. It signifies easy and early access to information, power to move decisions in their favour, heightened visibility, easy recognition and raised status. A centre such as ours is often put to the strain of explaining the tremendous work we do through the medium of our occasional reports. But words cannot fully explain deeds; it is not easy to reflect in these reports the full range, depth and extent of the centres exercises and the social transformation taking place, all the ups and downs of the journey. However hard it is to digest, one must admit that due to geographical distance, a centre is often left with no choice but to play second fiddle. When we asserted our worth for phase I in terms of our work and as evidenced by the UGC Review Committee's report, we were advised to merge both the department and the centre. We gave our consent and the UGC said a committee would be sent at the earliest, for which we have been waiting two years.

Need for strong shoes

Women's studies addresses a wide range of issues and hence a host of problems have to be faced. Treading on this thorny and wearisome path requires one to wear sturdy shoes. We have to grit our teeth and keep our spirits from flagging, moving up the hard way.

As we built up strong networking, gaining government recognition and social support, these became our safety nets. Besides the staff and students who are on the university records, our other powerful supportive constituency has been the hundreds of rural women who have worked with us. Sharing experiences with the directors and scholars of other centres is also a revitalising process. To this end, collective research and action programmes involving all centres are the need of the hour. When we faced a financial crunch due to delayed grants from the UGC and the centre's staff strength was dwindling, projects with external funds helped with human and financial resources. Moreover, as a member on many state strategic bodies, the director steps up the advocacy role of the centre.

The one unfinished work that makes us feel guilty is the inadequacy of our teaching and learning materials for which we plan amends invariably every year. But the heavy workload rarely gives us time of our own to attend to this. When we see new buildings come up for disciplines started after women's studies, we long for a godfather or godmother to give us a building with spacious rooms for our activities. Through projects and the UGC grant, we have improved our communication facilities. On the academic highway, we are fast runners, but with fettered feet.

Conclusion

Today, compared to the situation a decade ago, starting up women's studies does not entail the pioneering struggles of yesteryears. As

Bernard Shaw remarked, it is possible to be taller than Shakespeare when you stand on Shakespeare's shoulders. Similarly, when Alagappa University started women's studies, we capitalised on the efforts of people like Vina Mazumdar, Neera Desai, Maithreyi Krishnaraj, Pam Rajput, Leela Dube, Devaki Jain, Susheela Kaushik, etc. Even as I admit our debt to these heroic women, I also relive the pain of bringing forth something new, creative and pulsating with life. At times, there is an urge to flee with folded hands; at times, we have the satisfaction of mountain-climbers nearing the peak. Women's studies has been for us a complex experience with mixed blessings. We may not have achieved the full understanding of administrators who come for temporary periods and then depart. As the years go by, our direction will become clearer and our identity more visible.

My final words are: an empty sack will not stand; the sack that stands will not know the ease of emptiness but must bear the burden of hoarding.

Notes

1. See Government order dated 16 April 1991, Manuscript no. 461, Government of Tamil Nadu.
2. See Coyner (1983).

Reference

Sandra Coyner (1983), 'Women's Studies as an Academic Discipline: Why and How to Do it?' in Gloria Bowles and Renate Duelli Klein (eds), *Theories of Women's Studies*, London: Routledge and Kegan Paul.

10
Taking wings within a university:
Many struggles, a few successes

Women's Studies Research Centre,
Maharaja Sayaji Rao University

Amita Verma

The account that follows is less a factual and chronological case study of the creation and growth of the Women's Studies Research Centre (henceforth WSRC) at Maharaja Sayaji Rao University, Baroda, than a narrative describing my personal experience in this journey. Spanning almost two decades, this was an expedition undertaken to translate a dream into reality. It was an effort to locate and legitimise a physical and functional space for women's studies within the rigid structure of a large residential university. My narrative must also, perforce, speak of the inherent resistance of the university administration to even considering the possibility of making systemic and structural changes in its hierarchical and inflexible functioning to accommodate the requirements of this fledgling discipline.

The slow and painful steps we traversed in developing the WSRC are described in some detail to show how such endeavours seem to call for so much more struggle than seems warranted. The story may be a sad one in many ways, but it is a story of struggles won and ultimately a story of hope for the future.

Baroda is a complex city, at once old and new, shaped by complex transformations brought about through varied cultural infusions—Mughal, Maratha and British. The art and architecture, and the lifestyles of the people reflect the co-existence of the new highly industrialised, modern metropolitan culture and the medieval, basically feudal older order.

The freedom struggle may be taken as a point of change in the social fabric of Baroda. This affected all layers of society. Maharaja Sayaji Rao Gaekwad III was a nationalist and resisted British rule; his secretary was none other than Aurobindo Ghose!

In some ways, I can trace some fledgling roots of the Women's Studies Research Centre to the era of Maharaja Sayaji Rao Gaekwad III; he was a man who believed in making education free and compulsory for children up to the primary level. He even instituted a fine for parents who would not send their children to school. He set up a network of schools across the state, and as early as 1903, brought Montessori education to the state. He initiated a library movement. There was a well-stocked library in Baroda, with special books for children and women. A woman librarian would regularly take cases of books to the Maharani Chiman Bai Ladies' Club, where the wives of the gentry usually gathered to play cards, badminton, etc. Maharaja Sayaji Rao encouraged his Maharani to participate in the All India Women's Conference, of which she later became a President. He also set up a number of institutions for women's welfare.

The Maharaja Sayaji Rao University was established in 1949. Smt. Hansa Behn Mehta was its first vice-chancellor and credit goes to her for starting three new non-traditional colleges—College of Fine Arts, College of Home Science and College of Social Work—and for consciously creating more spaces for women on the campus. She invited scholars from other places to come and teach at the university, and was an inspiring mentor, so that many were able to use the opportunity to develop scholarship in their disciplines.

Sporadic efforts

There were a number of women-centred activities being undertaken by women's groups, academics and students, but these activities were not co-ordinated or sustained and could not lead to any concrete outcome. However, these activities served to unite different groups and interests and could be seen as one of the forces leading to the later establishment of the Women's Studies Research Centre.

For example, a forum was organised by women's groups to fight sex-selection and sex-determination tests and foeticide. This remained active over a fairly long period of time. These groups organised protests on the issue of sex-selection and sex-determination as well as against the Phase II clinical trials of Norplant carried out by the Indian Council of Medical Research (ICMR). Though some of us were put on an ICMR advisory committee, nothing came of it. We did not even get to see the report of the Phase I trials!

Women's groups such as Sahiyar, Swashray and Sahaj, were also active on issues such as the problems of rag pickers, domestic violence, displacement, etc., and involved students and teachers of the university in these, but again these too remained scattered, and unfocused.

Things shape up

Certain developments took place at M. S. University Baroda in the decade 1979–89, which finally led to the establishment of the Women's Studies Research Centre. During this period, the Government of Gujarat and the UNICEF invited me to do a situational analysis of women and children in two backward taluks of Baroda district, and to prepare a plan for social inputs for this group in the Area Development Plan for this district. I was at that time dean of the faculty of home science and was able to bring together a team of six senior faculty members from the departments of community resource management, nutrition development and extension, to jointly undertake the project. One important consequence of our involvement in this government plan was that we developed close linkages with the District Rural Development Agency (DRDA), officials of the District Planning Board and other government bodies. Following this, it became possible for us to develop a scheme of placements and action research for students from the departments to which these faculty members belonged.

The year 1984 saw my being appointed as acting vice-chancellor of M. S. University. One of the first things I did was to bring together women academics of the rank above research assistant, to encourage sharing of experiences—the pains and pleasures of working in the university. Thus was formed the Women's Academic Forum, a loose network of women academics.

It had been my hope that if such a large body of women united to chart a plan of work, it would be possible to make their presence felt in the university, with the attendant effect of moving towards gender equity. It had also been a hope that these women could be sensitised regarding gender issues in their own disciplinary frameworks, thus leading to more research on women's issues.

The Forum involved itself in some activities; one major campus event where forum members joined hands was a protest against a report that appeared in the local press portraying university women hostelites in a degrading and offensive light. We requested the university to take action, but this was ignored. The Forum then organised a protest march after which we handed over a memorandum to the press. When the students met members of the university syndicate, not only were they reprimanded, but allegations were heaped on the members of the Forum!

In 1985, a group of faculty members from the Women in Development (WID) office of the University of Illinois visited M. S. University and spent six weeks on campus working with members of the nucleus team formed to undertake the study for the Baroda Area Development Plan. These six weeks of fieldwork, discussion and review of literature resulted in a jointly authored monograph titled, *Household Resources and Their Changing Relationships: Case Studies in Gujarat*. Struck by the scarcity of literature in this area available at the university, I initiated a quick survey to identify the nature and extent of research being carried out in different departments of the university on aspects of women's development. The findings were disheartening. Small, scattered studies, mostly surveys, were found in the Centre for Advanced Studies in Education, the faculties of home science and social work and in the department of psychology. Furthermore, this was limited to student research at M.A. and Ph.D levels—samples were small, research design and methodology weak, and analytical framework unsupported by theoretical underpinnings. No research work was available on the basis of which generalisations could be made. It was clearly evident that women's issues were not a priority on the campus.

Women's studies research centre takes birth

In 1986, two of my colleagues and I were invited to attend the annual conference of the American Association for Women's Studies at the

University of Illinois, where we had the opportunity of meeting numerous feminist scholars and reading feminist literature from different parts of the USA, Africa and South Asia. It is here that the idea of developing a proposal for establishing a women's studies centre at M. S. University took a definite form.

A further impetus was provided by a collaborative project on 'Women and development' carried out by the M. S. University and the University of Illinois. The main objective of the project was to develop, clarify and share innovative methodology for research on Indian women as contributors to and beneficiaries of national, economic and social development. A number of modules were developed, which were discussed at two international seminars in Illinois and Baroda. A book based on these modules was published, titled *Capturing Complexities: An Interdisciplinary Look at Women and Households and Development.*

An ICSSR project to examine the women's studies component in selected home science colleges, and an in-house workshop at the Home Science College facilitated by Dr Neera Desai, resulted in our being able to draw up a core curriculum on 'women in development', which could be introduced in the Faculty of Home Science.

During this period, interactions with Neera Desai, Kamalini Bhansali, Kalpana Shah, Vina Mazumdar, Lotika Sarkar, Kamla Bhasin, Abha Bhaya—all of whom were involved in some aspect of women's studies and women's development—proved to be a source of inspiration.

The findings of the survey of 1985–86 highlighting the fact that there was almost no serious work on women's issues at the M. S. University, led to a group of women academics from diverse disciplines at the university submitting a proposal to the UGC for setting up a centre for women's studies. Such a proposal was submitted to the UGC in 1987–88 and again in 1988–89. The final approval and sanction of the grant was received in May 1990. The centre started its operation in November 1990.

These early beginnings are a reflection of how vision and commitment as well as a strong desire to find a space for women academics to come together could be facilitated using one's administrative position and power. The early concerns of the group related to ensuring that women on the campus, both students and faculty were not discriminated against, that their safety was ensured and that the physical facilities (i.e. toilets, recreation area, canteen, rest rooms, etc.) were improved.

It was planned that the process of examining the curricula of different disciplines so as to integrate a gender dimension into them would be started by questioning and debating on these issues.

When in May 1990, the sanction for the centre finally came through, I had just retired. The syndicate of the university approved my appointment as Honorary Director of the Women's Studies Research Centre, provided the UGC permitted, which it did, and I assumed charge in November 1990. At the same time, a proposal for setting up an information and documentation centre for household-level studies focusing on women was approved, with an accompanying grant from the Ford Foundation, I was appointed Director of this project.

At the time, I was 60 years of age and could not claim to be either a feminist scholar or an activist. However, what I did possess was the reputation of being what is called an 'institution builder', someone with both vision and the ability to take a firm stand on relevant issues. It was the life of my grandmother Sharada Mehta, that was my inspiration, for she had been a warm, considerate person as well as a determined and efficient organiser and worker, and was, in a way, the ideal role model for me in the work ahead.

The first steps

The WSRC was located in the department of human development and family studies of the faculty of home science. This decision seems to have been based on the logic that the proposal for the centre had been submitted by a professor of this department, and the developments that preceded the establishment of the centre had also taken place in this department. But perhaps the real logic was that a women's centre located in home science was more acceptable to the administration. Perhaps it seemed more appropriate to establish such a centre in home science and social work, given that within the existing scheme of things, it is in departments like home science and social work that a critical mass of the faculty and students interested in studying women are to be found.

Getting recognition and acceptance from scholars belonging to other disciplines, even those interested in gender issues, posed a real challenge. Many scholars viewed the centre's activities as 'all that women's stuff', having no theoretical base and hence not worth spending time on. While at an individual level many academics lent their support to the centre's programme, few departments acknowledged their commitment to become partners in building up an integrated and well co-ordinated programme of studies wherein the gender component is incorporated into diverse disciplines.

The absence of an interdisciplinary Board at the university level and the lack of statutory provisions for setting up fully independent autonomous centres or schools within the existing university structures has resulted in these centres hanging in the air like the proverbial Trishanku. At M. S. University, other centres facing similar problems are, the Population Research Centre, the Water Resource Management Centre and the Centre for Canadian Studies. Universities need to seriously consider making structural and systemic changes to provide space and legitimacy for such interdisciplinary programmes of study.

A proposal for providing faculty status to WSRC so that it does not have to be affiliated to the faculty of home science, was placed for consideration before the university syndicate in February 1998. The proposal was rejected on the grounds that the centre had no faculty positions, offered no courses and did not have a body of students. From the centre's point of view, unless faculty posts were created and government sanctions obtained, full-fledged courses could not be offered.

Being placed in Phase II by the UGC makes teaching mandatory for the centre. The academic or teaching programme of the centre can be developed only when a Board of Studies for women's studies is constituted. Such a Board has to be interdisciplinary in nature. Until statutory provisions are made for putting such a board in position, an inter- disciplinary committee for women's studies has to be appointed to consider and give approval to the courses being designed currently at the centre. Unless some statutory status is conferred upon the director of women's studies centres, the centres will not be given the kind of status that other institutions enjoy. For instance, the Director of the Centre for Continuing and Adult Education is an ex officio member of the university senate and has the opportunity of standing for elections to the syndicate, thus acquiring greater decision-making powers at the highest levels. The Director of the WSRC should rightfully be considered on par with the deans of faculties and attend the meetings of deans. A director without power can hardly be expected to negotiate with the deans of other departments for collaborative research or for involvement of faculty in teaching programmes etc.

Charting the course

Following the UGC Guidelines of 1986, we took a conscious decision to meet with deans, heads of departments (HoDs) and professors of various departments to try and introduce the basic concept of a women's studies centre. We also planned to stimulate discussions in various departments, with the specific purpose of introducing gender issues/concerns into their curriculum and to explore the possibility of doing collaborative research with faculty from these departments. We sought to identify how and where we could work with local women's organisations and groups.

Building up a library and documentation centre was a priority from the beginning and this was facilitated by a Ford Foundation grant for setting up an information-cum-documentation centre for studies on women, households and development.

We organised a number of seminars, workshops and gender awareness programmes, and resolved to bring out a quarterly newsletter on thematic grounds, to keep in touch with other UGC and non-UGC women's studies centres, in order to identify different schemes launched by the various departments of the government for women's development and for imparting gender training to the functionaries. On our agenda was also a plan to invite scholars visiting Baroda under the Fulbright–Shastri Indo-Canadian Studies fellowships, and other schemes.

Barriers and obstacles

Some of the problems we faced in our attempts to establish the centre as an integral part of the university included the inability to obtain even minimal functional autonomy, the absence of an interdisciplinary Board of Studies at the university level, the absence of any kind of statutory status conferred upon the centre, resulting in its being treated as a 'project' and not as a permanent institute within the university structure, the lack of recognition of the (Honorary) Director on par with the deans and HoDs of other institutions in the university, etc. It is no exaggeration when I say that we had to assert our rights even to have the centre's name and telephone number in the university diary and to include its activities in the University Annual Report! Financial auto-nomy was the only factor that worked in our favour in efforts to gain visibility on the campus, because we had the resources to organise pro-grammes and activities. It was against such odds that the centre had to work, in order to find a legitimate place for itself in the university system.

Building a teaching programme at the centre

During the first phase (1990–97), very many attempts were made to (a) introduce a foundation course in women's studies for undergraduate students of selected faculties, i.e., arts, commerce, home science etc., (b) design a special course for postgraduate students from different disciplines, who wished to work specifically on gender issues and (c) introduce special papers or topics on gender dimension in the curricula of other departments.

Visits to each HoD, meetings with senior faculty in different de-partments, official letters to chairpersons of the Boards of Study and the Faculty Boards of different disciplines, to consider the above pos-sibilities, all proved to be futile exercises. The Board of Postgraduate Studies was approached to explore the possibility of offering joint degrees in any one major discipline and women's studies, but it re-jected the proposal.

However, what the centre failed to achieve at the institutional level has been partially achieved at an individual level by academics sending those research students interested in looking at gender issues, to the centre, not only for reference but also to discuss proposed projects with the staff at the centre.

A major challenge in designing courses in women's studies arose out of the perception being increasingly fostered in universities, that all academic programmes must fulfill a market need. The centre has been attempting to meet this challenge by designing a range of courses from modular interdisciplinary courses which addressed the academic needs of both researchers and NGO activists, to courses which are more in the 'training' genre, catering to the specific needs of organisations such as the police, the judiciary, etc.

Some of the questions we have had to continuously ask ourselves are, 'who wants women's studies?', 'what is its marketability?', 'what relevance do these courses have?' and 'is there a balance between theory and practice?'

Success stories

The centre has had some remarkable successes in collaborative work, mainly arising out of the Ford Foundation-funded project 'Women, households and development studies and information centre' (WHODSIC).

The department of water resources management, a part of the department of civil engineering, participated in a collaborative venture to introduce a gender dimension into their training programme for students. An expert consultant was invited through the WHODSIC, to assist the faculty in developing a special course on 'Women in water management' and also to introduce a fieldwork programme to understand the role of women in agriculture and water management. The second success story relates to the involvement of two faculty members from the department of architecture who undertook projects on low-cost housing for the poor in the urban sector, keeping the gender perspective in mind. One of the two members has continued her involvement in the WSRC and has been instrumental in creating a core group of women architects in Gujarat.

The third instance is a two-day seminar jointly organised with the department of geography, with the aim of examining the geography curriculum of the department and to identify courses within which gender components could be integrated. Members from the departments of sociology and the Population Research Centre, as well as faculty members of department of geography participated in the seminar. Two experts from Jawaharlal Nehru University and Bombay University worked as resourcepersons and facilitated the discussion. This collaboration resulted in the WSRC's involvement in planning the international conference titled, 'Changing Patterns of Health in Developing Countries' organised by the department of geography, M. S. University, in February 1998. The fourth little success of the WSRC is the development of serious commitment on the part of some members of the department of banking to undertake studies on women and banking. Several Ph.D students in the department have already done significant work on these issues.

These are but a few examples of small scale exploratory efforts initiated by the WSRC which have had a 'ripple effect', resulting in expanding and opening up new vistas and visions of work in the departments of the university and in incorporating a gender perspective in teaching programmes.

Where are the teachers?

Since the inception of the centre, only one position i.e., that of a programme officer in the grade of lecturer, has been sanctioned. According to the 1986 UGC guidelines, the position of the director is to be filled by a senior faculty member from any one of the university departments. From 1990 to 1997, as (Hon.) Director, a retired professor from the department of human development and family studies was appointed. Since July 1997, a professor from the same department carries out the administrative functions, working for an average of four to six hours a week. The programme officer functions as a de facto head in terms of the academic planning and day-to-day functioning of the centre, as well as maintaining contacts with faculty of other departments, and planning the centre's programmes, but has no statutory mandate to do so. Also, considering that this post is the only sanctioned post, it should be made an academic one in Phase II.

Throughout the first seven years, it was not possible to institute any teaching positions in the centre and so the voluntary services of several faculty members from different departments were obtained. Their work was never recognised publicly or valued.

Providing for joint appointments between selected departments and the centre, making appointments of interested faculty from other departments, for periods ranging from six months to two years, would facilitate and strengthen the centre's programmes, and would also help in promoting the integration of the gender dimension into the other departmental programmes.

Where are the students?

In the initial stages (1990–97), the WSRC was a scheme for special assistance and had no 'academic standing' of its own. Since there were no teaching posts and no courses being offered, there was no 'student body' that regularly came to the centre. A single-credit postgraduate course on women's studies offered by the department of human development and family studies provided an entry point to the WSRC to interact with students, and this course, since the inception of the Centre, is being taught by a faculty member from the department and the programme officer of WSRC. The course being a seminar course affords the programme officer an opportunity to plan the readings, organise field-based small-scale studies and include discussions on contemporary issues of concern for women. The course has helped students to question existing assumptions and beliefs that they have derived from gender-blind, or at best, gender-neutral knowledge bases.

Student involvement has also been elicited through the various guest lectures, workshops, and seminars, organised at the centre, and a study circle, which meets periodically and provides a platform to those interested in gender issues. The documentation centre, set up under the aegis of a Ford Foundation grant, attracts students from many departments, who come to refer and to read for interest, the books, journals and documents available there. Celebration of International Women's Day and other similar events of importance for women, have also served to bring students to the centre.

In the Ninth Plan, a scheme of visiting lectures has been introduced under a series called 'Contemporary women's studies series'. This series is aimed at bringing the work of prominent feminist scholars to academics and research scholars at the M. S. University. By focusing on social science disciplines, it has been possible to discuss with scholars from concerned departments of the university and discuss possibilities for future collaborations.

Setting a research agenda

At a meeting of directors of UGC-supported women's studies centres organised at SNDT University, Bombay, in 1989, it was decided to carry out a multi-centre study 'Girl child and the family', using uniform research design and methodology. The project was supported by the Department of Women and Child Development of the government of India and co-ordinated by Dr Anandlaxmi and Dr Susheela Kaushik. The WSRC, Baroda, too, was identified as one of the centres to be involved in this study.

Since the programme officer at the centre carries a heavy burden of responsibilities, it is often not possible to take on independent research activities. However, some small-scale, need-based and action-linked studies have been carried out by the staff, and the centre has been encouraging faculty from other departments to carry out research studies in gender issues and has provided the necessary expertise.

In Phase II, it is planned to offer small fellowships to young members of the faculty and M.Phil and Ph.D students, to pursue studies on women's issues. The centre aims to focus on studying the struggles of the women of the region.

As indicated earlier, the Ford Foundation grant for the Information Centre also contained funding for a research component and under that, some faculty members carried out studies at the household level. The second Ford Foundation grant, received in 1995, provided funds to the Population Council for funding small research studies on various aspects of reproductive health. Several members of Maharaja Sayaji Rao University carried out research under this grant.

Receiving grants from outside sources is always a difficult proposition, and it is a tight rope walk to find a balance between the need for funds to carry out the centre's activities and the possibility of being co-opted into donor-driven research. Grants also bring other problems. For instance, though the Ford Foundation's grant for 'Women, Households and Development' was totally under my control and decisions regarding its use were taken by me, there was still some tension both inside as well as outside the centre, between the centre's staff and the staff for the project, for the project staff were better paid. We could pay them for a number of activities which the centre could not pay for and so there was also a feeling that the project was getting more attention and greater visibility on the campus.

A more serious matter was the kind of people we were taking on board for the projects, for while many were working on women's development projects, it turned out that they often did not have a wider perspective, or an understanding of women's issues. In spite of the projects being under the direction of the centre, the project staff could not take roots within the centre, and remained in semi-isolation from the staff of the centre, not only in terms of activities but also that of ideology.

Networking and advocacy

Networking with other groups has been one of the major strengths of the centre. The fact of a young woman who was actively involved in the women's movement and who was running a local women's organisation, being associated with the centre in the capacity of a junior fellow, facilitated the process of building alliances with various women's groups at the local as well as state level. Finding common ground for working together and preparing an agenda for action at the centre, which would be relevant to local needs, helped in strengthening the role of the centre vis-à-vis other women's organisations. Almost from its inception and throughout the eight years of its functioning, the centre has provided space to representatives of diverse groups to come together and work on issues of mutual concern and to give *voice* and *visibility* to these concerns.

The WSRC at Baroda, being the only UGC-supported centre in the state of Gujarat, assumed the responsibility of establishing relationships with academics and researchers working on gender issues in various departments of seven other universities in Gujarat. A two-day meeting was organised in 1992 to discuss ways and means of working together to strengthen teaching and research on women's issues within the various disciplines of these universities. It was also envisaged that curriculum development, faculty development, conceptualising collaborative multi-centric research studies, etc. would be carried out jointly. The need for setting up some structure or mechanism for working together was strongly felt and some meetings were held in Ahmedabad and Baroda to think of modalities for operationalising such programmes. Subsequently the Gujarat Forum for Women's Studies was formed. A major activity of the forum was the organisation of a two-day seminar to examine and evaluate various facets of the women's movement in Gujarat. Following the deliberations and discussions at this seminar, a feeling was expressed that the name of Gujarat Forum for Women's Studies should be changed to the Gujarat Forum for Women's Studies and Action.

The WSRC at Maharaja Sayaji Rao University became the headquarters of the Forum since there was already existing infrastructure and basic facilities. It has been extremely difficult to sustain such a loosely structured body with members scattered all over Gujarat but a small core group of women have worked persistently to keep minimal activities going. A *nyaya panch* was organised in February 1996 where minority groups, women's groups who supported women victims of domestic violence, state violence or state policies, as also those displaced by development projects, came together on a common platform and testified to their agonies. The response to the *nyaya panch* was extremely heartening. It also provided the centre an opportunity for releasing a booklet, jointly prepared with a local women's organisation, on violence against women. Though the Forum has been unable to plan and organise programmes on a large scale, it has responded to and taken stands on many socio-political and legal issues and matters of concern that have cropped up not only at the state level but also at the national level. Some of these have not necessarily been women's issues in a narrow sense but impinge on their lives in more than one way, such as privatisation of schools and health care, displacement, communal riots, violations of human rights of minorities, rising prices of essential commodities, etc.

Some exciting and thought-provoking experiences have resulted from activities jointly organised with other local, state-level or national-level bodies. In August 1997, a seminar on 'Fifty years of independence and women' was jointly organised by the Indian Association for Women's Studies, the Centre for Women's Development Studies (Delhi) and the Women's Studies Research Centre, Baroda. A one-day meeting on the National Women's Policy was organised by the centre at the behest of the Secretary, Department of Women and Child Development, Government of India. A two-day meeting was organised on amendments to the Constitution, under the sponsorship of the National Commission for Women. A one-day meeting on India's population policy was organised along with a local NGO. Such events, apart from giving visibility to the centre, also enabled it to engage with a wide audience in promoting debates on issues related to women.

Scholarship versus activism

This is perhaps the most persistent dilemma facing those involved in women's studies. Should they or should they not engage in activism? As scholars of women's studies in an academic institution, should they confine themselves to scholarly pursuits, maintaining objectivity, engaging in examining, analysing, interpreting and critiquing events and phenomena? Should scholars refrain from taking to the streets, waving banners and shouting slogans? Many events during the eight years of the WSRC's existence have required women both from the academic as well as the outside world to take a public stand and make their voices heard, in protest or in support, of one cause or another. Maintaining a judicious mix of scholarship and activism seems to be an appropriate answer to these dilemmas that confront women's studies scholars.

Has women's studies made a difference on the campus?

It would be unrealistic to answer this question in any definitive manner. For the central administration, the Women's Studies Research Centre has denoted 'nuisance value' because of its continued demands for flexibility, autonomy and restructuring of the existing systems of governance. The administration is unable to envisage an independent unit, closely linked with other units within the university, but not affiliated to any of the faculties.

Some teachers across the campus have become sensitised and have come to recognise the place of women's studies within the total academic programme of the university. The student body as a whole has hardly been affected by women's studies, though some of our women students have become sensitised enough to want to work with other women students to create more awareness. The opportunity of reaching male students has been very limited. The Ford Foundation-funded campus diversity initiative was conceptualised to include a strong gender dimension, focusing on a human rights approach but those responsible for implementation have shown total indifference in terms of including programmes that would lead to an understanding of gender differences and the need for gender equity in our social settings, more relevantly, in the university setting. Young, newly recruited faculty members, both men and women, could be reached effectively through the orientation course that they are required to take as a prerequisite for confirmation in service, but this opportunity too is being lost because the course director doesn't have the vision to include discussions on gender issues.

A suggestion made to the editorial board of the university journal (which brings out two issues, one on the social sciences and the other on science), to bring out a special issue on women's studies, met with a very negative reaction which bordered on hostility. Finally, the chief editor used his powers of persuasion and the Board agreed to devote one section to women's studies. Ironically, however, only one or two articles were submitted, but these were of such poor quality that they could not be included for publication. Perhaps the time was not ripe then, and the suggestion should be made again now as quite a few academics have started working on women's issues.

The survey undertaken in 1985–86 had indicated a paucity of research studies, in different disciplines, focusing on women. If such a survey were undertaken now, one would encounter a much larger body of research work on gender issues in different disciplines. While gendering of the curriculum has not met with a great deal of success, many departments have encouraged M. Sc, M. Phil and Ph. D students to take up research on women's issues. The Women's Studies Research Centre can thus take the credit for bringing women's issues to the centrestage.

On the positive side, if one views the kind of topics on which seminars and conferences have been organised by different faculties/departments across the campus, one is amazed by the fact that a substantial number of these have been on gender-related topics. The departments of English, linguistics, education, history and geography, and the Canadian Studies Centre, have all organised these meetings either independently or in association with the centre. In many instances, the centre has provided backup support by putting together resource materials and suchlike.

One development that the centre has been critically useful in facilitating is the University Forum for Women. Begun at the centre in March 1997, the Forum was envisaged as a body of members of the university community committed to building a woman-friendly campus. The Forum's activities got a fillip with the Supreme Court Judgment on sexual harassment in August 1997.

Does the Women's Studies Research Centre at the university have a large role to play, beyond the confines of the university campus? Ideally, the centre could play a vital role in helping the government to adopt a gender-sensitive development policy. It could carry out commissioned research, do evaluations of existing projects and schemes for women's development from various ministries, etc. The centre could also train supervisors and functionaries working in these schemes. The possibilities are immense but this can happen only when the centre has established its credibility and this, in turn, is possible only when it receives full support from the university administration and is in a position to demonstrate its ability to take on this expanded role. Currently, the centre is engaged in a struggle for existence as an independent unit within the university structure and hence its outreach is limited.

The role of the University Grants Commission

Reflecting on the various forces which have facilitated or acted as deterrents to the institutionalisation of women's studies in the universities, one cannot leave out the role and responsibility of the UGC, and the Standing Committee on Women's Studies at the UGC. Aside from providing financial assistance, the UGC has been rather negligent about its monetary role. The UGC simply seemed to take it for granted that once the grants are given to the university, it would disburse these without delay and red tape. The administration is not held accountable for ensuring that the centre functions as per the UGC guidelines. A set of guidelines was provided in 1986 and subsequently a new set, carefully formulated by the Standing Committee on Women's Studies, has also been provided. The new guidelines require the vice-chancellor to approve proposals sent by the directors of women's studies centres to the UGC. In spite of all this, when the funds come to the university, the bureaucratic red tape within the university system is so entrenched that funding to be used for developing and strengthening the women's studies centres is held up for months together.

Most vice-chancellors, pro vice-chancellors and registrars of the universities have no clue as to what women's studies is all about and therefore cannot play a proactive role in encouraging women's studies. The Women's Studies Advisory Committee meets only once a year and these experts, at least one of whom is a member of the Standing Committee, can do little to educate the administrators or make them more sensitive to women's studies. The most formidable opposition to any forward-looking changes in the university system is provided by the syndicates or the governing councils of the university. Since the UGC has only a recommendatory and advisory role, it cannot insist on strict adherence to the clauses/conditions contained in the guidelines. Can the University Grants Commission apply sanctions against those universities who flout the requirements stated in the guidelines? Perhaps the registrar and the vice-chancellor should be required to sign a contract in which they commit themselves to agree to specific conditions laid down in the guidelines. A quarterly report from the director, giving facts and figures indicating progress made according to the provisions in the guidelines should be required. Wherever there is non-compliance, the registrar should be asked to explain. Members of the Standing Committee of the UGC should make at least two visits during the year. During both the visits, a meeting with the local Standing/Steering Committee must be mandated. The University Grants Commission must organise meetings of vice-chancellors and senior administrators of the universities at a regional level to discuss the development of women's studies in the universities, and to clarify and resolve problems and arrive at agreements about steps to be adopted by the administration to support the growth of women's studies. Since it is the state governments that have to give concurrence for posts to the centres, the secretaries of state departments of education and finance must also be invited to these regional meetings.

Many states are now committing their support to women's education from the pre-primary to the collegiate level. The role of women's studies centres in training, research and development of training materials should be highlighted. These are just some random suggestions offered for the UGC to ensure greater accountability on the part of university administrators.

Some personal reflections

Since my retirement as (Hon.) Director of the Women's Studies Research Centre, I have had sufficient time to reflect on the growth and development of the centre from its inception and to evaluate my own contributions to this growth, and how the centre has in turn affected me.

My long years of experience of administering an educational institution stood me in good stead, but what may have been more important was the fact that I could and did take solid stances. I publicly acknowledged my support to various struggles that women were engaged in or even to larger struggles such as the Narmada Bachao Andolan, and various movements against the government's coercive population policy, human rights violations against minority populations and the injustice meted out to a poor Adivasi girl who had been raped by a politically influential head of an ashram. All this lent credibility not only to me as a person but also to the institution that I worked for, and countered the criticism that I was neither part of the active women's movement nor a feminist scholar. Being a 'non-political' and 'non-controversial' person has enabled my acceptance by diverse groups of women and organisations working on issues of women's and children's welfare and development.

The years of involvement in the centre's development have brought about a personal transformation, I have become more people-oriented, sensitive and responsive to the human situation. I find that there is a deepening of my own understanding of women's struggles for personal autonomy and for finding a place for themselves in this male-dominated society.

In my own assessment, my biggest contribution to the centre has been to give my younger colleagues the opportunity to design and give shape to the centre's programmes. This mutual trust and confidence has created an atmosphere of responsibility and accountability. Constant soul-searching about our programmes, and discussions on a variety of topics ranging from cinema to the changing face of the family have been a constant part of our activities at the centre. Growing saffronisation on the campus is a matter of grave concern. We, on our part, refused to take part in the conference on women's education organised by the Akhil Bharatiya Vidyarthi Parishad. There has also been a great deal of questioning on our part about whether the WSRC had a feminist orientation or not. We eventually came to the agreement that much of what was being done at the centre did have a feminist perspective and our continued interaction with the outside world, with sisters who were deeply involved in larger struggles kept us in touch with the reality of women's lives.

The debate regarding changing our title from 'women's studies' to 'gender studies' has been an ongoing one. Like Neera Desai, I too felt that this nomenclature acts more as a camouflage and is a way of gaining acceptance from people who feel a bit threatened by 'women's studies' and 'feminist studies'! Discussions and interactions with visiting feminists have shown that the line between 'women's studies' and 'feminist studies' is rather blurred anyway, and highlighted the fact that there are many shades and hues among feminists.

Today I believe that women have actually been able to stake a claim to space for women-centred concerns, for this it is crucial to reinforce a sense of sisterhood amongst women. In this struggle, women's groups, women activists and women academics, are all a crucial link, which sometimes falls prey to the divisiveness of politics and dogma. We come from different historical trajectories towards a common meeting point to share and mull over concerns and to shape an acceptable vision of the future. Let us continue to strengthen each other and ourselves in this common journey towards a future in which the future generations are also touched by our actions.

Reference

Borooah, Romy, Kathleen Cloud, Subadra Seshadri, T.S. Saraswathi, Jean T. Peterson and Amita Verma (1994), *Capturing Complexity: An Interdisciplinary Look at Women and Households and Development*, New Delhi: Sage Publications, 1994.

11

From presence to identity

Women's Studies Centre, Mysore University

Rameshwari Varma

The National Policy on Education (1986) had highlighted the need for setting up Women's Studies Centres (WSCs) in all universities, in the interest of promoting gender equality. The University Grants Commission (UGC) established these centres in several universities of this country. The UGC Guidelines, enunciated in 1986, spelt out the objectives of these centres, the most significant of which were:

- to promote awareness of the multifaceted roles of women and their contributions to society;
- to promote the equal participation of women in all spheres of life; and
- to act as a catalyst in ensuring women's rights and women's development.

In short, the objective was to work towards establishing gender equality in society, and the strategies/tools to achieve these objectives were identified as research, teaching, training, documentation, dissemination and extension.

The Women's Studies Centre at Mysore University was informally set up in 1989, and when this was announced by the then vice-chancellor of the University, Ms Selvie Das, it came as a dramatic surprise as there had been no indication of such a move. The announcement was made by the vice-chancellor while inaugurating a Seminar on 'Agricultural Marketing' organised by the Institute of Development Studies

(IDS)! However, for a handful of us at the university, who were much interested and involved in activist work, the surprise was a welcome one.

It was decided that the Women's Studies Centre (henceforth WSC) would be situated in and attached to the IDS. Since I was a faculty member of IDS and already involved in women's studies research, I was informally nominated the co-ordinator. When WSC submitted its proposal and it was formally sanctioned by the UGC in the mid-1990s, I was officially appointed the Director of WSC. My teaching duties in IDS were to continue. I was quite happy to shoulder the additional responsibilities.

This seems an appropriate place to go into a little digression as to how I developed an interest in women's studies and how my involvement with it grew. My interest in feminist theory was first kindled while I was collecting material for a lecture during the International Women's Year; in 1982, when I was in the USA on a Ford Foundation Fellowship and had the opportunity to visit several universities, I was already involved with women's activist organisations in Mysore. My interest in women's studies and women's issues prompted me to visit several women's studies departments and women's resource centres. I was also able to network with some women's studies scholars. After my return, I visited the Research Centre for Women's Studies in SNDT University, and apart from exploring the library and meeting some of the faculty, I also picked up a number of books which I read with increasing absorption. I realised that here was an area which I would like to be involved with and teach, if possible. All these factors enthused me into undertaking small-scale research in the areas of women and development, and women and work. I also sought to persuade students at IDS to take up project work/dissertations in topics related to women. Thus, some years later, the establishment of a women's studies centre in our university was a kind of dream come true as far as I was concerned.

When the Women's Studies Centre was first informally set up, we had no clearly articulated aims and objectives. We had only one direction—to sensitise people about gender justice and gender equality. A seminar that I attended in 1989 at SNDT University, jointly organised by the UGC and the university, gave me a clearer understanding of the aims, objectives and rationale of women's studies centres. At the same seminar, I was able to interact with the directors of a number of functional women's studies centres, which gave me a sense of the importance of linkages and networking.

As mentioned earlier, WSC was physically and functionally located in the Institute for Development Studies. Not all the faculty members of IDS were happy with this arrangement, some considering it an unnecessary addition, but many of the faculty members as well as the Director of IDS were quite supportive. The university order establishing the centre had simply stated that it was to be attached to IDS, without elaborating on the relationship between the two regarding how they were to function together.

In the initial stages, all the correspondence and financial matters of WSC had to go through the Director of IDS and all programmes had to be approved by the Faculty Council of IDS. At that point of time, this arrangement presented no problems, because, the then Director was supportive, but that could not be expected to continue as a norm because the directors changed on the principle of rotation and one did not know how supportive future directors would be.

Though being part of IDS was useful, gradually it became clear that WSC needed autonomy to function more effectively, but attempts to attain this were not totally successful as the university gave WSC only bare functional autonomy, which meant that the Director of WSC could make independent decisions only regarding correspondence and financial matters with and outside the university. This created a kind of uneasy relationship between the faculty at the WSC and the IDS. However, it was soon sorted out with the support of the vice-chancellor.

Though the IDS was in a big building, WSC could not be housed together in one compact area. Since I was a faculty member in IDS, I already had half a room to myself (I was sharing it with a colleague) and the rest of the staff of WSC were scattered in different places. The programme staff was in the rear portion of the building, whereas the office staff was on the second floor and the Director was 'in-between'! But we managed; being a part of IDS also gave us several advantages.

The centre got its own physical space and identity in mid-1994, but the umbilical cord was not fully cut as our diploma in women's studies was being offered by IDS, and, in all academic matters, we were still governed by IDS. The place allotted to us was right in the middle of the university campus in the humanities complex. It was strategically a good location, but the physical space was not sufficient for classrooms, lecture halls and seminar halls. Moving out of IDS was also problematic.

I had to divide my time between the two buildings that were separated by a long distance. I could, therefore, attend to its work only either in the forenoon or in the afternoon.

The earlier UGC guidelines had not been very clear about the status of women's studies centres. Like the centre at Mysore University, many others too were attached to a mainstream discipline. Being within IDS gave us direct access to students there, and through the IDS students we reached a large number of other students on campus, who attended our programmes in large numbers.

Since IDS worked with an interdisciplinary approach, when WSC adopted this approach in designing the curriculum for the diploma in women's studies, we did not meet with resistance. It was promising that WSC actually fitted in with the IDS philosophy of functioning. Being attached to the IDS (which functions like a department) was quite advantageous for the WSC. In the initial years, when the centre had just been set up, there were no financial resources at all but because we were attached to IDS, we could use their office for correspondence and secretarial work, and their classrooms for meetings, lectures etc. These advantages continued even after we received the UGC sanction. The staff of WSC was so small and the system of release of grants and appointments so rigid that the centre could not have had many programmes without the infrastructure and the supportive staff and students of IDS. This proved to be particularly helpful when the WSC hosted the Fourth National Conference on Women's Studies. The success of the conference owed much to the support of the Director, staff and students of IDS who very willingly and generously shared so much of the responsibilities and work. Thus, when we moved out of IDS we had already established a presence in the university campus and things were not very difficult.

An administrative problem of the early days was the shortage of programme staff. Even against the sanctioned positions of core staff, appointments could not be made before January 1992 due to the rigid appointment procedures. The temporary staff appointed during this period for the 'Project on girl child and family' facilitated our functioning.

Since the time WSC began to function under my charge, I cherished a dream that our centre should earn name and fame for its work and for its commitment. An early strategy I adopted was to enlist the support of as many people as possible, from within and outside the university and also from the local government administration. I had been in the university for a large number of years and could identify faculty members in different departments who were interested in women's issues and were ideologically committed to gender equality. I knew I could enlist their support and that they would always be 'friends' of WSC; I could also identify faculty members in the university who were known for their progressive outlook. I knew from experience that enlisting the co-operation of the Government Administrative Staff Training Institute, the Regional College of Education, the Chief Secretary of the Zila Panchayat etc., and including them in the Advisory Board would be strategically advantageous to WSC. Finally, there were so many that they exceeded the numbers suggested in the guidelines, though the actual selection of members was more or less based on the logic of the guidelines.

It is now 10 years since the Women's Studies Centre, Mysore, was established. How do we look back on the experience? To what extent have we succeeded in our objectives? Have we been able to carry out all the activities suggested in the guidelines? What were the landmarks in the life of the centre? What kind of impact have we made? What were the supportive factors? What were the limitations and constraints and what strategies did we adopt to overcome them? The rest of this paper addresses these questions.

The initial UGC guidelines had suggested a big agenda of activities, but considering that the core staff for the programme were only three and the recurring grant a mere Rs 50,000, it was well nigh impossible to take up all these. What we did was to concentrate on those aspects in which we had inherent strengths like teaching, research, training, etc. while also trying to have programmes aimed at addressing special target groups. In order to supplement our finances, we took up activities for which funding was available. A few examples will explain our attempts.

The year 1990 was declared as the Year of the Girl Child, and the UNICEF, the Department of Women and Child Development and various other organisations were promoting and supporting advocacy for the girl child as well as girl child sensitisation programmes. The WSC took advantage of this fact to approach the UNICEF for a series of workshops and programmes, which brought the centre much visibility.

Since there was a paucity of publicity material in Kannada we organised a workshop for preparing material for advocacy and sensitisation on the girl child. Several well-known visual artists, creative writers, dramatists, NGOs and activists participated in the workshop. The material that resulted from this workshop was in the form of posters, slogans, plays, songs, *harikathas*, skits etc. These are being used not only by WSC but also by various other organisations, for *anganwadi* workers, field-level functionaries of government and NGOs. The literacy mission in the district also used some of the material.

The WSC also attracted notice through its week-long orientation course conducted in 1992, 'Women's studies: what and why?', which was mainly in response to several people on the university campus and outside wanting to know what the centre did and what women's studies was all about. We charged no fee, gave wide publicity to the course and finally selected 30 people from various walks of life—students, teachers, activists, NGOs, homemakers and others to attend the course, many of whom later renewed contact with us by attending our subsequent programmes.

In 1993, WSC hosted the Fourth National Conference on Women's Studies, following a suggestion from Dr Vina Mazumdar. The organisation of the conference was a challenge to us, a stupendous task, as more than 500 delegates were expected to attend. While the required financial resources were mobilised by the IAWS, we at the WSC needed to gather 'human power' and goodwill from various quarters. At this point the fact that the centre was attached to IDS, gave us a lot of support. The conference brought us fame and helped put the Women's Studies Centre, Mysore on the women's studies map of India.

Keeping to the UGC Guidelines, the centre organised several workshops and seminars addressing important women's issues, two of which deserve special mention. One was a three-day gender sensitisation workshop for undergraduate lecturers. This was organised jointly with the Government Administrative Training Institute at Mysore. I mention the workshop here because, though the problems involved in organising such an event are innumerable (and often very tedious, as for example getting permission for the deputation of teachers), their impact is far reaching.

The other exciting workshop was the one with well-known Kannada women writers, organised jointly with the Karnataka Women Writers' Sangha, which sought to document the lives of these writers, their support systems, factors influencing their lives and writing, their struggles and achievements, etc. in the form of case histories, using the personal narrative form. The writers were candid in their narration and the uniqueness of the workshop was much appreciated. The narratives were documented and have been published by the Karnataka Women Writers' Sangha as *Leka Loka*.

Curriculum development and teaching were two of our main activities. We sought to treat the fact that we were part of the university as one of our strengths and followed the 'integrationist' approach to curriculum development suggested in the UGC guidelines, rather than starting postgraduate degree or diploma courses of our own. As a beginning, we offered an elective paper on 'Women and Development' for the postgraduate degree in development planning in IDS. Since I was already teaching development studies and had forayed into women's studies, I developed the curriculum as well as taught the course.

In 1992, we decided to start a PG diploma course in women's studies. According to the rules of Mysore University, any diploma/degree course can be started only after the relevant Board of Studies passes the syllabus with its recommendation and it receives sanction from all other academic bodies as well. The WSC at Mysore did not, and still does not, have a separate Board of Studies, and is still attached to the IDS for all academic purposes.

After receiving the vice-chancellor's approval (the VC also being the President of the Advisory Committee), we approached the Registrar for nominating at least two women's studies experts to the Board of Studies for Development Studies so that they could scrutinise the syllabus for the diploma course.

The preparation of the syllabus for this diploma is an experience worth recalling here. We visualised the diploma course as being of an interdisciplinary nature, including legal, social, cultural, political and developmental perspectives, and a number of teachers from the different departments, got together in an informal workshop to prepare the syllabus. These teachers who participated in this workshop had always been allies of the WSC, and agreed to teach the different papers related to their main discipline though they were senior teachers already busy with activities in their own parent department. To date, more than 40–50 students (boys and girls) have completed this course. After teaching this diploma course for three years, we found that, in our initial enthusiasm we had overloaded the course and therefore organised a formal workshop to revise the syllabus. It was heartening to observe that even teachers who had not had much 'gender sensitivity' in the beginning had developed insights after three years of interaction with the WSC.

The workshop also reflected on how women's studies should ideally be very different from conventional mainstream courses, in classroom pedagogic methods and in the orientation to learning through fieldwork as opposed to learning from books, etc. The workshop also explored the constraints in offering such a course within the university system, chief among which is that women's studies questions norms and conventions and perspectives which are well-established, not only 'out there' but also in the functioning of the university. My experience has shown that teaching women's studies is a worthwhile exercise, particularly in smaller cities and towns where students come largely from middle and lower middle classes and castes, and such a course creates awareness, brings gender sensitivity and in many cases is empowering.

After we conducted the orientation course for college teachers there was a demand from them to introduce women's studies as an elective subject at the undergraduate level. The university set up an expert committee to formulate a syllabus for women's studies at the B.A. level, which was cleared by various academic bodies for introduction at the undergraduate level in colleges.

WSC, Mysore was a part of the multi-centre study on 'Girl child and family', sponsored by the Department of Women and Child Development in 1990. The experience of this project is memorable particularly the 'planning' workshop in Trivandrum and the coding workshops, one of which was hosted by us. I look upon this project as a landmark in the development of women's studies in India for several reasons:

- It offered an opportunity to research, network and build linkages in a large national project. The project afforded a good chance for an interdisciplinary approach, since the directors were drawn from various disciplines.
- One outcome of the networking was a multi-centre (this time about five centres) project on 'Child labour in the *beedi* manufacturing industry'.

While the WSC, Mysore succeeded in establishing networks and linkages, it encountered difficulty into carrying on field-level activities. One of the main reasons for this was the lack of finances. The rigidities in the university system regarding field-level activities and working towards social change were also a constraint.

What has been the impact of the centre on its various constituencies, within and outside the university? The different kinds of impact are as follows:

- Few members of the university community, teachers and students were aware of women's studies as a discipline prior to the establishment of the centre; in fact it would be no exaggeration to say that few were even aware of issues related to women. To some extent, the WSC has been able to create gender sensitisation among the university community.
- Though many students and teachers may not be fully conversant with the aims and objectives of WSC, they are now aware that its work is related to women's issues and that it is proactive about women. I describe two incidents here. One is related to a student and another, to a teacher, in the university. There was a character assassination campaign against one of the IDS girl students who was a little bolder than others. Graffiti appeared on the walls with the aim of maligning her character. At this point, many of the girl students turned to WSC for condemning these acts and punishing the culprits. Though WSC could not punish the culprits, the centre held a meeting and condemned the act. Following this, a number of male students came to us and expressed their anguish over such acts and voluntarily erased all the writing. A similar thing happened to one of the female teachers from another department, and WSC, along with a women's activist organisation, took out a procession in the campus, and presented a memorandum to the university authorities, asking that the culprits be punished. All these incidents have given us a reputation for not taking misdemeanour towards women lightly!
- WSC has certainly been successful in creating a 'space' for exchange of thoughts and for holding discussions for people both inside and outside the university, particularly NGOs and activists.
- Both scholars and laypersons use the WSC, Mysore as a resource and information centre on women's issues. Material prepared by

the centre is widely used by various organisations. Not only the university community and the public, but the Zila Panchayat, the Government Administrative Training Institute, the District Training Institute, the Literacy missions, the District Primary Education Programme units and many others turn to the centre for organising training and research. An example is the 'Study on female infanticide' requested by the Zila Panchayat of Mysore when it came upon alleged cases of female infanticide in a particular taluk.

• A large number of girl students who have completed the diploma in women's studies courses have admitted that the course changed their outlook and empowered them. To quote one of them, 'though we knew we did not have the same rights as boys, though we knew that we were disadvantaged and faced constraints and taboos, we thought that it was natural and normal. This course has opened our eyes and has made us look at our situation and other things differently. We have now become bolder. We have started questioning. In future we want to have control over at least those things that affect our lives.'

• The WSC, Mysore has also been able to motivate many scholars in IDS and in other departments to take up research in women's studies.

• The fact that several women's studies scholars from within and outside India are requesting affiliation to the WSC, Mysore indicates that it has carved a niche for itself in the world of women's studies.

WSC, Mysore has also faced several constraints and problems that have acted as limitations. One of the most persistent problems is related to finances. The UGC has to sanction grants and release them to the Mysore University and in turn the Mysore University releases money to the centre. This flow is never smooth. Not only are there time lags, there are also communication gaps regarding the formalities to be followed, and the distance makes it difficult to bridge these gaps. As a result of this time lag, whenever the grants are received, they get adjusted against salary advances from the university and the money available for programmes gets affected. If we depended solely on the UGC, the WSC could have organised very few activities indeed. Therefore, we adopted a few strategies to overcome this hurdle.

- We looked outside the university for joint sponsorship of program-mes. We approached the government, NGOs, the Zila Panchayat and the Administrative Training Institute for sponsorships. These have been quite willing to collaborate because they often have the money but lack in expertise and organisational capabilities.
- We took advantage of women's studies scholars and activists vis-iting Mysore on the invitation of other institutions and approached them to lecture, or speak at seminars in the centre, thereby saving on travel expenses.
- Though we planned our activities in the beginning of the year, we were always ready to accommodate initiatives from NGOs and others.
- Using the goodwill we had already earned, we managed to enlist the support of the press and Akashvani, which always gave wide publicity to our activities. This helped us in getting a larger par-ticipation of people in our activities at no extra cost.
- We did not confine ourselves to the social sciences or humanities alone. We spread our net over the field of culture as well by de-signing programmes for visual artists, writers, etc.
- WSC's director and staff made it a point to participate in rallies, meetings and seminars organised by other progressive groups and NGOs, thus building up solidarity.

There were constraints other than the financial ones. For any organi-sation to function successfully a full-time head is necessary, but the pre-vious guidelines of the UGC were not clear on this point. Therefore, directors of women's studies centres, including myself, had to serve two masters—the centre and their own parent department. Often the parent department would demand its pound of flesh by not giving any concessions in the teaching load and other responsibilities. After all, the salary of the director came from there. Even with regard to filling up positions at the centre, small towns face a problem. Since the posts are temporary, the problem gets compounded.

Though feminism places importance on functioning in a non-hierarchical manner, and I myself dreamed of creating such an atmo-sphere in WSC Mysore, it is never easy to carve out a different path amidst pressures from a well-established system. It was a disadvantage that the WSC did not have its own Board of Studies. Ph.D research scholars in women's studies get their degree in development studies and not in women's studies because there is no Board of Studies and the CWS is still a part of IDS. Even though the vice-chancellors of universities may be supportive, unless they are convinced that women's studies centres are central and not peripheral, the status of the centre within the university may not improve much.

In spite of all these hurdles and constraints, the WSC also received support from various sources including the successive vice-chancellors of Mysore University. The centre owes its existence to the vice-chancellor who took the initiative and who kept up her involvement with the centre as long as she held office. The next vice-chancellor was equally supportive.

I want to end this paper on a personal note. My experience as Director of the Women's Studies Centre, Mysore has been enriching and enlightening. I have enjoyed every bit of the process. Building up an organisation requires much interaction with people, earning support and goodwill from fellow workers, authorities and the various constituencies it serves. I have found that this process demands tucking away one's ego and bending over backwards, but always with dignity.

Section II

Case Studies of Women's Studies Centres Outside the University

12
Building a service station brick by brick
Institute of Social Studies Trust

Devaki Jain

Institute of Social Studies Trust (ISST) is a product of the times. Started in the bedroom of our flat in Jorbagh in 1975–76, using a dead file which gave the original registration papers of an organisation called ISS which had been set up in 1965, it carried itself forward on the momentum provided by the many energies and events leading to and followed by 1975, the International Women's Year.

Looking back, it seems that the shape it took, the initiatives it launched and its particular character at the end of 20 years—1975 to 1995—just happened, brick by brick, without any architectural plan, without any initial financial back-up and without even a suggestion of what it was all about and what it was going to unleash. While initially it looked as if it was taking one step at a time, an approach that certainly one man, namely Gandhiji, would have approved, this gave way to many steps in many directions simultaneously most of the time. In one sense it could be said that ISST burst open on the scene, with all the good and bad aspects of bursting.

One of the points that ISST proves, among others, is that it is possible to go from nowhere to somewhere, if the ears and the mind are constantly on the alert for signals from the ground and the feet have no hesitation or encumbrance to follow that signal to its source. It responded to issues and needs that emerged from the public domain, be it from the state, academy or the women's movement. This pulsation attracted support of all kinds needed for making the bricks into a house. And indeed a house it became as by 1992, ISST owned its own office space in two cities—Delhi and Bangalore—which in turn housed activities ranging from family counselling to a marketing facility centre for women producers and a select library service, apart from the research and administrative teams.

Over the same period, more than 40 young women, some fresh from university, some young fellows of other mainstream research centres, and some wives of civil servants and activists, passed through the Trust's portals, as researchers. A few stayed on to become well-known gender specialists. Many organisations and networks were born or facilitated by this house. Over the same period, the house prepared more than 100 reports, six books, several project proposals for NGOs, and many policy and programme advice notes.

ISST's history suggests that the women's movement as well as developmental government agencies, require and support a service station which can provide researched, data-based reports and reference material, and follow up on crises and tackle problems after studying these reports. A kind of technical support group, as it is called nowadays. It also proves that government constantly uses and can use policy and programme advice, evaluation and project design advice from outside, but does not see the importance of supporting such technical services with capacity-building finance.

What follows is an attempt to move from ISST's genesis, to a description of the various roles which the organisation tried to play as a service station, some of the features of its governance and finance, the synergy that this produced as well as the strains, its tentative attempts at practising what it perceived as the feminist method, the research methodology and some of the innovative management ideas that evolved out of that experience. We will dwell on how the inside is affected by the outside, on leadership and transition, and ponder over what all this suggests for the future.

The political and the personal

While the need for an institutional vehicle for doing research is what made me in 1976, pull out the file, the idea and thrust of the research was born out of two 'feminist' calls.

First was the experience of compiling and editing a volume for 3 years during 1971–74, called *Indian Women*,[1] for the Publications Division of the Government of India. The invitation to compile this book had its genesis in a 'feminist take-off'. I had written an article in a special issue of *Seminar* devoted to the theme of 'Indian Woman'. In this article, I had argued the need to replace the reigning goddesses who provided role models in the Tamil Brahmin tradition into which I was born—namely, the images of Ahalya, Sita, Draupadi, Tara and Mandodari, called the *panchakanyas*—by other role models, namely, Ambapali, Gargi and Avvaiyar. Looking back, I would say that this piece is the first stirring of feminist consciousness in me. I was perhaps unknowingly freeing myself from the Ahalyas and Sitas.

This exposure plunged me into concern for the inequality between men and women and made me aware of the huge deficiencies in knowledge about that inequality. The introduction to that volume, the first piece in that book, is the beginning of my travels into understanding the dynamics of gender. In short, it caused my rebirth.

The book was released in January 1975, even as Vina Mazumdar, Lotika Sarkar and Kumud Sharma were trying to complete the CSWI report—from an office in ICSSR—and we had many discussions, especially with Kumud Sharma who was drafting the chapter on economics. These visits to ICSSR brought me in touch with the inimitable J. P. Naik, changing the course of my life and giving a new lease of life to ISST, as the ICSSR funded the first piece of research that I undertook.

The second call was the first UN World Conference on Women held in Mexico in 1975. This conference was a turning point, an overwhelming experience for anyone who attended it, in its sheer physical size and 'aura'. Nearly 8,000 women gathered in one place and challenged every proposition that determined history, economics, politics and development. In some sense, it was a larger, less divided (official versus NGO), more political (as different from technical) space, than those that followed. At a panel chaired by the famous Ester Boserup on women outside the GNP, I presented a paper on 'measurement failure' in the counting of women workers and the analysis of their roles in the economy—drawn from our Indian time-use study.

Research for advocacy

The entry point was a time-allocation study of men and women in rural households in six villages, conducted during 1975–77, and supported by the ICSSR. The hypothesis of this study was that female work participation rates are underestimated in India due to methodological incorrectness or what can be called measurement failure. This study in a sense, was a pioneering study for many reasons. While the first field trial was conducted by Prof Ashok Rudra, then at Shantiniketan, in a village called Muluk, and established that women and girls were earning their daily bread by subterfuge and were certainly uncounted, the study also had the partnership of the National Sample Survey Organisation (NSSO). Investigators, all the way up to the Chairman and the Chief Executive Officer, were totally absorbed in both the implementation and the outcome of the study.

The study revealed that amongst the poor, the work participation rate of women was greater than that of men and that children, especially girl children, between the age of eight and twelve were engaged in significant economic activity. It also showed that the activity code, namely 'domestic activity code', as canvassed in the opening block of the NSSO schedule was a stumbling block for women due to their self-perception that the activity in which they were engaged most regularly over the year was household work (even if they worked for four hours a day weeding, or for six hours a day looking after animals and milking, or for twelve hours a day chopping mulberry and feeding it to the silkworms). The study not only pointed out the invisibility of women workers, but also made inroads into how to change the methodology of the survey in order to make visible what was invisible.

The study's conclusion that amongst the poorest, defined as the landless households, women's work participation rates were higher than that of men, led us to understand that 'all poor women are women workers', since no poor woman cannot work, as she and her family would perish. Women provided the survival kit to the household and would do anything, including selling their bodies, to find that daily bread.

ISST teams led by our first and most worthy research assistant Malini Chand (now Sheth) lived in the villages for a year and recorded what poor people—women, men and children—actually did.[2] The information was shocking. Women and girls were working 18 hours out of 24. Boys played or went to school while girls cooked, cleaned, and carried. Girls were often breadwinners for the whole household amongst the poor. Women's work often increased as a result of a 'development' intervention without any increase in either income or convenience. Men preferred to be idle rather than work for poor wages. Intriguing data like the low female participation rate in West Bengal, was uncovered. Poor women and girls in West Bengal were working too but 'under cover' in 'feminine' work—such as domestic help, even begging—often for non-monetary rewards.

The hypothesis underlying the time-use study, challenging the measurement of women's economic contribution, and concentrating on the poorest, attracted the interest of many of the most well-known economists and social scientists of that time. Apart from Prof Ashok Rudra, Professors Pranab Bardhan, Pradhan Prasad and Ashok Mitra gave suggestions on how to stratify the sample by class; Prof V.M. Dandekar directed the NSSO to partner with us, both in selection of villages and households and later to give us the questionnaire of the 32nd Round to canvass with the same households that the NSSO visited for this Round, and also access to the raw schedules of the NSSO itself.

Thus, we were not only able to present our data in columns alongside NSSO data for the 27th and 32nd rounds (though not at all strictly comparable) but also in columns alongside tabulated NSSO 32nd round questionnaires—making our case on under-enumeration as well as the reason for it, stronger.

ISST drew extraordinary mileage from this one study as the study got known by a constituency of persons known for their expertise in data collection and use, especially on employment, both outside and inside the official system. We were included in all the NSSO, CSO and Census conferences and began systematically to establish ourselves as the focal point, both in redesigning data collection and in action related to women and work concerns.

The Invitation to give the Padmaja Naidu Memorial Lecture[3] in 1982 gave us a chance to wave these facts from the rooftops so to speak and to challenge social scientists. What was this sociological family they were talking about? What were all these kinship organisations in India and their rules and regulations? These were fragmented non- families in which women battled for life. What was this counting of workers and hierarchy of work that the statisticians were putting forth? Women among the asset-less households had higher work participation rates than men from the same households.

This differentiation between men and women, amongst the poor, now known as gender differentiation, became the basis of all the research and advocacy of ISST. The uncovering of women within the poverty sets as a 'class' by themselves was of crucial importance to the journey, as it challenged political ideology as well as economic programmes.[4]

The second entry point was to look for situations in which women were the predominant workers and their engagement in that work had been recognised and organised in order to improve their economic and social strength. This search was initiated because of news of SEWA as an organisation of self-employed workers in the informal sector, but whose unionisation had transformed their negotiating power. At that time, SEWA was the women's wing of the Textile Labour Association, a trade union with a strong presence in Ahmedabad. An ICSSR funded case study of SEWA led to a search for similar organisational experiences of large masses of women. A survey of India, looking for such success-ful endeavours led to the book *Women's Quest for Power*.[5]

The book and its design opened up a new style of writing case studies—taking a ground level experience, bringing in a primary data profile with an on-the-spot household survey, followed by the narrative, voices of women. It also established another proposition, namely that poor women were able to identify spaces where they could eke out a livelihood even if only at a survival level but, providing backward and forward linkages to them, such as organisation, market intelligence and access to raw materials or wholesale goods through collective purchase, could enhance their income by many times. This amounted to a critique and a revision of the mode of developing income-generating projects for women, a pattern that was at that time the norm and also supported by the govern-ment and even agencies like CSWD, UNICEF or DWCRA. Our suggest-ion was that the survival strategies of poor women can teach development design.

Thus began the search for clusters of women who were already in a particular occupation. Our effort was to expand that space. This in turn led to a Government of India national programme called STEP (Sup-port Team for Employment Promotion). The experience also led to the birth of Mahila Haat, a marketing window for women producers at ISST. The idea was to start with the traditional *haats* as viable market-places where the trade turnover would be greater than that of modern markets, and where women could sell what they produced. Moreover the idea of what to produce came directly from the market place.

The fact that ISST's first study was partnered with mainstream statistical agencies including the Planning Commission, enabled ISST to have a Round Table in 1980, with 50 to 60 senior economists (some of whom were initially skeptical). This was called 'statistical dialogue between micro and macro' at the Institute of Economic Growth, University of Delhi. Micro studies from different agencies were presented to the official data system which in turn led to the inclusion of a gender focus, both in the CSO, the NSSO and the National Board of Statistics as well as the Registrar General. This partnership with the official data collection systems continued and ISST was part of the delegation from India for the first International conference on Household Survey convened by ESCAP in Bangkok. We carried the day, arguing that women as a subject should not only feature, as it usually did, in the category of social welfare but in their economic and social roles. It was also the beginning of the recognition that the household cannot be the ultimate unit of sampling as individuals within households not only held different occupations but often experienced development differently. These micro-macro interactions on data encouraged us to initiate a network of economists—men and women who were involved in gendered research, called EIWIG (Economists Interested in Women's Issues Group), a clumsy title but intended to be inclusive of men.

Many studies revolving around poor women's work—in different industries and sectors such as forest-based industry, marine products, in handloom industry, khadi and village industry, sericulture (both mulberry and tassar), and public works programmes—all requiring field-work with household surveys, where households were stratified according to class as revealed by landlessness modules, became the core of our work. We did the most elaborate study to understand female-headedness in households, choosing the areas for field study to reflect different 'sources' or 'causes' of female-headedness.[6] Most of these were commissioned by the government or the UN agencies.

We had such a collection of studies, as well as knowledge of the various data sources that we decided to provide a service station for information on women and work, and published a three-volume bibliography on women and work in India, published by Sage Publications. This was to be updated every year, and we produced a second, and later a selective third. Around this time, we also published the first catalogue of women studies centres in India. These bibliographies and catalogues were in continuous demand by all agencies as it was the time when there was a quest to find the organisational base for engendering both development and databases.

In those days (1975–85), the environment was such that these ideas and findings were taken seriously by the 'mainstream'. Women were identified as a subset of the poor, for statistical and programmatic responses. Their occupational characteristics, often a man and woman having different sources of income within a poor family, was taken note of by the Planning Commission and Rural Development Departments. The sixth Five-Year Plan of the Government of India (1976–81), for the first time, had a separate section on women's employment, with tables showing the sectors where women were bunched and their responses to this phenomena. For example, women were often in the least paid and the most tedious occupations, apart from the fact that the many tasks they performed in the process of manufacture, which were also income-earning, were not even notified as occupations. Therefore, neither was it counted nor was there a wage fixation. The government's response was to set up many structures—from statistics improvement to labour laws to the promotion of the organisation of women workers around their occupation. They also reserved 25 per cent of the IRDP loans for female-headed households, amongst the poor, in some states. ISST then argued that public works programmes were a basic amenity for poor women and that the women's movement needs to recognise that broad-based employment programmes were a more important project for poor women than the micro-income generating projects which were the fashion of the day. This led to ISST's advocacy for the 'right to work' as a national programme and the calling of a national conference on the 'right to work' in collaboration with the Institute of Applied Manpower Research and SEWA and with support from the Planning Commission, in 1991.

Responding to the notion of integrating women into development, as well as a message from the UN's 1975 World Conference on Women (Mexico) and the concern for women in poverty, ISST undertook a study of the planning process of the Government of Karnataka, calling it 'Integrating women into a state five-year plan'. Today this would be called an attempt at mainstreaming. The government funded this study and there began a continuing partnership with the Government of Karnataka.

This study raised the whole question not only of development transfers to the poor but also on the context within which poor women could be enabled out of their poverty. Development design and development transfer was flawed—the removal of women's poverty had to be located in a broader critique of the system, the method and the local, macroeconomic, political and social contexts.

Simultaneously, we were critiquing the sericulture development project of the World Bank and did a 'tasks' format showing what women did in sericulture, removing the myth that they could only make garlands with the broken cocoons. Women were awake all night feeding the greedy silk worms whose trays occupied all the huts, cleaning their dirt and cutting leaves from the mulberry bushes. Men hardly did any work except selling the cocoons! As a result the Government of Karnataka set up a Task Force on Women in Sericulture which later informed the World Bank. The gender dimension of these projects became a part of the process. One woman from Kanakapura was to become the sole trader in the cocoon market. This led to a number of such studies where we exposed the myths as well as showed what interventions could overcome the exclusion of women from the pre-project profile.

ISST as networker

Along the way, in the same period, ISST enabled the birth of many new organisations. It was at ISST that Kali for Women drafted its first proposal for support. Ritu Menon had been editing our *Women's Quest for Power*. When she and Urvashi Butalia decided to start their own publishing house, ISST personnel provided the knowhow for registering the society, drafting a proposal for the publication of *Speaking of Faith*, Kali for Women's first publication, funded by NORAD. ISST also enabled the birth of many more SEWAs, such as SEWA (Delhi) and SEWA (Lucknow), and identified agencies through the Gandhian Women's Network, which then went on to become SEWAs, such as SEWA (Bhagalpur). From this emerged SEWA Bharat, a network of SEWAs. We even tried with the Dastkar Anjuman, a co-operative society that Gandhiji had established, to develop a SEWA in Kashmir to enable women in the carpet industry.

ISST also laid the foundation for other networks. The Gandhian Women's Network, now dormant, was initiated with a meeting of about 30 women drawn from Gandhian ashrams all over India. The study of SEWA, whose ethic was strongly Gandhian and revolutionary, the close association with Lakshmi Ashram in Kausani, whose head, Radha Bhatt was a Trustee, and who helped us to understand Gandhian practice and pedagogy, roused our curiosity. Could there be a Gandhian feminism? With impulses and ideological premises different from, say, Marxist feminism? The best way, we thought, of finding out was to ask women in the Gandhian ashrams. We encouraged each woman to narrate her own story and locate what in it was the touch of Gandhi and what in it was irksome to her as a woman. It was a first for the women, and the network continued to meet, seeking to delineate its own perspective on women and economy.

The EIWIG convened three more seminars, such as on 'Women and industry' by U. Kalpagam at the Madras Institute of Development Studies (MIDS), 'Women in poverty' by Nirmala Banerjee at CSSS in Calcutta and one by Pravin Visaria from GIAP in Ahmedabad. ISST was the energiser and helped in raising funds from the Ministry of Labour and the Planning Commission, depending on the theme for these seminars. The four seminars of EIWIG yielded another ISST Volume, *Tyranny of the Household*, drawing attention to all aspects of women and work.[7]

A service station for networks

Development Alternatives with Women for a New Era (DAWN), a network of third world women engaged in development concerns, was launched at a meeting in August 1984, called by ISST, at Tharangavana in Bangalore, where ISST and the Singamma Sreenivasan Foundation had their offices. The idea of holding a brainstorming session for women from the south came out of many experiences and initiatives ranging from a study ISST had done of integrating women into five-year plans, to the lecture I was invited to give at the Organisation for Economic Cooperation and Development (OECD) at Paris called 'Development as if women mattered or can women build a new paradigm?'[8] The bonding of women economists, enabled by EIWIG, the conversations and experiences of women from the developing countries and most of all the advent of the third UN world conference on women, planned for June 1985 in Nairobi contributed to the launching of DAWN.

It also seemed a natural consequence of all the work of ISST, as described in a report prepared by C. P. Sujaya and Vimala Ramachandran (called 'Strategic Planning' for a Ford Foundation review of ISST). To quote,

ISST has been a pioneer in critiquing existing development models and paradigms from the women's perspective. The development theories and approaches taken up from time to time (social welfare vs. development, 'women only' projects, 'mainstreaming' women in development etc.) have been the subject of analysis in ISST's research. Many lines of argument, sometimes overlapping, sometimes converging, have been followed. Thus, 'politics of development' has become an important dimension of ISST research. It seeks to provide an ideological base for ISST's work through a vision of alternative growth patterns 'appropriate' for women in poor households. One argument that ISST has been able to float convincingly is that—when conventional 'development' has had such a devastating effect on the livelihoods of poor marginalised women, the concept of bringing them into the 'mainstream' does not make a lot of sense. In the mining study, for example, an ecology—friendly approach has been favoured even at the cost of foregoing new employment opportunities in the villages created by the mining operation. ISST's interest, in this case, is in sustainable development. At the same time, ISST's basic efforts have been to give poor women a voice in local governance and decision-making, so that services and programmes are better delivered and answer women's specific needs and questions. The major contribution of ISST to creating an alternative paradigm for women's development has been the DAWN network.

Women from the developing countries in international conferences, and in other North-led forums during 1975–84 experienced moments of distance and discomfort. There was an inevitable bunching together and the almost tedious reference to 'third world women'. Agendas as well as knowledge bases came from the Northern women. When asked if I had any ideas for Nairobi, I suggested a consultation, in a place in the South, far away from New York, where we could put our act together, before going to a world conference.

In three unforgettable days in Bangalore, 20–24 August 1984, the group, comprising of one woman each from Africa, West Asia, Latin America, the Caribbean, the Pacific, South Asia, as well as one from Europe and the USA as donors, each person a friend whom I had known from my overseas meetings in the 1970s and early 1980s and several from India, transformed the framework given by the UN for Nairobi, and as we often recalled later, transformed each individual.

For about two years ISST was a service station for DAWN—taking care of finances and communication, and drawing in other networks and agencies. We held meetings in Delhi to share the project. ISST became a hub for Nairobi and supported nearly 40 women from grass-roots and academia to attend the Nairobi conference, including some now famous names like Bina Aggarwal, Srilata Batlivala, Ritu Menon and Urvashi Butalia of Kali for Women, and Kumud Sharma ISST was also drafting two chapters for the official GoI report for Nairobi.

At Nairobi, DAWN presented a book, the now famous *Development Crises and Alternative, Visions: Third World Women's Perspective* by Gita Sen and Karen Grown, as well as several panels, and emerged as the most significant new actor in the international fora.[9] Upon return, ISST initiated a process in India—it organised the translation of the DAWN book summary into eight Indian languages, had workshops with grassroot organisations to spread the analysis, tried to establish a DAWN India movement to politicise the Indian women's movement around development, and initiated a new framework, a new paradigm. The international focal point for DAWN, was moved to Latin America, from where it moved to the Carribean and now is in Fiji, in a process that was part of the DAWN ethic that it should not become a power structure around any individual or organisation, but share the power and advantages of location by shifting to different regions every three or five years.

Once again another asset of ISST, its international linkages, the reputation with donors due to its research, and the ethic of facilitating made it possible for us to undertake anything as ambitious as launching an international development network. Alongside DAWN, ISST began to provide material to the South Commission, a commission of economists chaired by the late Julius Nyerere, of which I was a member. In collaboration with the South Commission and DAWN, ISST organised a consultation on African Debt at Ibadan University. ISST was slowly growing into a service station for the South.

Aspects of research methodology— A balancing act

Our beginnings—women and work in statistics, women workers in organisation, women in poverty, women within the household, and women in struggle, determined the course of our journey. Since our work involved identifying large organisations which were economically active, and since our thesis was that that it was remunerated work which was the first need of poor women, we were engaged to identify five projects in which large numbers of poor women were involved and whose work could be furthered. We decided to do an all-India scan, using the help of our already-in-place partners such as SEWA for Gujarat and the west, Lakshmi Ashram in Almora for Uttar Pradesh and the North, Santiniketan for West Bengal and the east and our own branch in Bangalore for south. From these five projects, proposals were developed in a design workshop with the organisations that were funded. This exercise developed our skills in designing fundable projects for small NGOs, enabling us to provide a kind of technical service for lesser known organisations. We thus became a service station for the grassroots.

Our knowledge base on grass-roots organisations whose special focus or participation was with women became our special asset. Though the word 'best practices' has emerged only now, we had begun to uncover what we called successful endeavours; and our next set of case studies was of effective endeavours in adult education of women—a kind of analysis of types of pedagogy rather than organisational histories. Dr Madhuri Shah, Chairperson of the UGC at that time, not only used it but took the larger list from which we selected five. Thus the wagon rolled on, with our case studies being supplied to the Ministries of Education, Labour, etc. We were a focal point for the uncovering of ground-level work.

This asset then defined the methodology for our research. Since we were also doing studies, especially in data collection—whether it was of workers in the Khadi and Village Industries network, *bidi*-rolling, seri-culture, prawn-peeling, minor forest produce, mining or a dozen other occupations—we always partnered with a grassroots agency and this became our methodology. This asset also yielded documents, such as ISST's contribution to the International Conference on Population and Development (ICPD) in Cairo, which was called 'Voices of poor women on population policies'.

There were many spaces for joint endeavours in advocacy. The various advisory committees of government and the working groups for the plans brought together CWDS, ISST and SEWA. For example, Scarlet Epstein organised the first ever programme on gender, a three month course during 1976–77 at IDS, Sussex called 'Women in rural development'. She invited Vina Muzumdar and myself as co-directors and ICSSR sponsored Ela Bhatt and Padma Ramachandran (then the Joint Secretary Bureau for Women, Government of India). We also worked together on different issues, and protests: it could be said that all of us knew all of us. If it was Development of Women and Children in Rural Areas (DWCRA), then it was SEWA , ISST and some others who designed the scheme and then monitored it. If it was the Equal Remuneration Act, CWDS and ISST were selected by the Ministry of Labour to be the Inspectors. When Dr M. S. Swaminathan wanted to follow up the 1975 conference, with a focus on women, he invited Vina Mazumdar and me to review the Agricultural Universities from the perspective of women as economic agents, and not just as recipients of home science education. Vina Mazumdar and I were also delegates to the first and only NAM conference on women, convened before the UN World Conference at Mexico.

Our twin journey—academic as well as grass-roots—was not always an advantage, however morally satisfying. We could neither claim to be a research centre nor a strong action-oriented women's organisation. The response to this kind of research was not always supportive either. The catalogue and the selection process caused irritation as much because of inclusion as for exclusion, inviting the abuse that we were brokers for the donors. The work on interventions in development design, our work with the Sericulture Project and with the Dairy programme, which we presented as a paper in the preparations for the 1980 Copenhagen conference, was seen as reformist, and not revolutionary.

These criticisms made us learn and we grew out of this mode of work as we too began to challenge the existing structures and processes, top-down projects and the World Bank itself. On the whole, the research journey of ISST has been exciting and there was a sense of pioneering in both the revelations and their follow-up.

Organisation

ISST invented itself as an organisation beginning with one researcher in 1975, then acquired another, with a few in the field and by 1994 had as many as 30 researchers between Delhi and Bangalore. Sometimes a person came in and we gave her a place, then set about finding a role and finances for her. The Counselling Centre, for example, was started that way. Most of our personnel came in through friends asking if there was some work they could do and often we took her in, and a project grew around her. For example, one of the pillars, the late Pushpa Rani, a physically challenged woman started that way on Rs 300 a month and later became the Administrator, the central pivot, the knowledge base, the Public Relations Officer (PRO), the everything of ISST. So did Manju Misra, now Associate Director. Raj Virdi came as mother of Mallika Virdi but is now the life of the Counselling Centre. G.R.N. Moorthy, another ISST stalwart and Revathi Narayanan, now with Mahila Samakhya are similar examples. The ISST family got built by these people who sought it out.

The question then became how to provide. The constant end-of-the-month scramble for salaries was exhausting. This led us to seek freedom from the market which in turn led to fund-raising for the endowment. This required enormous performance, output and individual energy towards writing, lecturing and travelling. The effort was rewarded. By 1994 we had an Endowment Fund that enabled us to start a Provident Fund type of scheme. This was a great achievement for us. We also had a building fund and a publications fund (with the royalties of books), and hoped to start a pension fund.

We also went to the government and this is a story that must be recorded. We argued with the government that while they denounce

274 ❦ Devaki Jain

the fact that NGOs take money from foreigners; (the Kudal Commission and similar witch hunts had been going on India in the late seventies and early eighties leading to FCRA etc.) they were not willing to support NGOs except in the meanest of ways. The government had a scheme for organisations like ISST, where they would give Rs 50,000 a year if we could show that our expenditure was more than our income, and at the level of Rs 1 lakh a year. For two years we tried to write proposals and schemes which would help them to move beyond this margin, since our budget was at least 3 lakhs per year by then. We then took up the case for 10 agencies like us—Anveshi, Chetana and Vimochana are some of them.

We wrote up a case for Rs 5 crores for a five-year plan with Rs 1 crore set aside per year for 10 agencies, which were to be given Rs 10 lakhs each as a grant-in-aid. We could provide meaningful service to social, economical and political agencies, who were working towards justice. The scheme was not only finalised, even an Expenditure Finance Committee (ESC) was drafted, but it just did not go through. Even to-day, organisations like ISST do not have any regular scheme of support and are driven by projects which can often exhaust the office and most of all, its leader or director.

The establishment of the Bangalore branch in 1981 was a major milestone in the evolution of the organisation. Beginning with a study commissioned by the government of Karnataka, the initial nucleus of this team consisted of the recently retired Director of the Department Women's Welfare as it was called then, and a retired accountant from the Hindustan Machine Tools factory! We were given a room in the Secretariat, in the Planning Department. As our team grew and space became an issue, we moved to the premises of the Singamma Sreenivasan Foundation, and stayed there till 1993. A series of research projects were initiated with the Government of Karnataka being the end user. Some of these projects involved intensive fieldwork and large sample surveys that compelled research teams to camp in the field. This approach to fieldwork differed from that of the Delhi office which invariably organised its fieldwork in partnership with a local NGO, largely because it was difficult to find young educated women who were willing to live in villages for long periods. Young scholars like Dr U. Kalpagam, Dr Gita Sen and Dr Srilata Batlivala joined as resource-persons, guided by the eminent macro-economist Dr K.S. Krishnaswamy.

Over the years 1975–85, ISST's Board of Trustees was built around various types of interest and expertise. A pioneer in child health and discrimination against female infants, two women activists, a mainstream academic economist, a diplomat and a specialist in rural management formed our Board. Trustees here were often an additional 'staff' resource 'on call', not only identifying areas of research but enabling the research and offering their time to the organisation. For example, two of the Bangalore trustees would visit the office every week to guide the team there. In Delhi, trustees were in charge of management, developing the salary scale and even the financial system. They often led meetings, and skill development, and represented us in other fora.

The balance sheet

In assessing the ISST experience it seems best to see it in two time phases, as well as in terms of 'issues'.

Between 1977 and 1985–87, ISST was in fast forward mode—its output of research, its outreach to grass-roots organisations of women and its organisational strength, both in finance and team workers, multiplied by ten. The advantages of this overdrive are easy to guess—the organisation reached a pinnacle of visibility and reputation. The personnel had high exposure including at the Nairobi World Conference in 1985, but more importantly, to the various luminaries in the women's movement both in India and abroad, with whom they mingled.

However, there was a flip side to the activities, especially the more exciting as well as ambitious ones such as the birth and nurturing of DAWN in the little office at 5, Deen Dayal Upadhyaya Marg. DAWN was like a hurricane which swept the organisation in its wake, but it also, in a sense, cracked it. It was too much for each one. The energy, the writing as well as the mobilising that is required of the individual, namely myself, was too much and led to incompetence in handling the outcome and the post-outcome period. I felt a strong sense of withdrawal and it was this sense of 'it is too much, I cannot bear it' that started at Nairobi and persisted post-Nairobi for the next nine years which even led me to 'retire myself'. Simultaneously, it put team members into a spin which, while giving them the opportunity to participate, also exposed them to a form of hierarchy and levels of experience and competence which disturbed what was a quiet evolution within the small space of the organisation. Fast forward also meant stress for the administrative and financial managers. Many projects, most of them small, required enormous jigsaw puzzle fitting to come out at the end of the year.

Fast forward also meant that while much research was being done, much time was also taken up in advocacy, which meant that reports did not get published or put into high quality formats like papers. At every meeting of the collectivity and every meeting of the trustees, these ideas were put forward so as 'to be done', but they did not get done. Many valuable manuscripts, like the case studies on Adult Education for Women, the report on the women workers in the Maharashtra Employment Guarantee Sites, the Study of Mining in the Himalayas, and many more lay unprinted and unpublished despite decisions to have a series of working papers and books. There was no money for hiring outside skills.

One important aspect of our character, was the multiple roles each of us took on. There was no peace, as we had to hop from being researcher to manager to lobbyist. Suggestions such as that an administrator was required, turned out to be unsatisfactory as he/she could not understand the needs of the project coordinator. So we settled on another innovative structure called the CoC, the Committee of Co-ordinators, consisting of our own researchers, who would take collective decisions on most managerial issues.

Apart from multiple roles for the individuals there were also the multiple roles of ISST—research, documentation service, preparing notes for policy-making bodies, being the nucleus of a network, advocacy, counselling and action. While this fits in with the main characteristic of ISST mentioned earlier, as growing in response to the demands expressed in the outside space, in retrospect I would say this kind of multiple presence is unwise and untenable. Yet because most women studies centres have a commitment to social justice, there is also a compulsion, moral or political, to take the shape the 'customer' demands. A point to consider.

The next phase, i.e., 1985–94, a period of consolidation, was also mixed in its pleasures and pains. The flow of income and visibility continued, there was greater security and managerial innovations. Quite a few of the team had opportunities to go abroad for improving specific skills and due to the overseas experience, a middle cadre emerged which had its own place both in the house and outside, as the ISST people. Bangalore–Delhi connections were deepened. A second line of leadership emerged naturally in both places consisting of persons who had worked in the organisation for more than, say, three years and had begun to identify themselves with it.

However these were also the years of strain in relationships between part-timers and full-timers, between those who came with a long background in research and those who had learned it hands-on at ISST, those who provided consultancy for specific papers and those who provided the fodder for that exercise. Our heterogeneity, our meagre space and our overstretched means, were tiring us out.

The breakdowns of 'fast forward' revealed the need to settle the organisation with rules, regulations, finance and a few focus projects. Thus, 85/87–94 saw fewer but better-financed projects and recruitment of staff through advertisements and selection committees. Pay scales, grades, increments, provident fund, leave rules, etc. were settled. The reputation of the previous period was sufficient to cause donors to give larger grants. Also the momentum of the decade and the visibility and importance of the inclusion of gender in all development analysis and projects, made a large market for organisations like ISST.

Even as we were thus stabilising, there was a real debate within the organisation, especially initiated by the trustees, questioning the direction the organisation was taking in terms of becoming an 'office' and not a service station. Trustees at ISST had always been strong partners and one important aspect of our pioneering stage, which is perhaps true of other beginnings, is the involvement of trustees. Several of our trustees came from voluntary organisations and saw ISST as a service organisation, and wanted to keep its ethic as a service station for the 'Women in poverty' movement. However, the team had other demands on its time—the regimenting and time inputs that project-driven work demanded, such as timely reports, constant hopping-on-toes for the next month's wherewithal, and meeting the monetary needs of women who were supporting their families and therefore were looking for employment and not voluntary work.

This issue of identity and ethic remained an unresolved aspect of ISST's evolution and location in the landscape of non-governmental organisations. We were everywhere and nowhere because of this lack of definition. The scholars respected and befriended us but we were not considered part of the academic cohort. We did not teach, or offer courses of any kind, nor could we. The activists also regarded us well, but we were not in the core of any activist forum for public action as, for example, the Seven Sisters, or the all-India campaigns spearheaded by the Left or the autonomous women's centres' networks. Perhaps our closest allies were the Gandhian organisations and networks as we did use and partner a great deal with the Gandhi Peace Foundation, the Gandhian Ashrams and their movements, including SEWA a great deal. Nevertheless, we could not adopt the Gandhian ethic either in our clothing or consumer behaviour, as they did.

Though initially the founding call was feminist in nature, the team could not identify itself with that label—partly because they came from diverse backgrounds. The move towards a commitment to women's rights emerged out of the work and not because of a prior ideological impulse. We were a curious place, attempting many feminist methods, but singularly non-ideological as a group. We were not a homogenous group either ideologically, or in terms of a category such as academic or card-holding members of a party or a trade union. Yet we were a team and looking back, a racing, productive team.

We attempted, however, or perhaps experimented with what we considered, or may be, what I considered, were feminist ideals. How should one deal with power, as it relates to hierarchies and permanence? So, in order to reduce the inequalities in power as they are related to income, we kept the distance between us in salaries, short, with the highest not more than Rs 3,500 and the lowest at Rs 500 per month. In retrospect, it is interesting to recall how we felt somewhat shocked when in 1985 a consultant wanted Rs 5,000 per month. However small the space, we all sat together with no partitions—both in Delhi and Bangalore, this was an often noted feature of ISST which reduced the distances created by cubicles and the difference in roles. For example, usually typists and accountants are separated from the academic or the 'literate'. But we thought we were being feminist if we mixed up those distances and there was no particular table or space belonging to the director. Sitting in one hall close to each other meant that everybody knew everything— visitors, letters, discussions—so that there was rarely any need for writing notes or 'file' movement. It was again an interpretation of feminism, the 'ideal' of detachment from power-centricity, the image of a 'collective' rather than an 'ikon' that led me to move out of directorship.

The flip side of this is that, many of those who had to concentrate on reading and writing found the 'marketplace-like' atmosphere of one crowded gallery, irritating and disturbing. Not everyone felt there was a method in the madness. The ethic was not one that had emerged through any form of group therapy or political background. In any case, as we had grown on an 'as and when basis', we were too heterogeneous even to try to build that common purpose.

In the period 1975–85, the mode of formation of women's organisations had a certain ideological and emotional content which required it to be self-conscious about its institutional structure. The fashion was to have collectivities. Feminism connoted a voluntary spirit, non-hierarchical collectivities and ideal centres (such as Vimochana in Bangalore). Many others who were also making their mark, were the ideals. There were another set of organisations—mass-based as for example SEWA, where the cadres were drawn by the desire to 'serve the poor' and identified themselves with the working class. The 'institutes' (like ISST) would intersect with these other more ideologically drawn organisations, and this pushed them into thinking of their internal format and issues. Discussions always left the team at ISST unhappy because the collectivity seemed to be more attractive, less hierarchical and less encumbered with the pressures of 'leader' and 'led' that they were suffering from. On the other hand, the overall pressure of delivering reports and papers in return for the funding was pushing these centres into becoming more 'boxed'. Strict demands by the organisation instigated strict demands by the 'workers'.

But we could not stop discussing what we were. A professional organisation like Institute of Economic Growth or Centre for Women's Development Studies? Or a consultancy organisation such as Industrial Development Services, on a smaller scale? Or a feminist collective or voluntary organisation of the old days where the spirit of service and voluntariness made moral demands with no remuneration? It seemed important to sort this out, as on that depended our organisational rules, salaries, allowances, holidays, entitlements, etc. These were some of our internal debates and stresses.

This ambiguity of 'shape' and 'location', if we can use that term instead of identity, was also a factor in what can be called the nature of continuity in the organisation. Although a second line of leadership emerged which was self-confident and competent, the organisation could not hold them. It is not surprising that it is the brightest of the professionals who left, while the 'solid' workers remained. By the 1990s, this exit could also be due to changes external to the organisation. The organisation's role and purpose was not embedded in any specific guidelines or orientation. It was in people and their lived experience.

By the 1990s, gendering of development had become a strong presence, especially among donors and international agencies, including the World Bank. The opportunities as well as the demand for gender specialists and the reward structures had expanded by ten or more times and many of the best of our teams either married and had to change residence or left due to the frenzy of activity, or had better offers and looked for a change. This emptied the vessel just when it was full.

There was both a recognition that there was something called gender analysis of everything under the sun, as well as a demand for those who had soiled their hands with the issue. There were also many more small and big organisations and networks amongst them, engaged in the domain of women's rights and concerns of so many typologies. The excitement of discovery and argument, the movement driving the organisations was perhaps overshadowed by the market demand for gendering. The clients were different, as was the predominant environment. In a strange way this made for more structured space, more critique of ourselves from inside and from outside, more professionalisation, and perhaps less open spaces.

I would guess that this also determined the internal dynamics, losses and gains of ISST. It also shaped the outcome of the transition to a new leadership, as change had to take place in a different kind of space. In retrospect the experiment with feminist 'ways', rewarding as it was, had not taken enough root to survive change. But the institutional structure was strong, as was the track record and core staff who stayed on. The outside had changed, and the organisation was small and flexible enough to adapt to that change.

The space today is larger, it is more populated and more diverse and the biennial NCWS proves this each time. However, the space is also demanding more structure and more specificity—partitioning and 'specialisation'. Within universities, the centres are perhaps responding to the kind of education the market needs right now, whether it is a commercial or an academic market. Outside, in the spaces that organisations like ISST occupy, finding a niche is probably more necessary and also more difficult.

With the maturity and distance of hindsight, it could be said that the ISST experience was an experiment in institution building. We grew into a 'something', our shape emerging out of practice and not planning. There were many undefined characteristics because of this type of growth, a growth which seemed to be a response to the outside, rather than an internally-defined shape with a mandate drawn from a pattern of assistance either from the UGC or from the ICSSR or from an ideology like that of a political party or a philosophy whether drawn from Marx or Gandhi or a spiritual fold.

The ISST story shows that it is possible to invent an organisation, out of commitment as well as the enthusiasm and demand from the outside environment. It also shows how much space there is to be filled, and how much technical services are in demand. But it also reveals the lack of recognition of the value of such services by the government as not only did they not develop a scheme or a pattern of assistance which would have strengthened such inventions, but instead tried to set up their own resource centres and research organisations, as if such skills and services can be 'set up' or constructed.

'Once we were warriors' is a gripping film, which tells the story of Maoris in New Zealand, who moved to the cities, lived on the margins and got embedded and associated with a low life on the lower side. They were once 'warriors'. There is no matching story here. But we, who drew on and took further the threads of women's studies, were 'once warriors'—at the forefront of the debates on equality, on the neglected sectors like unorganised labour and rural areas, on administrative and legal restructuring. We were 'free'—free of organisational tethers, free to move around in the space of justice movements. It could be Marianad one day—the fishing village in Kerala which taught us about community-led resistance to every dominating force, be it the paradigm of development, the terrorism of livelihood-displacing technology or of caste and religious oppressions. It could be the Mathura case on another day. But we were there in some informal or formal way.

I do not then want to go on to say 'once were...but not now', as whatever we are now, is also the natural concomitant of the passage of time. I would leave it at 'once we were warriors' but would call attention to the importance of witnessing the 'birthing' and growth of these centres, from the point of view of the outer space and the mood of the times in which we pioneered, keeping in mind the present scenario.

Appendix

Publications of ISST (1975–94)

1977, *Impact of Women's Employment: A Case Study on the Modernization of the Traditional Handloom Weaving Industry in the Kashmir Valley*, ISST.

1977, *Field Investigation of Rural Households, Especially Their Time Disposition*, ISST.

1977, *Country Paper: India, Network on Information Exchange and Transfer of Technology*, ISST.

1978, *Development Planning for Women: India Case Study*, ISST.

1979, *Impact on Women Workers—Maharashtra Employment Guarantee Scheme, A Study sponsored by ILO, Geneva*, ISST.

1979, *Monitoring and Evaluation of Social Development Planning: Implication for Women's Question*, ISST.

1979, *Case Study on the Modernization of the Traditional Handloom Weaving Industry in the Kashmir Valley*, ISST.

1979, *Folk Artists of Mithila—Some Notes*, ISST.

1980, *Developing a Single Prototype for a Child Welfare Programme*, ISST.

1980, *Exercise in Project Development for Women*, ISST.

1980, *Women's Employment as Related to Rural Areas*, ISST.

1980, *Profiles of Some Voluntary Agencies and Women's Development Projects*, ISST.

1980, *Technology for Rural Development—Some Issues*, ISST.

1981, *Providing Comprehensive Child and Family Welfare Services—A paper from India* (Vols. 1 and 2), ISST.

1981, *Women in the Labour Force*, paper presented at seminar on women in the labour force, organised by Asian Regional Team for Employment Promotion (ARTEP) and International Labor Organization (ILO), Trivandrum.

1981, *Working Child—A Guide to the Literature*, ISST.

1982, *Inter-state Tasar Project, Report on a field survey Chandrapur District of Maharastra*, ISST.

1982, *Taluk level Conference in Gulbarga*, ISST.

1982, *Assessment of Women's Roles—The Karnataka Sericulture Development Project*, ISST.

1983, *Grass Without Roots—Rural Development under Government Auspices*, ISST.

1983, *Integrating Women's Interest into a State Five-Year Plan* (Vols 1 and 2), ISST.

1983, *Statistics on Women, Children, and Aged in Agriculture in India*, ISST.

1983, *Women's Roles in Large Employment Systems*, ISST.

1983, *Visit of the Swedish Women's Council to India*, ISST.

1983, *Women's Employment as Related to Rural Areas*, ISST.

1983, *Development as a Platform*, paper for 1985 women's conference, Nairobi.

1984, *Development of Women and Children in Rural Areas* (Vols 1 and 2), DWCRA, ISST.

1984, *Preliminary Report on Marketing Study,* ISST.

1984, *Adult Education for Women: Eight Case Studies,* ISST.

1984, *Employment of Women from Kerala in the Fish Processing Units of Gujarat,* ISST.

1984, *Women's Development and Institutional Changes,* ISST.

1984–85, *Preliminary Report on Marketing Study,* ISST.

1985, *Marine Fish Marketing Study: Indo-Danish Fisheries Project,* ISST.

1985, *Fisher Women of Tadri: A Socio-Economic Survey,* ISST.

1985, *Role of Women's Organizations in Third World and ECDS,* second RIS conference theme paper, ISST.

1985, *Utilization of Child Development Services—A Field Study,* ISST.

1986, *Moonlight in Mithila: A Feasibility Report* (Vols 1 and 2), ISST.

1987, *Women Migrant Workers from Kerala in Fish Processing Units of Tamil Nadu, Maharastra and Karnataka,* ISST.

1987, *Small-Scale Forest-based Enterprises in India, with Special Reference to Women Case Studies—Material Review Paper,* ISST.

1987, *Small-Scale Forest-based Enterprises in India, with Special Reference to Women Case Studies—Karnataka State level paper,* ISST.

1987, *Fertility and Socio-economic Activity of Rural Women,* ISST.

1987, *Linking Fertility and the Socio-economic Activities of Rural Women—A Case-study on the Malur Rural Project of the Family Planning Association of India,* ISST.

1987, *Rural Sanitation—Technology Options.*

1987, *Survival Strategies of the Poor, Traditional Wisdom—A Reflection,* ISST.

1988, *Linking Vienna with Villages—Recruiting a Part of Science and Technology for Development,* ISST.

1989, *Impacts of Sericulture Pilot Project in Karnataka—An Evaluation,* ISST.

1989, *Small-scale Forest-based Activities in Karnataka with Special Reference to Women* (Vols 1 and 2), ISST.

1990, *Radical Possibilities of Conservative Institutions—An Analysis of Demographic Changes in Malur Taluk, Kolar District,* ISST.

1990, *Raj Krishna Memorial Seminar on Labor and Employment,* ISST.

1990, *Indian Women's Experience of Development – An Analysis,* ISST.

1991, *Mining in the Himalaya—Report on a Field Study in Almora and Pithorgrah Districts,* ISST.

1992, *The Role of Mahila Mandals in Locally Managed Rural Development Programmes with Reference to Panchayat Raj System,* New Delhi, ISST.

1992, *Rural Women—Leadership in Development,* ISST.

1992, *Employment Opportunities for Women in Village Industries in Selected Districts of Uttar Pradesh and Rajasthan,* ISST.

1993, *Concern and Conflict—Women, Work and Child Health and Development,* ISST.

1993, *Women's Studies in India—A Directory of Research Instituitions.*
1993, *New Economic Policy and Women,* prepared for the Sixth National Conference of the Indian Association for Women's Studies, ISST.
1994, *Income and Nutrition Effects of Shifts from Subsistence to Cash Cropping Especially on the Poor Farmers, Women and Children,* Vol 1, and 2, ISST.
1994, *Sustainable Development through Natural Resource Utilization,* ISST.
1994, *Women's Development Corporation—An Assessment,* ISST.
1994, *Report on Sustainable Development Through Natural Resources Utilization—A Case-study in Karnataka,* ISST.
1994, *Listening to Women: Evolving a Women-Sensitive Population Policy through Consultations with Rural Women in India,* final report of the first phase, ISST.
1994, *Evaluation Report on NORAD-assisted Programme in Madhya Pradesh for Training and Income-generating Activities,* ISST.

Other articles: (1975–94)

Devaki Jain (1975), *India's Effort in International Women's Year,* Statement made at International Round Table, UNESCO, Paris.
———, 'Organizing Women Workers (on SEWA)' in *The Times of India,* 31 August 1975.
——— (ed.)(1975), *Indian Women,* New Delhi: Publications Division, Ministry of Education and Broadcasting, Government of India.
——— (1977), 'Measuring Women's Work: Some Methodological Issues' in Rounaq Jehan and Hanna Papanek (eds) *Women in Development: Perspectives from South and South East Asia.* Dacca: Bangladesh Institute of Law and International Affairs.
——— (1978), 'Are women a separate issue?' in *Populi* (Journal of the United Nations' Fund for Population Activities, New York) November issue (Republished in *Mainstream, Yojana* and *Development Forum*).
——— (1978), 'Can feminism be a global ideology?'in *Quest* (Washington), Winter issue.
——— (1978), ' Role of rural women in community life: a case study from India' in Nalini Singh and Abha Bhaiya (eds) *Economic Bulletin for Asia and the Pacific.* Bangkok: ESCAP.
——— (1979), 'The subordination of women: Analysis needs new categories' in *Mainstream.*
Devaki Jain, N. Singh and M. Chand (1979), *Women's Quest for Power: Five Case Studies* sponsored by ICSSR, New Delhi: Vikas.
Devaki Jain (1980), 'Importance of Age and Sex-specific Data Collection in Household Surveys', paper presented at the Regional Conference on Household Survey, organised by Economic and Social Commission for Asia and Pacific (ESCAP), Bangkok.

Devaki Jain and Malini Chand (1981), 'Patterns of Female Work: Implication for Statistical Design, Economic Classification and Social Priorities', paper presented at the National Conference on Women's Studies, Bombay.

Devaki Jain (1982), Background note for the Technical Seminar on Women's Work and Employment organised by ISST, New Delhi,

Devaki Jain and Malini Chand (1982), 'Report on time allocation study', Technical Seminar on Women's Work and Employment, ISST.

Devaki Jain (1982), 'Indian Women—Today and Tomorrow', Padmaja Naidu Memorial Lecture, Nehru Memorial Museum and Library, Teen Murti House, New Delhi.

———— (1984), 'Female and Child Workers—A Case for Methodological Revision', Working Paper, Asian Development Centre, Boston.

———— (1985), Role of Women's Organizations in Third World, ISST.

————, 'Voluntary Agencies and Their Role' in *The Financial Express*, 1 July 1985.

Devaki Jain and Banerjee N. (1985), *Tyranny of the Household—Investigative Essays on Women's Work*, New Delhi: Shakti Books.

Devaki Jain (1986), 'Advances in Feminist Theory: An Indian Perspective', Lecture delivered at the International Conference on Anthropological and Ethnographical Sciences, Delhi.

———— (1986), 'Alternative Development for Women: Mediterranean Women's Studies', ISST.

Devaki Jain and Diana L. Eck (ed.) (1987), *Speaking of Faith—Global Perspectives on Women, Religion and Social Change*, Philadelphia: New Society Publishers.

Devaki Jain (1987), 'Through the Looking Glass of Feminism', paper presented at the symposium on the Gender of Power, Leiden, University of Leiden.

———— (1987), 'Healing the Wounds of Development Curriculum Requirements', paper presented at the conference on Worldwide Education for Women's Progress, Prospects and Agenda for Future, Massachusetts, USA.

————, 'Remembering Kamaladevi' in *The Indian Express*, 3 November 1985.

———— (1989), ' The Culture of the Poor—Is Equitable Development Possible?', in K.M Braganza and S. Peeradina (eds), *Cultural Forces Shaping India*, New Delhi: Macmillan.

———— (1990), 'Development theory and practice—Insights emerging from women's experiences' in *Economic and Political Weekly* 7 July 1990.

———— (1990), Radical Possibilities of Conservative Institutions—An Analysis of Demographic Changes in Malur Taluk, ISST.

———— (1992), 'Global Forum for Women: New Visions of Leadership' Speech delivered at the Global Forum for Women, Dublin.

———— (1992), 'Women in Extreme Poverty and the Global Political Economy—The Intersection', ISST, Vienna.

———— (1993), 'The Leadership: Challenge to Feminists', Presidential Address, Indian Association of Women's Studies Conference, Mysore.

———— (1994), Karnataka State Planning Board, Social Development Plan.

Notes

1. See Jain (1975).
2. See Jain and Chand (1982).
3. See Jain (1982).
4. See Jain (1981).
5. See Jain, Singh and Chand (1979).
6. See Jain, Singh and Chand (1979).
7. See Jain and Banerjee (eds) (1985).
8. See Jain (1983b).
9. See Sen and Grown (1987).

References

Devaki Jain (1975), *Indian Women*, New Delhi: Publications Division, Ministry of Information and Broadcasting, Government of India.

——— (1985), 'The Household Trap: Report on a Field Survey of Female Activity Patterns', in Devaki Jain and Nirmala Banerjee (eds), *Tyranny of the Household*, New Delhi: Vikas.

——— (1996), 'Valuing Work: 'Time as a Measure' in *Economic and Political Weekly*.

——— (1982), 'Indian Women: Today and Tomorrow', Padmaja Naidu Memorial Lecture.

——— (1981), 'Patterns of Female Work: Implications for Statistical Design, Economic Classification and Social Priorities', paper prepared for National Conference on Women's Studies, Bombay.

——— (1978), 'Are Women a Separate Issue?' in *Mainstream*, August issue on *Women as a Subset of the Poor*.

Devaki Jain, N. Singh, and M. Chand (1979), *Women's Quest for Power—Five Case Studies*, sponsored by the Indian Council for Social Science Research (ICSSR), New Delhi: Vikas.

Devaki Jain (1983a), *Integrating Women's Interest into a State Five Year Plan* (3 volumes), Sponsored by Ministry of Social Welfare, Government of India, A Study Conducted by ISST.

——— (1983b), *Development as if women mattered: can women build a new paradigm?* Paris: OECD.

Gita Sen and Karen Grown (1987), 'Development Crises and Alternatives Visions: Third World Women's Perspective' in *Monthly Review Press*.

13

Nurturing links between scholarship and activism

The Story of Anveshi

Anveshi Research Centre for Women's Studies[1]

Anveshi Research Centre for Women's Studies was founded in 1985 by a small group of women activists, many of whom were academics and professionals. Their involvement in the women's movement had changed their lives and work. The movement had clarified for them the need to study, document and analyse the various dimensions of the Indian situation and its impact on women's lives. Such research was fundamental to the objectives of the women's movement.

Anveshi was thus born out of the productive interaction of practice and theory which was made possible by women's movements worldwide. The desire was to create an institutional forum in which activists and academics could work together. These forums were rare in mainstream institutions—activist or academic. The decision to set up Anveshi as an autonomous organisation, despite the fact that many of the founder-members worked within the framework of the university, was influenced by many factors. As a child of the women's movement, women's studies had started with a special intimacy to both activism and scholarship. Universities and academic institutions were not structured to facilitate it. Mainstream organisations, at best, 'allowed' research on women. They did not have the interdisciplinary structure essential for women's studies. Moreover, many of the activist women who wanted to do research did not have the educational qualifications required by universities. Remaining outside the rigid frameworks of mainstream organisations would also permit the flexibility needed for a continued engagement with the public sphere in an effort to infuse the gender question into the entire scope of public discussion and renew the social force of scholarship.

The late 20th-century re-emergence of the women's question can be thought of as powered by two revolutionary insights, viz., (*a*) that the principal forms of patriarchal power operate in civil society through institutions such as the family, the school, religion, the arts and so on. Furthermore, in these institutions, power operates through consent, not force; (*b*) that there is a mutually endorsing relationship between power and knowledge. Consequently, the representation of women and the discourses in which women's issues are studied or discussed, be it in academic disciplines or in the public sphere, are of critical importance. These discourses determine the way in which the women's question is analysed and acted on in everyday life as much as in government or institutional policy.

The health and vigour of the public domain is obviously vital to the growth of democracy. This is only too evident in India today where a number of new constituencies—women, Dalits, tribal people, regional groups, communities of various kinds—use this domain to voice their aspirations and press their demands. From the very outset, therefore, Anveshi has regarded researchers and theorists on women's issues as activists in the public sphere, committed to reworking civil society institutions and to redirecting the thrust of theory and practice.

The dynamic nature of this group is reflected in the people who are associated with Anveshi. In the early years the organisation was largely identified with its founder-members, their work and spheres of influence. From about the early 1990s onwards, a number of very articulate and capable students and younger activists became involved with Anveshi. They were largely attracted by the fresh and meaningful perspectives on issues that were agitating the public imagination— reservations, caste violence, the curriculum, the popular media—and were emerging in our public initiatives, writings, discussions and study groups. A third phase might be identified in the new groups, issues and constituencies (Dalits, land, life-prisoners, family violence, a Telugu reading public) that over the last 3–4 years have increasingly found place in Anveshi's work.

The work of the organisation over the last 16 years has consistently addressed the concerns that led to the formation of Anveshi, outlined in the earlier section. Anveshi has grappled with questions of gender in the very midst of issues that inflect contemporary life—secularism, caste discrimination, liberalisation, globalisation and the media revolution.

Significantly, Anveshi takes creative initiatives in setting up discussions in the public domain on a variety of issues, produces a number of very influential publications, collaborates and networks with other organisations, and takes up research projects that have substantially changed the understanding of several issues. We have developed a library that is reputed for its careful selection of books and documents in English and Telugu. The library specialises in gender studies, but also has a considerable collection of material on literature, media, mental health and law.

Initiatives in the public domain

Initiatives in setting up discussions in the public domain have taken various forms. Given the context of discussions provided by Anveshi, groups tend to emerge spontaneously around public issues. These groups initiate and organise many of the discussions. Anveshi actively supports such efforts through interventions, networking and creating issue-based alliances with other groups as well as through creating critical and informed public discussions. For instance, Anveshi collaborated with other organisations in issues like targeted sterilisations (1998–99), the central government's proposal to legislate death sentence as punishment for rape (2000), and tribal land rights (2000–2001).

Anveshi was an active participant in the debate over the Uniform Civil Code (1997–98) and the inclusion of caste alongside race in UN categorisations of discrimination (2001). A recent example is the response to the Domestic Violence Bill (2001). Anveshi took issue with several aspects of the Bill. These were expressed in a response which was sent to various women's groups. On 6 April 2002, Anveshi organised a workshop, 'Domestic Violence Bill 2001: Issues at Stake.' The workshop bought together many individuals and groups working with and concerned about the role of the law (and order) machinery on issues of violence against women in the family.

These activities not only contribute in addressing the issue on hand, but also help in the formation of sustained study groups and result in the publication of scholarly articles of public interest.

As an organisation too, Anveshi involves itself in movements in the public sphere. Our part in the historic anti-arrack movement of 1992–93 is an example. A team of nine members from Anveshi visited 12 villages of Nellore district where the movement was most intensive. With the help of Jana Vignana Vedika (a voluntary body involved in literacy programmes), the team met many women who spoke to them of their concerns and indicted the government involvement in the sale of liquor. In public forums, the movement was being described and documented in a stereotypical and moralistic manner in terms of women's purity and their efforts at tidying up the body-politic of the nation. Anveshi's report and analysis sought to refocus the attention on the political demands being made by the women, especially about drinking water supply and the sale price of rice.[2]

The findings of this team were publicised through meetings with different women's and Dalit groups in Hyderabad. Reports of the visit were also published in Telugu and English. Since the literacy programmes were widely regarded as catalysts for the anti-arrack movement, the group recognised the importance of developing post-literacy readers. Therefore, at the request of Jana Vignana Vedika, Anveshi developed readers on topics such as women's health, women's work, women's rights and legal issues.

Reaching out to a larger audience: Publications

The interests of individual Anveshi members in their spheres of activity, the discussions in Anveshi and the political potential and topicality of issues in the public forums have paved way for the publication of several books from Anveshi. One good example is the Telugu health book *Savaalaksha Sandehaalu (One Hundred Thousand Doubts)*.[3] The book grew out of ongoing discussions and research on women's health. The group working on the book included members of Anveshi who were doctors, other health care providers, researchers and critical users of the health care system. Activists and academics worked together to produce a rigorous and impassioned critique of the system as it exists.

It is interesting to take a look at how the book was received. It has run into two editions. It has been used in the mass literacy campaigns of the mid-1990s, by self-help groups, by *anganwadi* supervisors in the Integrated Child Development Services (ICDS) programme, social welfare residential schools, NGOs, Andhra Pradesh State Women's Welfare Department and so on. The largest sale was to individuals. Men bought it for their wives, women for their husbands. Patients clutched copies when they went to meet doctors. The renowned folk balladeer, Gaddar, composed a song titled 'Savaalaksha…' drawing on material of the book, creating, in the process, a new life for some of the feminist issues raised by the book. The Telugu poet Jayaprabha composed a poem that became part of a landmark debate in the history of Telugu literature on appropriate topics for poetry and feminist poets' violation of the decorum of Telugu poetry.

In short, *Savaalaksha Sandehaalu* is not just a women's health book. It has reconfigured the whole question of health and the politics of health care systems, and carried its critical essence into other forums. A similar story marks the production, reception and circulation of *Women Writing in India: 600 B.C. to the Present,* edited by Susie Tharu and K. Lalita. Anveshi provided the institutional and intellectual support in the making of this path-breaking two-volume collection of women's literature translated from 14 languages.[4] This archival project emerged out of the critiques of literature syllabi and teaching in the universities. Its impact on literature and literary criticism is evident from the many laudatory reviews it has received. Selections from the book have appeared in the syllabi of NCERT, universities of Bombay, Delhi, Baroda, Kerala, the North-East and those in the USA and UK. Emerging as they do from a feminist context, many of the other books published from Anveshi have made an impact in more than one discipline.

Working together: Collaborations and networking

Initiatives in both the public sphere and critical research that provide inputs for publications, have been enriched by collaborations with other organisations concerned with issues of democracy, gender, community, minority and education.[5] Collaborations make possible the wider dissemination of the programmes, productive co-operation between academics and activists and support for women from the mainstream.

One of the main collaborative efforts is the organisation of seminars and conferences. These often bring together different approaches to similar concerns. In 1993, in collaboration with the Subaltern Studies Collective, Anveshi organised an international conference on 'Subalternity and culture'. This conference highlighted the convergence of concerns between the project of the subaltern studies perspective and that of feminism in the questioning of mainstream history. Collaboration on a workshop on the 'Cultural politics of translation' with the Central Institute of English and Foreign Languages, Hyderabad and Sahitya Akademi, New Delhi arose out of the recognition of the importance of developing a theory of translation. The political tradition of producing translations from different languages into Telugu has enabled a number of intense debates in Andhra Pradesh. Anveshi has handled some major translation projects like *Women Writing in India*, *We Were Making History* (the oral histories of women involved in the Telengana struggle) and the health books. These experiences led to the realisation that while the usefulness of translations is generally accepted, it continues to remain an undertheorised area. Issues relating to the cultural and political contexts of the translation process still needed to be studied. The collaboration brought together a large and diverse group of people including practising translators, literary theorists, philosophers, linguists, political theorists, sociologists, medical practitioners, film theorists and students from different disciplines.

Collaborations have also been issue-specific. In March 1999, Anveshi was involved in a campaign against the Andhra Pradesh Government's proposal to conduct family planning camps in the twin cities of Hyderabad and Secunderabad. Since the objective of these camps was to meet the targets that the government had set itself, many groups in the city objected to the manner in which they were being conducted. These groups came together to form the 'Group Against Targeted Sterilisations' (GATS). Anveshi's involvement with the post-communal riot activities, organised by the Confederation of Voluntary Organisation in the old city of Hyderabad is another example issue-specific collaboration. Collaborations have also resulted in long-term and intensive discussions on a particular theme even after the immediate issue has been addressed. An example is the formation of the Anveshi Law Committee around the debate over the Uniform Civil Code.[6] The Law Committee continued to meet and had several discussions and presentations on critical legal theory and practice. The activities of the group led to the organisation of an international seminar on 'Gender, law and citizenship: Issues in India and the US' in 2000 in collaboration with the Indo-American Centre for International Studies in (IACIS) Hyderabad. The Committee continues to discuss and comment on topical issues, the latest being the rustication of 10 Dalit students in the University of Hyderabad.[7]

Breaking new grounds: Research projects

Experiences from many of the short-term initiatives highlight the need for a sustained and focused study of issues. These translate into proposals for projects. A good example is the project on 'Institutional responses to domestic violence'. The project grew out of the experience of addressing the issue of civil societal violence, especially family violence, in the context of civil liberties. Campaigns of the women's movement have highlighted anew the pervasiveness and intensity of violence against women within the family. Anveshi's study aims to look at family violence in relation to the situation in Andhra Pradesh with a view to set up a legal aid centre. The project aims to understand the response of the legal system, supportive agencies and institutions and explore the context of violence as experienced by women in the domestic sphere.

Research initiatives also consider the specific skills and interests of one or more members. An ongoing project which addresses dropouts and curricular transactions in primary schools, for example, emerged from two strands of our earlier work, (*a*) extending our involvement with gender to issues of caste and other forms of marginalization and subalternity, and (*b*) the interest that some members have had in the theory and practice of literacy. The need to initiate interest in specific areas and to add to the interest concretely is also reflected in the kind of projects designed. The Telugu Material Production Project is an example of this kind of activity. Andhra Pradesh continues to witness a variety of movements that challenge earlier formations of the polity. Questions of caste, minority, region and sexuality are major concerns in the political and cultural life of contemporary Andhra Pradesh. Through the production of serious reading material, the project undertakes to add quality and range to the resources available in what is, by any standards, a very active regional public sphere.

Research projects also arise from the need to investigate trends in public life. It has been noted that as a result of the intense social change that marked the last decade, the number of children from minority communities and marginalised sections of the society attending schools has increased. But statistics show that the number of dropouts, especially of children belonging to SC/ST communities, is also increasing. We found that in Andhra Pradesh, only 1 per cent of the children aged had between 6–13 belonging to these communities, had completed Class Five. A large percentage of these children were girls. These observations have led to a project studying the curricular transactions in government schools in Andhra Pradesh. The project will also record the life stories of school children and narratives of schooling, which will provide insights into their experiences of school life and the reasons for dropping out.

Specialised anthologies have been part of the building up of the scholarship of all radical movements. In the past few years, we have seen the release of many feminist and Dalit anthologies. However, conspicuous by their absence are collections of Dalit women's writings. In keeping with its objective to recover women's history, literature and art, Anveshi has initiated a project which will result in the collection of Dalit women's writings that will feature the works of over 40 writers. The significance of this project lies in the fact that it will provide Dalit women artists and intellectuals a new self-image and develop a strong critique of the middle-class/upper caste nature of the Indian women's movement.

Thinking together: Seminars and conferences

Over the years, Anveshi has organised a number of seminars, workshops and conferences on a variety of issues, Local workshops in which individuals and groups in Hyderabad participate are a regular feature and are often forums where current issues or concerns from projects are discussed. Workshops are also held for special interest groups, like the workshop on domestic violence for counsellors. Seminars often have a national participation and bring together interested people from various fields. One good example is the national seminar on 'Women and mental health' organised in 1996. The seminar brought together and professionals from the fields of psychiatry and psychology, feminists, literary theorists, health professionals, sociologists, political theorists and users of the mental health care system. Active discussions on various topics that problematise psychological and psychiatric theory and practice from the perspective of gender came up for discussion. The feedback showed that the perspectives that came out of the seminar were a revelation for both feminists and mental health professionals, and have led to further work both within and outside Anveshi.[8]

In recent years, Anveshi has organised various such events both in collaboration with other organisations and on its own. Significant among these are the symposium on 'Gender, law and citizenship' (with the IACIS, Hyderabad, 1999), workshop on Telugu cinema (with the Centre for the Study of Culture and Society, Bangalore, 1999), plenary session on 'Tribal issues and women's movement' for the 9th national conference of the Indian Association of Women's Studies (Hyderabad, 2000), etc.

In 2001, Anveshi, in collaboration with the Hyderabad Women's Collective, organised a South Indian young feminists' conference, 'Listening together, talking differences'. This was an attempt to bring together the newer generation of feminists from various parts of South India. True to the title, various discussions brought forth the differences in both their concerns and approaches to questions of gender. It was clear that future theorisations of gender and feminism would have to find ways of working with these differences.

Looking back

Looking back, it is possible to see that the work done by the organisation since its inception has been considerable and significant. However, Anveshi has also had its share of problems. At the organisational level, Anveshi worked with a small staff for a number of years. It is primarily known for its discussion forums, outreach programmes and projects. However, in a context where funding is available only for projects rather than for core institutional activities, Anveshi's work too has been affected.

Presently, Anveshi is carrying out three major projects, (*a*) study of institutional response to domestic violence, (*b*) curricular transactions in government schools, and (*c*) Telugu materials production. Undoubtedly, we obtained significant benefits by taking up the projects, in terms of the increased number of people working full-time at Anveshi, expanded areas of interest and work, effective intervention in more areas, and increased publications. However, the focus on projects in this initial phase marked a shift in Anveshi's functioning. Our engagement with the constituency that involved themselves in the different discussions of Anveshi became more infrequent over time. In spite of the several and rather hectic project-related activities that were taking place at Anveshi, there was a sense among this group that Anveshi activities were at a standstill! We have sought to address this problem by striking a balance between project-related work and our work with the larger community of activists and scholars. The experience we have acquired over the last couple of years of working on projects too is helping us address this task better.

A few years ago, in 2000, Anveshi faced a rather difficult situation. The question of relocating ourselves—office and library—seemed to loom large before us. Osmania University, which, since 1989, had supported Anveshi's activities and had given us office space on the campus, withdrew this support. Location on the university had enabled interaction with various departments and also helped involve the campus students in discussions and other activities. Members of Anveshi in turn were invited to participate in the academic meetings held on the university campus. This mutually beneficial arrangement ended when the administration asked Anveshi to vacate its premises in 2000 'as part of their new policy.' While the incident might seem like an isolated case, it also reflects what women's studies means to academic institutions. The positive feedback from the public was gratifying, but the attitude of the university which chose to audit us in economic rather than academic terms was quite saddening. Thereafter we were forced to relocate ourselves. While affecting this shift, we were particularly mindful of the fact that Anveshi's location should be easily accessible to our many members.

The occasional crises apart, Anveshi has consistently tried to meet its objectives. We owe the success of our programmes and the effectiveness of its presence to the contributions of the large number of academics, activists, students and other people who make use of its resources and space. There is an active local participation in the regular meetings, study groups and campaigns. These, along with the library, provide a significant resource base to the advancement of women's studies, the articulation of gender in the public sphere and the politicisation of various other issues. But equally important is the *space* that Anveshi provides, to plan activities, to hold discussions, to read, to meet people, or to just hang around. It is a space defined by support and togetherness. The atmosphere of the place, the culture it has evolved and the friendships it enables makes available a domain where the personal can become political.

Appendix

Publications from Anveshi Research Centre for Women's Studies

Stree Shakti Sangatana (1986), *Manaku Teliyani Mana Charitra* (Telugu). Hyderabad: Stree Shakti Sangatana.

Stree Shakti Sangatana (1989), *We Were Making History: Life Stories of Women in the Telangana People's Struggle*, New Delhi: Kali for Women.

Tejaswini Niranjana (1992), *Siting Translation: History, Post Structuralism and the Colonial Context*, California: University of California Press.

K. Lalita (trans.) (1993), *Mantrajalam Daktarlada Mantrasaanuda (Is the Magic Doctor's or Midwife's)*, Hyderabad: Charita Publications.

Sheela Prasad (1995), *Urban Health Care: A Study of Public and Corporate Hospitals*, New Delhi: Delta Publishers.

Shodhini (1995), *Touch Me, Touch Me Not: Women, Plants and Healing*, New Delhi: Kali for Women.

Susie Tharu (1996), *Antonio Gramsci: Jeevitam-Krishi (The Life and Thought of Antonio Gramsci)*, Vijaywada: Sameeksha Publications.

Bhargavi Davar (ed.) (1996), *Women and Mental Health: A Select Bibliography*, Hyderabad: Anveshi Research Centre for Women's Studies.

Mary E. John (1996), *Discrepant Dislocations: Feminism, Theory and Postcolonial History*, New Delhi: Oxford University Press.

Susie Tharu (ed.) (1998), *Subject to Change: Teaching Literature in the Nineties*, Hyderabad: Orient Longman.

Bhargavi Davar (1999), *Mental Health of Indian Women: A Feminist Agenda*, New Delhi: Sage Publications.

D. Vasanta and D. Samrajya Lakshmi (2001), *Pasupattccha Wallpaper* (A translation of Charlotte Perkins Gilman's *The Yellow Wallpaper*), Hyderabad: Vishalandhra Publishing House.

Bhargavi Davar (ed.) (2001), *Mental Health from a Gender Perspective*, New Delhi: Sage Publications.

Anveshi Research Centre for Women's Studies, Forthcoming, *Women's Health Matters: What the Doctors Don't Tell Us*, New Delhi: Penguin.

Notes

1. An earlier version of this paper was presented by K. Lalita at the Workshop on Women's Studies organised by the University Grants Commission in Chandigarh in 1999.
2. The Anveshi Team's report of this visit has been published in Telugu and English. See Anveshi (1993a), Anveshi (1993b) and Anveshi (1993c).
3. See Hyderabad Women's Health Group (1991).
4. See Tharu and Lalita (1991).
5. We have collaborated with the Subaltern Studies Collective; the National Institute of Mental Health and Neurosciences, Bangalore; Sahitya Akademi, New Delhi; Indian Council of Social Science Research, New Delhi; Satyashodhak, Hyderabad; the Central Institute of English and Foreign Languages, Hyderabad; Centre for the Study of Culture and Society, Bangalore; Hyderabad Book Trust, Hyderabad; Osmania University, Hyderabad; University of Hyderabad, Hyderabad; the Indo-American Centre for International Studies, Hyderabad; Jana Vignana Vedika, Nellore and other organisations.
6. For Anveshi's position on the Uniform Civil Code, see Anveshi Law Committee (1997).
7. See Anveshi Law Committee (2002).
8. The papers presented at the seminar have been published as Davar (2001).

References

Anveshi (1993a), 'Maa Vuriki Saara Vaddu: Oka Visleshana', *Bhumika*, Inaugural Issue.

Anveshi (1993b), 'Reworking Gender Relations, Redefining Politics: Nellore Village Women Against Arrack', *Economic and Political Weekly*, January 16–23.

Anveshi (1993c), 'Stemming the Tide: A Report from the Anveshi Women's Centre', *The Women's Review of Books*, 10.

Hyderabad Women's Health Group (1991), *Savaalaksha Sandehaalu*, Hyderabad: Stree Shakti Sangatana.

Susie Tharu and K. Lalita, (eds.) (1991), *Women Writing in India: 600 B.C. to the Present*, New York: The Feminist Press.

Anveshi Law Committee (1999), 'Is Gender Justice only a Legal Issue?: The Political Stakes in the Uniform Civil Code Debate', *Economic and Political Weekly*, 32(4).

Anveshi Law Committee (2002), 'Caste and the Metropolitan University', *Economic and Political Weekly*, 36 (1).

Bhargavi Davar (ed.) (2001), *Mental Health from a Gender Perspective*, New Delhi: Sage Publications.

14

The discourse between studies, institutions and critical pedagogy

Centre for Women's Development Studies

Kumud Sharma

The discourse and political practice of women's studies with its attendant complexities and dilemmas is a reflection of the heterogeneity of its knowledge bases and its multiple centres of dialogue and action. The significant strides made by women's studies during the last two and a half decades, can be ascribed to the contributions made by a variety of institutions, individuals and an active women's movement. Institutions are important not only for exploring and building a knowledge base from positions within the academy, but also for continuing the dialogue with diverse institutions and groups. Women's studies found an institutional foothold in the 1970s (SNDT University, ICSSR and ISST). This institutionalisation gave women's studies a new identity within the higher education system, although none of these three institutions was teaching women's studies.

This paper brings forth my own locational experiences within the Indian Council of Social Science Research (ICSSR) and later with the Centre for Women's Development Studies (henceforth CWDS), of being a quintessential part of the women's studies discourse for more than two decades. The paper tries to encapsulate the key concerns and dilemmas of CWDS, in mainstreaming women's studies within the social science discourse—its critique of social science concepts and methods, the linking of theory and practice, its tackling of the economic and look social developments affecting women by calling into question policies, development planning and practice. The promotional role played by the ICSSR (both in the CSWI's work and later in supporting the CWDS initiative) through its sponsored programme on women's studies, succeeded in generating policy debates, promoting research in priority areas (women's work and occupational pattern, migration, family, socialisation practices and the women's movement) and in developing fresh analytical perspectives. The ICSSR's women's studies programme planned two series: 'Women in a developing economy' and 'Women in society'. The Advisory Committee also suggested a series on sources of data on women, under the joint editorship of Prof B.N. Ganguli and Prof Ashok Mitra.

The ICSSR Advisory Committee on Women's Studies, (chaired by Prof B.N. Ganguli and later by Prof Ashok Mitra) at this point, while congratulating the institution for its contribution to policy debates and for expanding the cadre of social scientists interested in women's issues, also pointed out a general lack of impact on social science research in general.[1] The Committee recommended the need for 'an autonomous institution to build on existing knowledge but with broader mandate and resources'.

CWDS's initial work plan evolved from the experiences of some of its founding members who were involved with investigations of the CSWI and with the ICSSR women's studies programme. The founding Director of CWDS, Vina Mazumdar was Member-Secretary, CSWI and later, Director of the ICSSR women's studies programme. A rebel within the higher education system, she has remained a strong critic of the notion of 'academic neutrality' and an ardent advocate of participation by the academic community in shaping human and social values and acting as the 'conscience of the nation'. This philosophy continues to guide this centre's work and processes of learning.

The genesis

CWDS, established in 1980 under the Societies Registration Act, described itself in its programme brochure as 'a group of research professionals striving for the realisation of women's equality and development in all spheres of life'. It was further stated 'the main objective of the Centre is to help in the promotion, development and dissemination of knowledge, regarding the evolution of women's role in society and trends in social, economic and political organisations which impinge on their lives and status.'

CWDS saw its role primarily as a catalyst, not only through its own actions but also through various institutional networks and sub-systems in society. Right at the beginning, it realised that 'policy change would not come about as a result of research, nor could the goals of women's equality be achieved through government actions alone. It was equally important to counter the forces of reaction, create active mechanisms to help translate into reality the constitutional goals of women's equality and equal participation...'.[2] The centre's evolution during the last two decades reflects this philosophy, as it has reached out to various groups and forged links with various networks while continuing to form alliances on different issues.

CWDS planned to undertake new research on women, particularly in the context of socio-economic transformation and population dynamics. It also planned to re-examine the existing body of knowledge about women and to introduce a differentiated approach to the multi-faceted and multi-dimensional problems of women in different socio-economic groups. It was argued, in this context, that much of the distortion, complexity, invisibility and marginality could be eliminated by determined acquisition and dissemination of knowledge about and for women. Research, training and documentation, it was felt, could thus become a method, not only for promoting and assisting women's struggles against inequality and injustice, but also for supportive action for women. Such action is undertaken at different levels of society—among women's groups, co-operatives, trade unions, people's participatory organisations, within government and its agencies, in the legal and medical professions, educational and communication agencies, as well as among the exponents of creative and interpretive arts—in short, involving all those who help to shape the social ideas, skills and values that ultimately affect the views of society—both men and women—about women's roles. In conceptualising and exploring development terrain in terms of an interwoven set of policies and practice, the work of CWDS has covered broad fields and multiple themes.

In 1984–85, when the ICSSR's first Visiting Committee came to CWDS, it noted that, 'being a new and complex area of research, ready-made models are not available within which research can be programmed and interdisciplinary connections found'. During 1991–96, CWDS drew up a five-year plan to work in two core programme areas—women's right to land and other productive resources; and political participation. It made the connection between economic and political empowerment of women. The plan emphasised the need for consolidating the knowledge and insights gained from its research and action projects. It also planned to expand the scope of action research projects, extend collaborative exercises and develop the role of CWDS as a training institution in collaboration with other training/teaching institutions. The second work plan also emphasises consolidation rather than expansion.

The journey

The journey of discovery of the Centre for Women's Development Studies, Delhi, has been rewarding, challenging and at times terribly frustrating. In the initial stages, the centre visualised its role primarily as a research institution, developing a clearing-house for information and ideas, and promoting training and action programmes for women, in collaboration with academic institutions. Its work also emphasised the need for major policy dialogues to arrest the process of marginalisation of women. CWDS's concern with major demographic indices, particularly the declining sex-ratio and economic participation, was placed before the members of the Planning Commission in a symposium organised in 1980, jointly with some women's organisations ('Women in the eighties: development imperatives'). The initiative did result in the incorporation of a chapter entitled 'Women and development' in the Sixth Five-Year Plan—a milestone in the history of planning in India.

The centre's interventionist role was not clearly articulated as the emphasis was on recovery of women's knowledge to change perspectives in social science research and teaching, and systematising knowledge. As the founder-director, Vina Mazumdar, pointed out, CWDS was founded by a group that did not accept prevalent ideas about the limited role of academic institutions. Its intention was to work for change, using all the skills and tools acquired during years within educational institutions—research, communication and rational persuasion with hard data. In the process, we learnt to use new tools, techniques and forms of activism. However, we did not surrender our identity as an academic institution whose primary business was to generate, disseminate and apply knowledge.[3] Recovery and incorporation of the unheard voices and submerged knowledge of invisible women into critical scholarship, has remained our biggest challenge. In attempting to balance research and action and seeking ways to apply knowledge, CWDS has rescripted its research agenda. However, the tensions are lodged deep within academic discourse.

Action research

CWDS's involvement in International Labour Organisation (ILO)-supported action research projects in Bankura District (West Bengal) and Jalandhar (Punjab) changed its thrust and perspectives on the role of educational institutions in social transformation. The seeds of our ideas for action/intervention met with strong resistance from a few Executive Council members, who thought of CWDS primarily as a research institution and believed that its members did not have the skills and expertise required for intervention/action. They were of the opinion that if the centre had to undertake such a responsibility, it should have been designed differently, with a clear mandate and a different set of people.[4] However, in the Executive Council, there were also a few ardent advocates of academic interventionism. Reviewing the work of CWDS in its initial phase, its founder-director questioned the notion of academic neutrality in social science research and teaching. She argued,

> Scholarship in teaching and research has become increasingly confined to classrooms, campuses and seminars where the issue of participation by the academic community in the process of shaping human values is considered an outdated shibboleth. For those looking for a socially more meaningful role, academic activism, academic interventionism or academic entrepreneurism does not sound questionable.

The challenge thrown up by the centre's action research project in Bankura, and the resurgence of the women's movement in exploring alternative ways of learning and generating knowledge, and developing alliances with women's groups and networks, gave a new dimension to the work of the centre. Conscious of the political aspirations of women's studies and the need to have active links with the women's movement, its perspectives have been shaped by time. In the mid-1980s, a Standing Committee on Action Research was constituted to guide, monitor and give direction to wide-ranging activities in the area of action projects. The lively debates within the centre on the vital links between research, action and advocacy have continued. The centre has also continued to strive to combine research concerns and the interventionist approach within its organisational framework. Social scientists, state structures, grass-roots organisations and social movements, were identified as key actors. The fluid nature of governments and policies, which make it possible to find within its ranks, individual allies, but not always a systemic response, forced us to look to other fora or pressure groups. The formation of Seven Sisters in the 1980s was a response to a sense of disillusionment about the working of bureaucratic structures. The alliances we built also influenced our partnership with the Bankura women's groups.

The anti-rape march of 1980, the Mathura Case agitation, and the increasing number of anti-dowry campaigns indicated a new mood within the women's movement and within educational institutions. These developments were of immense significance in the politicising of women's studies.

CWDS, while maintaining its identity as an academic institution, did not limit its role to working within the conventional mould of a social science research institution. It has drawn strength and inspiration from diverse sources and tried to reach out to a variety of institutions as well as grass-roots and action groups. This interaction has, on the one hand, provided valuable inputs for research, and, on the other, promoted collaborative action and research, laying the foundation for new research initiatives. Exploring the process of erosion of women's customary rights, women's role in management of natural resources and in forest protection committees, the impact of globalisation and market economy on women's lives and livelihood and so on, have redefined our frameworks for research and action. This learning process has not only transformed our research agenda, but also to some extent, the very personalities of those whose interventionist work brought them into intimate contact with the lives of peasant women. Vina Mazumdar sums up the experience, '...their capacity to learn, their wisdom and their courage has destroyed our arrogance of learning and class, and helped us to develop new forms of learning'.

A review of the first five years of the centre's involvement in these action research projects points out that,

> This has proved to be a tremendous learning experience for us, providing insights into the hidden structures of power in rural society, the extraordinary potential displayed by the poorest sections of rural women in collective action, leadership and learning skills, the diversities as well as commonalities in rural women's experience of the processes of change and the essential and vital links between participatory development of women and the attainment of broader development objectives stated in the national policies... . This process of learning through trial and error—of how to plan new economic activities which could be viable and still produce the desired results from participatory collective development; of how to match the needs of human resource development with the needs for economic growth; of how to manage human and power relations within the collective organisations and with the power structures outside—the panchayat, the bureaucracy and various sources of funds, expertise, technology etc; and eventually, to understand our own role transformation as intermediaries, from mobilisers, leaders and managers to teachers, helpers and advisors, has provided a most rewarding experience to all those involved in these projects.[5]

The recent Annual Report (1997–98) further elucidates that the centre's initial engagement in action-research with peasant women was an outcome of policy/programme strategies identified between 1977 and 1980, with which some of the founder-members were closely associated—working groups on employment, training, rural women's organisations and adult education. The idea was to demonstrate the feasibility of such strategies in the rural context.

The peasant women from Bankura have participated in Asian regional workshops, national consultations and in the Earth Summit at Rio (1992). They are key actors in this drama of 'sustainable development' and their voices are recorded in the series, *Voices of Peasant Women*, brought out by CWDS. The presence of peasant women in workshops held at Vidyasagar University, Midnapur, West Bengal and at the UGC-sponsored refresher course on women's studies at Jadavpur University, is a critical acknowledgement of 'other' epistemological bases of knowledge formation and the relevance of grass-roots learning and experience to academic feminism.

Research, advocacy, networking, communication and information sharing

Over the years, at CWDS, there has been more research than teaching in women's studies. In the early years, research was classified into four categories—evaluative research, action research, critical issues research and exploratory research on issues of women's identity, self-perception and inner consciousness. Research at CWDS is diverse, wide-ranging and reflects the individual interests of a multidisciplinary faculty, as well as institutional responses to contemporary debates and challenges. The opening out of research interests and the diversity of themes has necessitated collaborative arrangements that have provided opportunity for academic networking and linkages with a range of institutions.

The issues of mainstreaming women's studies within academia, the responses of academic communities to women's studies, the relevance and legitimacy of women's studies, the link of academicians with activists, the interface between theory and praxis, the concept and dimensions of women's empowerment, the promises and pitfalls of advocacy and networking, the ideological dimensions and dilemmas of new ways of generating knowledge, have all been part of the active debate within CWDS. Knowledge and knowledge establishments have been instruments of dominance and in the struggle to use knowledge for women's empowerment, CWDS has to continuously examine its research priorities and methods and contextualise knowledge. Many of these debates are far from being settled, but women's studies has created a space for dialogue. The struggle of women's studies within higher education is part of women's struggle to redefine the nature, purpose and social relevance of educational institutions. It is also a struggle of all marginalised discourses against knowledge hegemonies.

CWDS has kept these debates alive through research, action, publication and networking. CWDS initiated a debate on the role of higher education as an instrument for social transformation through its journal *Samya Shakti*. The first editorial stated, 'We want women's studies to grow on a broad base, and do not want to impose any ideological boundaries to constrict its development. We want no renewal of purdah—in any form. We do believe in equality for all human beings, and power as an essential dimension without which equality would be unreal and meaningless'.[6]

The first issue focused on the relevance, the experience and the future of women's studies. CWDS has continued to be an active participant in debates on the socio-political context of women's studies. Its philosophy, its objectives, its work and its eagerness to create a common forum for interaction between women's studies centres and the women's movement are reflected in its approach. By choice, CWDS opted for the role of a catalyst—in promoting research, teaching, action and policy debates. It has worked to create a forum for policy research and dialogue. It has actively participated in working groups, task force, standing committees set up by the government to look into different issues of women's development, articulating its criticism as well as offering constructive suggestions.

The 1990s have been years of new challenges. Global trade technology, decline of the welfare state and the ascent of market ideology, have made the world a markedly different place. While the old and persistent problems of gender, poverty, violence and attack on women's rights by reactionary forces remain unyielding as ever, fresh challenges pose a bigger threat to the ideals of democracy, gender equality, equity and social justice. Women's studies needs to focus on these new challenges and examine its research and action frameworks. The 'gender and development' debate has to deepen and continue in this changing global context, particularly, of ideological conflicts in the field of human rights, culture and gender.

To discuss the work of CWDS in terms of projects, programmes and approaches is a difficult task, for the work and interests of the Centre are not always predetermined but emerge from a perspective that seeks to understand and analyse the transformation of gender relations, the spaces women create to confront their subordination, the development approaches which respond to the multiple, flexible and

changing interests of women, and the strategies women adopt to define their own agenda and enhance their power.

The terrain: Issues and challenges

What are the organisational dilemmas that the centre has to continuously address? Despite repeated emphasis on consolidation, the mandate to intervene in the debate on contemporary issues and respond
through research and action has kept our staff preoccupied, leaving
little time for basic research. Some of us, who have been with CWDS
since its inception, have evolved methods for coping with the multiple demands and pressures of academic work and activism, but some
of our younger colleagues feel, at times, a sense of unease about the
interface between these two. CWDS has the identity of a research institution, not that of an NGO, and operates from a different institutional framework, where scholarship and activism are both valued.
Over the last two decades, the growth and expansion of CWDS has
brought into focus a renewed discussion on scholarship, priorities,
credibility, identity and ideology. The compulsions of history and the
compulsions of an academic institution merge with the compulsions
of women's studies as an intellectual as well as political enterprise.

Resource mobilisation remains a major source of worry. While some
of these concerns are common to all ICSSR-supported research institutions, the need to raise project grants as a survival strategy, is a real
drain on the energy and time otherwise invested in consolidation and
reflection. International funding for women's studies centres remains
inescapable though it is controversial and a cause of heated debate
among women's studies scholars and activists. Does international funding erode the autonomy of these institutions? Not in our experience, for
the few attempts made were effective. Does it distort research priorities?

Issues of autonomy, agenda setting and the distortion of research
and action priorities due to external funding (donor-driven) have
remained highly contentious issues. The crisis in higher education and
increasing pressure from historically subjugated and marginalised
groups to reshape knowledge and systems of higher education, continue
to pose a challenge. Access to power and authority in the production

of knowledge go a long way in explaining the institutional factors that constrain attempts to bring about significant changes in the educational system.

Women's studies centres have continued to broaden the scope of their enquiry but this has remained largely outside or parallel to mainstream academic debate. While university-based women's studies centres face patriarchal bureaucracies, low budgets and the rigidities of academic structures and disciplinary boundaries, those institutions that are not part of the university system and enjoy a degree of autonomy, remain outside the centres of academic power.

CWDS has always had a dual loyalty to the social sciences and the women's movement. This has not been without tensions, for if academicians consider that much of the empirical work in women's studies is devoid of academic rigour, more informative and less theoretical, activists within the women's movement feel that the academic jargon of women's studies is alienating and often lacks understanding of grassroots realities. Caught in the theory-praxis dilemma, personal experiences of trying to negotiate the complex and often contradictory terrain of middle-class women's studies academicians and the knowledge and voices of poor peasant and working class women, creates its own conflicts and dilemmas.

Women's studies, as an intellectual enterprise oriented to the women's movement, has been a constant arena of tensions. Theoretical debates within women's studies have not been insensitive to non-academic forms of feminist knowledge and discourses. Women's studies scholars value the experiences of grass-roots organisations, and these have received critical acknowledgement by others. However, their impact on academic discourses has not been very demonstrable. The location of women's studies scholars and activists in a variety of institutions indicates the broad base from which we are trying to understand the processes of development and change; however, transgressions across disciplines and occasional encounters with non-women's studies academic discourses are not always rewarded. In a recent refresher course on sociology, with a focus on gender studies, sparks started flying on the first day between purists and those arguing for women's studies as an interdisciplinary area. We often feel that we speak in two voices—one for academic discourse and the other in an activist idiom and expression. Tensions between academicians and activists persist. Which identity does one represent, who can speak for whom? The questions of identity, diversity, plurality, solidarity and sisterhood—how are they to be confronted? The identity of a women's studies scholar has its own underpinning of dilemmas. Several times, I have been asked whether I am a gender expert or a feminist! Within general academic discourse, some scholars prefer to remain outsiders, though addressing women's studies questions, rather than be labelled 'women's studies-*wallahs*'. Independent research institutions, as extra-university constituencies, have shared academic spaces and linkages with women's studies centres and the women's movement. Have these two homes (or maybe the multiple homes) of women's studies blurred the boundaries defined by the conventional higher education system or have they become little ghettos in the academic wilderness? What has been the impact of this intellectual rebellion on the higher education system? While women's studies has brought new resources for teaching, research and action, has it posed a threat to traditional disciplines, their methodologies, tools and perspectives? The strength of organised and entrenched disciplinary boundaries never gets undermined. How does one mainstream or integrate women's studies? Does mainstreaming mean losing the radical thrust of women's studies? How does the interdisciplinary research and scholarship within women's studies interface with other interdisciplinary programmes of research and teaching?

Are independent women's studies centres more policy-oriented and less academically oriented as they are often accused of being? The ability of such centres to respond to issues, both contextually and strategically, varies and depends on human resources, their competence in building institutional linkages and in-house capacity. What is the role of apex bodies like the ICSSR and UGC in supporting, funding and promoting women's studies research and teaching? The ICSSR women's studies programme became defunct after the two functionaries constituting the Women's Studies Unit migrated to CWDS. The Advisory Committee functioned for some time but the environment built over a period of five years gradually disintegrated. ICSSR is still providing financial support to research projects and research fellows. However, there is no planned approach despite the fact that it funds CWDS; occasionally it tells CWDS not to duplicate research already undertaken by UGC centres and to be better co-ordinated with them.

Despite the impressive growth of research, women's studies is faced with several challenges. The educational system suffers from much structural rigidities, which create obstacles in the development of women's studies as an interdisciplinary area. One has also to guard against what has been termed 'false specialisation and a new sexual division of labour', in which women's studies becomes the exclusive preserve of women, since it was never visualised as a parallel branch of knowledge, but aimed to review, question and revise the content and methods of the social sciences. The UGC's earlier guidelines also said, 'women's studies should not be organised as a separate discipline or department.... . However, it admits that this would not be possible in the present context, without an institutional mechanism to act as a catalyst and support system'. What is the mechanism we need to discuss and create? Is getting legitimacy within academia an end in itself?

Some women's studies practitioners caution against the dangers of 'institutionalising and academising a non-conformist area of study'[7]. With the growing professionalisation of women's studies centres, tensions have also grown between those whose primary interest is scholarship and those who swear by the inherently political nature of women's studies. Is there a fundamental difference between women's studies and gender studies? There are many issues confronting us. We need to work out a common agenda for debate and mobilisation. Women's studies, if it is to retain its dynamism and avoid ghettoisation within academia, needs to grow on a broad base without diluting its main drive or getting trapped in narrow ideological moulds.

Notes

1. See CWDS (1987).
2. Ibid.
3. See Preface, CWDS (1987).
4. This information was obtained through personal communication with the founder-director.
5. See file report prepared for the first meeting of the Standing Committee on Action Research Projects of CWDS in November 1986.
6. See *Samya Shakti* (1983).
7. See Desai and Patel (1983).

References

CWDS (1987), *First Six Years and Forward*, New Delhi: CWDS.

Neera Desai and Vibhuti Patel (1989), 'Critical Review of Research in Women's Studies 1975–1988' (mimeo), New Delhi: ICSSR.

———— (1983), 'Editorial', *Samya Shakti*, Vol 1(1).

Section III

Individual Scholars

15
My journey into women's studies

V.S. Elizabeth

I begin by confessing that I feel out of place in this group of writers, who have all been so much a part of the history of the women's movement and women's studies in India, as my own association with both, is in contrast, very recent. What I want to do here is to briefly write about my introduction to feminism, and to women and law issues, after my association with the Centre for Women and Law, and the consequent birth of interest and active involvement in the area of women's studies. A brief history of the centre and its activities will show how it aided the growth of my interest in areas related to women and law. Ever since it was started, the centre has been involved with the work of various women's organisations, but for me, its importance derives from the fact that it opened up a whole new world of exciting interests and activities that have at the same time also been the cause of so much inner turmoil.

The birth of my interest in feminism

I have no claims to being a feminist or a member of the women's movement in India. I have never been formally associated with the latter, though I have read about it and even met some of its more illustrious members. It was during my brief stay at the Mangalore University, while reading for a doctorate in history, that I first became consciously aware of feminist writing and studies. The departments of Kannada and English of the university were housed in the same building as the department of history, and in the library, books on English literature were stacked in racks adjacent to the racks of history books. My interest in literature brought me into contact with students of literature and I found myself drawn to those books more than to books of history. It was then that I heard of and began to read feminist theory, which immediately formed connections with my own feelings, evoking the resistance I had been putting up since the days of childhood, to the injustice and unfairness of gender biases.[1] But even then, I did not take my liking for feminist literature any further, in that I never really sat down and tried to read my way to an understanding of feminist theory, but I did get involved in the discussions and arguments of my friends from the literature departments.

As these friends worked on dissertations and bounced off ideas against my mind, I began to perceive a whole new way of approaching the past. One of my closest friends, Veena Bannanje was working on the verse of Akka Mahadevi, the 12th-century woman saint, for an M. Phil in Kannada. It was the familiar mode of resistance, and the same themes of woman versus society, but looked at with a totally new approach, which opened up immense potential for perceiving not only the thoughts of Akka Mahadevi, but also the possibility of looking into India's past for the origins of protest by women. The writings of Black feminists, similarly, opened up new avenues, and suddenly, there just seemed to be so much more to life and thought than I had hitherto imagined.

In September 1991, I joined the National Law School of India University, (NLSIU), to teach history to law students. One of my friends there, Ms Geeta Devi, was the then co-ordinator of the Centre for Women and Law (CWL). Whenever she organised training programmes she would automatically rope me in to assist, and thus began my journey into the activities of the Centre for Women and Law. In October 1994, the then Director, Dr N. R. Madhava Menon, asked me to take charge of the Centre for Women and Law. There has been no looking back since then, and now, even if I were to cease to be the co-ordinator of the CWL, it would not mean the end of my association with women's issues.

I knew so little about 'women and law' at that point of time. My attempts in this field had been so inconsequential, that I wasn't very sure I would be able to handle the responsibilities and work of the centre. But Dr Menon was more confident of my abilities than I was! He assured me that I would be able to do a good job. The first few years were spent in trying to understand the numerous activities of the centre and the work which was carried on with the assistance of students and colleagues. My role seemed to be only that of a facilitator, i.e., identifying appropriate people to handle the tasks at hand; I was literally what my designation said—a 'co-ordinator'. There was almost no initiative at all of my own, and I merely continued with activities charted out by those who had been there before me, trying to fulfill the tasks assigned by various agencies. The general expectations from the centre were high because of the work done hitherto under the very able guidance of Dr Madhava Menon, Ms Sita Anagol, Ms Geeta Devi and Ms Asha Bajpai.

At that point of time, I did not possess a law degree, but it did not seem difficult to recognise inequalities in the law, or help to formulate proposals for law reform with the assistance of those already involved in this work—my colleagues, women's organisations, the funding agencies and freelance researchers. It was only an innate sensitivity to the concerns of the marginalised, particularly women, that enabled me in those early years to find my way through assignments, without messing up. I have since then, of course, acquired a degree in law to assist me in my endeavours.

The truth is, however, that one doesn't need a law degree to recognise that law and the legal system are not neutral. The Constitution of India guarantees to all its citizens, equality under Article 14, but in reality, the experience of many Indians is far from it. What exists is merely equality of opportunity in a context where people do not start from the same point at all—women and other marginalised sections of our society are weighed down by a number of handicaps, as a result of various events in history. The Indian Constitution has made provisions to counter these handicaps, through Article 15, Section 3.[2] But when a woman goes to a court of law she is hardly likely to find justice because of the gender bias of judges.[3]

All one has to do is to examine the judgements of the courts in cases relating to crimes against women—be it rape or dowry harassment. The insensitivity of the judiciary is blatantly evident in the sentencing policy and the high level of acquittals.[4] By and large, the entire legal system, from the police station to the courtroom, does not take women's issues seriously. If a woman goes to the police station to complain of harassment within the household, she is sent away with the advice to tolerate and 'adjust', which are supposed to be the qualities of 'good' women. The courtroom is not any friendlier. All of this makes it very difficult for a woman to access justice. Then there are the family laws that are unjust, by and large, whether the issue awaiting judgment is marriage, divorce, property rights, custody or adoption. Man-made laws in the name of religion, have been a continued cause of oppression and exploitation of women. Even a casual perusal would show that these laws are not based on the scriptures of any religion, but are the traditionally accepted means of discriminating against women. A deeper study of the laws, and a degree in law enables one to appreciate the means by which changes can be brought about and how to use the existing system to the advantage of women.

My very first assignment, after becoming the co-ordinator of the Centre for Women and Law, was to attend a Round Table Conference organised by the United States Information Services (USIS) and the National Law School of India University on 'Empowerment of women through the courts'. The guest speaker at this meeting was Justice Sandra O'Connor, a judge in the United States Supreme Court. Many women activists and writers attended this conference. This was my first real encounter with those who had been working on women's issues in various ways, and by the end of the conference, my desire to work on women's issues, and the confidence in my ability to do so, were strengthened. Here, I found, I was feeling at home and although the discussions did not go over my head, I became conscious of the fact that I was ignorant of the nitty-gritty of the laws, but this seemed to be less an insurmountable difficulty than a minor obstacle that could be overcome with minimal effort. I was sure now that I had my heart in the right place and decided to acquire a degree in law, which enabled me to continue as co-ordinator of CWL.

In March 1995, I had the opportunity to participate in a seminar on 'Women, law, culture and tradition' organised by the British Council and the School of Law, University of Warwick, at their campus in the UK. The seminar brought me into contact with women from all over the world—women who were members of their governments, lawyers, activists etc., who were passionately involved in their work and who had been able to achieve so much in spite of the many obstacles and limitations that confronted them daily. Their successes were heartwarming and inspired the feeling that any one of us could achieve the same if we were as committed. The women from the African continent particularly, caught my imagination. They were well-organised and had built up links with one another in order to continue their women-centred work, in a very unique way that did not involve sacrificing their culture or aping the West. They had been working with ethnic legal systems that were as complex as our own, and yet had managed to make headway in helping women access their rights. In addition, they were warm, friendly and so full of life—none of their struggles and disappointments had daunted them, or dampened their spirits.

Interacting with these women inspired those of us who were from South Asia to think of networking on similar lines, and it was this that led to the birth of the Women and Law South Asia Network (with the assistance of the British Council), in August 1995, with its headquarters in Kathmandu. It was our work here that brought home to us the fact that above all differences in culture, history, class, caste, race and religion, and there are certain experiences which are common to women all over the world. The differences cannot be ignored, if we are to really empower women throughout the world, but these common experiences can help us unite and march together in the struggle for justice. However, this network has not been able to fulfil its agenda or carry out any of the tasks it set for itself, simply due to the lack of sufficient funds. Today the network remains only in name; all it needs to be brought back to life is some money. It has the potential to be the starting point of collaboration between women's groups and academicians in the South Asian region.

For me, there was absolutely no looking back after this seminar. I continued to teach history to law students, and at the same time coordinate the activities of the CWL. But the journey has not been easy; being a historian by training, it is difficult to think of turning away from the past to commit myself totally to teaching, talking and researching on women's issues. Though the struggle has not ceased completely, I am more confident today of my own need and the ability to continue working in this area. This conviction was inspired by two women— Dr Ann Stewart of the School of Law, and Dr Parita Mukta of the School of Sociology, both from the University of Warwick. They are responsible for making me see how I could actually use my learning and experience to contribute to the academic discipline of history as well as the area of women and law, without giving up either area of involvement, but actually enriching both, for the inequalities of law are best understood with the help of an understanding history and the evolution of society. The emergence of patriarchy in the context of private property and the experience of discrimination and oppression universal to women are best explained by placing these in the context of history.

My voyages into history have not ceased with the completion of my Ph.D. I read continuously for the sake of teaching at the law school and because of my own interest in the area. It is clear that research and writing in history have been strongly determined by the interests of those who have been working in this field, but although there has been a growing awareness of the need for feminist history in the West, there has been very little endeavour in this direction in India, especially in the English language. Historians like Gayatri Spivak have begun the process, but there is much to be done. We have a rich and complex history which has not been sufficiently documented or written about. There is also the need to understand the present status of women from the context of an undoctored history. This becomes crucial in the situation of women's demand for equal rights being countered with questions and statements such as 'what have women done?', 'where does history reveal the singular contributions of women?' and 'women's role has always been in the domestic arena'. In the face of such statements, one has to turn to the past for corroboration. Is it true that women have made no significant contributions to society? If it is not true, then why is it that the texts do not speak of the role of women in shaping human history? In the quest to find answers to today's questions and to shape a better tomorrow, people have customarily turned to the past and its lessons. Women need so much more to venture into serious historical research to provide the data and tools for legitimising their claims.

In teaching history at the National Law School, I have already begun to create an interface between history and women's studies. I teach three courses in history. The first course is meant to provide an understanding of history as a discipline, as most of the students come from science and commerce backgrounds; to enable this process I have incorporated a study of the development of history writing and the various schools of historiography which includes a chapter on the feminist perspective of history. While teaching Indian history, I steer analysis towards the status and role of women in the different periods, and examine the medieval bhakti movement as an example of a movement of dissent. To me, the women bhakti saints represent that phase of Indian history where a definite attempt was made to break the stereotyped roles assigned to women in society—that of daughter, wife and mother. In the third course, divided into three modules, I have included a section on the emergence of the women's movement in the West, the various schools of feminism and the evolution of women's rights within the discourse on rights. Through these three courses, my goal is to sensitise students to an appreciation of women's issues in the larger context of society. I hope that through an understanding of women's history, they will be able to appreciate the role of law in the oppression of women and get enthused enough to make contributions to the reform of law.

My skills as a historian have definitely enabled me to understand the current status of women; it has helped me to comprehend the similarities in women's experiences around the world, while at the same time enabling me to note the uniqueness of these experiences. Patriarchy, after all, is almost completely universal as an institution of oppression. While its origins are yet to be identified and described satisfactorily, it definitely helps to understand why discrimination against women and the problems of domestic violence, rape, etc. are so universal. There is vast scope for study in this area. I have only begun at the tip of this huge iceberg, but in the intermingling of my mixed interests in law and history, I find that the experiences of my work in law colour my writing on history and whatever lessons history has taught me form a kind of contextual underpinning to my reading of law.

As the co-ordinator of the Centre for Women and Law, I have been actively involved in teaching an optional seminar course, 'Women and law', for the fifth year students in the National Law School of India University. This has facilitated my own reading and understanding of the relationship between women's issues and law, and has, at the same time, provided an opportunity to those among the final year students who are interested in pursuing a career in this area of study, to gain a basic foundation.

My work at the centre brought me into interaction with women activists, NGOs, academicians, lawyers and feminist researchers which widened my perspective in many ways (least of which is the recognition accorded to me today as someone in a position to make positive contribution to the area of women's issues).[5] Sometimes it still seems unbelievable that I have travelled so far, and achieved this much, but actual events and successes show them to be real, and I am grateful to all the wonderful women who have contributed to my learning, from my

Mangalore University days to date. My involvement with the activities of the Centre for Women and Law have brought me not only more opportunities to share concerns and interests with a wider group of people, but also to learn many new skills.

In 1998, I had two opportunities to extend my area of work; first, a chance to visit the School of Law, University of Warwick for two months on an exchange programme that exists between them and the National Law School of India University; second, I was approached by Nata Duvurry of the International Centre for Research on Women, based in Washington DC, to take up a project on domestic violence, under the Programme for Women in Development (PROWID). Both these opportunities opened up new vistas of study and research for me, and through the centre, for some of the students of the National Law School.

The exchange programme led to my attending Dr Ann Stewart's classes for postgraduate students on 'Gender and law'. These classes were a thrilling experience. Here were students from different parts of the world with their particular experiences and perspectives, sharing their thoughts on a wide range of issues affecting women around the world. I too was given the opportunity to speak about issues paramount in India, with reference to women. I took the opportunity to discuss marriage, dowry harassment and the increasing number of dowry deaths. Some very interesting questions and reflections emerged from the discussion.

Another aspect of the exchange programme was the training in how to conduct training programmes in gender sensitisation, particularly for the judiciary. Dr Ann Stewart, with the support of the British Council, has been conducting these training programmes for the judiciary for a while now. The National Law School is keen to duplicate this process so as to ensure better justice for women. This study period fructified in a training programme for the judges of the subordinate courts in March–April 1998 at Bangalore. We were able to develop some material for training programmes as well as some specific skills necessary for the education of adults, very specifically developed by Ms Joanna Liddle, Centre for Gender Studies, University of Warwick— an amazing person whose tact, patience and skills are worth emulating. I hope to duplicate the exercise in the future.

The research project for ICRW plunged me into a totally new area— domestic violence. This project provided a meeting point for those working on women's issues, and for me, the chance to interact with people who had been using the legal system to access justice for women. This was very valuable, particularly since these were people with practical knowledge of the limitations of the legal system, who had still managed to keep faith in it as one of the possible means of empowering women. It was heartening to see that they believed that with appropriate changes in law enforcement and training of personnel involved and law reform, the law could be successful in ensuring justice and non-discrimination for women.

I learnt first-hand about the frustrating delays and other problems that are very often caused only by loopholes in the law, the gender bias or the lackadaisical attitude of medical personnel, the police and the judiciary. This experience has so spurred my interest in the issue of domestic violence that I continue to read and learn, to collaborate with NGOs, lawyers and others who work with women subjected to domestic violence. This was how I made the transition from being confined to areas of theory to a more practical area, which has actually strengthened the theoretical base.

The Centre for Women and Law

The centre was started in 1987 along with the National Law School of India University. It was then known as women and the law centre. It was envisioned as working 'under a Faculty Committee and a Research Advisory Board, to endeavour to look at law and the legal process from the perspective of gender justice and administer programmes directed towards equal justice for women in Indian society.' From the very beginning it was expected to work in close association with the Legal Services Clinic, another extension centre of the National Law School of India University. The Centre for Women and Law was also expected to act as a law reform group, trying to liaison with social activists and women's organisations. Legal assistance was one of the major aims of the centre.

It was then financed by a grant from the Ford Foundation under its Rights and Social Justice Programme. (The grant has now been exhausted and the attempt is on to find new sources of finance for its ongoing projects as well as to take up new ones.)

The activities of the CWL are wide-ranging and include the following:

- Legal awareness programmes for girl students in schools and colleges, and short-term workshops for activists, on laws affecting women.
- Legal aid and advice, in collaboration with the Legal Services Clinic at the University's city legal aid office and in the rural mediation centre at Ramanagaram. Legal service is also rendered to women's groups in Bangalore and its neighbourhood, with whom the National Law School has been working for the last few years.
- Legal empowerment, attempted through para-legal training programmes for women activists and NGOs, followed up by legal advice and research assistance.
- Law reform, an activity through which the centre hopes to bring about necessary and appropriate changes in law so as to make legal institutions a tool for empowering women.
- Gender sensitisation, a continuing activity aimed at sensitising all sections of the public as well as civil servants in order to make equality for women a reality.
- Legal education, to promote equality, dignity and non-discrimination through necessary changes in the curriculum, teaching materials, teaching methods, etc., in keeping with which an optional seminar course on 'Women and law' is offered to students together with the attempt to examine various laws from a gender perspective.
- *Gender Justice Reporter*, the journal published annually by the centre in order to bring developments in law, whether statutory or decisional, to women activists, NGOs, and the public at large. It also provides space for critiquing and generating opinion in favour of gender justice in society.

The first co-ordinator of the Centre for Women and Law was Ms Sita Anagol, under whose guidance the Centre began efforts to carry out at least the first five activities of the CWL. She laid the foundations of the work that the CWL is today involved in. She was followed by Ms Geeta Devi, who joined the CWL in 1991 and further built up its activities and networking, systematised record keeping and encouraged student involvement in the centre's activities till 1993 when she left. It was during her tenure that a workshop was organised with the support of the British Council, Chennai, on reform in the laws connected to rape, immoral trafficking in women and indecent representation of women and obscenity. The centre also helped draft the State Commission for Women Bill for Karnataka (though when the Act was finally passed it hardly reflected any part of the draft made by the centre). For a brief period, Ms Asha Bajpai looked after the centre, especially the Legal Literacy Programmes, in which she got the students of the National Law School involved in taking classes and doing street plays. In October 1994, I was asked to take charge.

Taking charge of the Centre for Women and Law has changed my life, and I am fortunate to have come in at a time when the centre's involvements were beginning to mushroom with the efforts of the previous co-ordinators. Their contacts and the goodwill they had earned, won this young centre the recognition to launch it on the map of women's issues as a result of which expectations from the centre were very high. The task of fulfilling them was tough indeed!

The Centre for Women and Law is expected to fulfill a number of expectations, which range from legal assistance, to research on various issues. It is not easy to meet these, as we are faced with a constant shortage of both monetary as well as human resources. For all activities of the centre, it has been mostly the faculty of the National Law School that have been the main resource persons, be it legal literacy classes, para-legal training programmes, sensitisation programmes or just providing moral and legal support.

The Ford Foundation, the British Council of India, Chennai and the National Commission for Women, then under the Chairpersonship of Ms Mohini Giri and Padma Seth, its Law Member, not only provided us with financial support, but also reposed in us much confidence, which was a major factor in making possible the various activities of the Centre since 1987.

It was the grant from the Ford Foundation that put the CWL back on its feet, for it was this grant that made possible the birth of the centre and its legal aid activities, especially in the rural mediation centre. In fact, the legal literacy and the para-legal training programmes would not have been possible without this grant either.

The British Council has helped in conducting workshops on law reform, in the launching of the Women and Law South Asia Network and financing the participation of faculty in international seminars and training programmes. They have been especially helpful in facilitating the inter-university exchange programme with the School of Law, University of Warwick. It was with British Council support that the gender sensitisation programme for judges was undertaken.

The National Commission for Women together with the then Director of the National Law School, Dr N. R. Madhava Menon, conceived the *Gender Justice Reporter*. In fact the first journal was published with the financial support of the NCW. The NCW also gave the CWL and NLSIU some projects for research, of which one was to survey the existing laws, which affect women, especially the various policies and programmes of the government at the central and state levels, initiated since Independence. The purpose of this exercise was to follow up these government initiatives, see what had actually been achieved and try to revive those that had not worked for one or the other reason. The other project was to look into existing laws affecting women, in order to provide a background for the Women's Code. These research projects helped the process of documentation, which in turn facilitated further research and assistance for future projects.

The National Commission for Women was greatly impressed by the legal literacy programme for women students being carried out by the centre. They suggested that the National Law School alone disseminating information to one college at a time was too slow a process, and suggested that we train representatives of the various women's colleges in India to co-ordinate similar programmes for their own colleges. As a result a training programme for trainers was organised, funded by the NCW, which also provided some seed money for colleges that required funds to start off the programme. Many more colleges have conveyed their interest in sending faculty to be trained. In fact, the legal literacy programme of the National Law School has been one of its more successful activities, which has from the beginning brought success as well as satisfaction. We are now regularly involved in conducting legal literacy classes for women students, women employees in the public sector companies, etc.

None of these activities could have worked so well without the support of the student body of the National Law School. It is they who provided the research inputs and their active involvement went a long way in successfully completing project assignments. Interaction with the student body on gender issues has been an extraordinarily enriching experience; their insights and knowledge have been a source of inspiration to others and me. This is not to say that the whole student body is gender-sensitive. What we have is a small group of gender-sensitive students who have organised their own Gender Study Circle, which organises discussions, film shows, paper presentations, guest talks, etc., in order to widen their own knowledge and make more students sensitive to gender issues.

The most pressing problem that the centre, like many other institutions, faces is one of funds. This means that we are dependent on student involvement to see our projects and assignments through, as we cannot afford to recruit regular staff, especially clerical and research staff. Lack of funds also creates the problem of our research and the activities being directed by funding agencies. However, all this has not stopped our work. There is even a positive aspect to this obstacle—the active involvement of students, as a result of which, knowledge, experience and commitment, not only for them, but for us too, have deepened. These are rare opportunities for them to learn on the job, as it were. Especially for those of them who may not in the future take up such work, this could be the only chance of first-hand knowledge of women's problems and their legal remedies. This has been successful in sensitising the student body to women's issues.

One of the more recent occasions when the student body was involved in a CWL project was the 'Truth Commission' organised by Vimochana, a women's organisation in Bangalore. The purpose of this commission was to focus attention on the huge numbers of women who have died or are being harassed for dowry or other reasons and who have at the same time failed to secure justice. At least 40 students from the National Law School were involved in the documentation process so as to facilitate the presentation of these cases to the eminent jury that had been put together for this occasion and to give them a glimpse into the enormity of the situation.

The Centre for Women and Law has benefited immensely from interaction with a number of feminist scholars who have visited the National Law School. Amongst these are Ms Ratna Kapur, from the Centre for Feminist Legal Research and Ms Brenda Cossman, from the University of Toronto. They provided a feminist perspective to the study of law within the classrooms, through their interaction in all classes, from the first year to the final year. It was through their efforts that the students and faculty of the National Law School were exposed to feminist jurisprudence. Together with some of the faculty and students they brought out one issue of the *National Law School Journal*, devoted to feminism and law. Their classes provoked heated debates and for the students, it was probably the first point of contact with the feminist perspective on law. In fact it was these interactions, which helped the Gender Study Circle to grow and attract more student attention to serious issues affecting women students, on campus in particular, and in the wider world. The CWL has always tried to be supportive of the work of the Gender Study Circle in its efforts to sensitise a larger body of students within the Law School. This exposure motivated the students to do their vacation placements with NGOs and lawyers working on women's issues, and to add substance to the Legal Services Clinic's efforts to bring legal aid to women through its extension activities. This sensitisation to women's issues resulted in the students of the National Law School incorporating a feminist approach to their case studies for the Law Reform Competition that the National Law School organises once in two years. They actually chose to study the property rights of women in one of the villages in Karnataka, for one of these competitions and even used feminist methodology.

The optional seminar course offered to fifth year students at the National Law School has been one means of encouraging students seriously interested in pursuing further studies or even a career in 'women and law'. The focus of this course has often been in accordance with the current concerns of the centre in this area. Through the seminar courses, it has been possible to get feedback from students about many of the projects undertaken by the centre and also to find research support for some its ongoing projects. The focus of the course has ranged from issues of prostitution and trafficking in women to domestic violence. At one point, Ms Flavia Agnes, the activist lawyer from Mumbai, offered a course on 'Effects of Marriage on Women's Rights', as part of the fulfillment required for her M.Phil degree from the National Law School. The institution and students benefitted from this exercise.

My contributions to the centre's work included the introduction of training of co-ordinators for legal awareness programmes, which has ensured that legal literacy is spread fast and amongst a wider group of women over a larger geographical area; networking, both within the country and outside, which has enabled the exchange of information, pursuit of need-based research and documentation; gender sensitisation training for judges; preparation of study material that provides a slot for creating sensitivity to women's issues, in the training of judges;

gender sensitisation of faculty in the National Law School, so as to mould resource persons for training programmes and at the same time to ensure some sensitivity to women's issues in the teaching of law at the National Law School; providing basic information in laws related to women, for trainees who are working for organisations dealing with women's issues, as a regular part of their training programme; and publication of The *Gender Justice Reporter* since 1995.

All these measures aimed at empowering women through an awareness of rights brought about by providing appropriate information about laws. While it is important for women to be aware of their rights within the existing legal system, it is also imperative that they realise the limitations of the legal system. Through our training programme for judges, lawyers and others, the effort is to create a more woman-friendly environment, particularly within the legal system.

Learning from the past

As for my own or the centre's ideological location, there has not really been any clarity. As far as the centre is concerned, this has been largely due to the fact that the orientation of the centre depends almost entirely on the orientation of the co-ordinator. In the early years of its existence it also depended on the ideology of the Director of the National Law School of India University. The very first Director, Dr N.R. Madhava Menon, was the spirit behind the setting up of the centre and the moving force behind all its activities even when he did not agree with the ideas and thoughts of the people he assigned tasks to. He was himself no feminist, but as a law person he believed in the use of the constitutional provisions for the empowerment of women. But like most of us, he too had his limitations, especially when it came to the question of the appropriate ideology for the centre, as well as its role with reference to the women's movement. He did not want the centre to take on an activist orientation, but rather, wanted it to provide support for activists through research and documentation.

I cannot speak about the ideological orientation of former co-ordinators, but for myself, I know that I cannot call myself a feminist, for in spite of all I have learned on this journey, I find that I do not have an intellectual or experiential grounding in any school of feminism. What

I am clear about is that I want to work on issues affecting women, from the women's perspective. Somehow the use of the word 'feminist' seems too restrictive; my own approach appears to come close to that of the socialist feminists of the West. Since I have not got a foothold on feminist methodology, I would not claim to be using it in my research.

I would like to return now to the point of where the Centre for Women and Law becomes significant in the dialogue on women, on women's issues, and by implication, to women's studies. The CWL's own experience, though brief, has shown the potential that such centres have to help policy makers and planners achieve the goal of a just and equal society. We have become a part of the global, economically liberalised community. At the same time funding agencies and governments have been made increasingly aware of the need to examine and focus on the gender component of their policies, programmes and expenditure. We have definitely contributed to the success in creating interest in the area of women and law, and been instrumental in creating the conviction that if we can build similar centres in other institutions teaching law, it would mean wider legal awareness, greater empowerment and speedier rendering of justice for women.

There is a great need for linkages at different levels between such centres and other organisations working for the empowerment of women. What I mean is the need for networks to be set up at the state, regional, national and international levels. For through such linkages we can assist one another, share our experiences, prevent duplication of research and avoid wasting precious time and funds. The documentation of work done till now and identifying areas for future research and action, need to be taken up.

For example, my own exchanges with people like Shaheen Sardar Ali, an academician from Pakistan, made me realise how much we could learn from each other. Women's groups in Pakistan have often worked for reform from within the system, using Islam. Whereas here in India, our efforts to bring about reform are so often thwarted by resistance from religious or community leaders, all in the name of protecting their identities. Similarly, we could use our common experience as colonised countries, which have been bequeathed the common law system, to bring about reform in our laws.

Were I to continue as the co-ordinator of the centre, I would certainly like to bring in more of the woman's perspective. I would like to introduce one more optional seminar course on 'women and law', to deal with women, law, development and violence against women; to evolve a policy on sexual harassment for the National Law School campus through a participatory process so as to prevent sexual harassment and at the same time, to provide for a mechanism to deal with cases of sexual harassment; to develop gender sensitisation training programmes for the police, judiciary, lawyers and law teachers; to continue documentation and analysis of domestic violence; and to spread legal awareness amongst women of different backgrounds (as of now we largely focus on women students in schools and colleges).

In conclusion I would like to say that for me, it has been a gratifying trip down memory lane, as I tried to re-enact my passage into the world of women's studies. It has also enabled me to reflect deeply on all that has been done and at the same time to dwell on what still remains to be done. I would like to end by acknowledging the gratitude I feel to the Centre for Women and Law, which has been, for me and many others like me, a spur constantly urging us forward towards a society with equal opportunities for all, irrespective of gender.

Notes

1. Even as a child, I remember resenting my mother's efforts to teach me to sit 'properly', in a 'ladylike' manner, nor did I like being asked to do household work when I would rather have read a storybook. The harassment of conductors in the bus, their stares and comments, made me hate men. I taught myself how to manoeuvre my body along; in fact as I physically matured, my one desire was to keep a low profile so as to avoid unwanted attention from any male; not that it did any good. The myth that women who are dressed provocatively are the ones who get harassed is simply not true. It was impossible to comprehend that I was subjected to all these intolerable experiences merely because I was female. When I started menstruating I thought that it was the worst form of oppression. It was only as I became an adult that I learnt to pride myself on being a woman and tried to inculcate some part of this pride into my younger sister.
2. Article 15 (3) allows legislation in favour of women and children.
3. In the study conducted by Sakshi, it was found that 34 per cent of the judges felt women should share some of the blame in cases of violence inflicted on them. In the case of sexual violence this blame was defined in

334 ⊠ **V.S. Elizabeth**

terms of 'her dress and behaviour', 'her failure to take precautions' and 'her provocative nature' to name a few. Often there was even an opinion that 'if she wasn't a virgin, no harm was done.' See Sakshi (1996).

4. 'In the context of dowry related deaths, the all-India figures show that there were 6917 reported cases in 1998, of which 3407 cases ended in conviction. Karnataka had the dubious distinction of having a high number of dowry related deaths while the rate of conviction was disproportionately low. 570 cases of dowry deaths had been reported between 1996 and 1998, in Karnataka, and only 22 persons were convicted. See *The New Indian Express* (1999).

In a study conducted by them in June 1995, of the sexual assault cases pending before the Supreme Court at that time, Sakshi found that 'in approximately 80 of the 94 reported cases surveyed, the trial court convicted the accused. Acquittals were awarded in five cases. On appeal however, the High Court acquitted in 41 per cent cases, reduced sentences in 53 per cent and increased sentences in 6 per cent of the cases that came before it in appeal.

The following myths/prejudices influenced the outcome of these cases either in terms of acquittals or reduction of sentence:

(a) The victim (irrespective of age) is 'habitual of sexual intercourse' (Lawrence Kannadas v. St. of Maharashtra, 1983, Cri LJ 1819; Bharath v. St. of M.P, 1992, Cri LH 3218) or is of 'easy virtue' (Balwinder Singh v. St. of M.P, 1992, Cri LJ 715; State of Punjab v. Gurmit Singh 1996 2 SCC 384 in which Supreme Court refers to a trial court reference to the 'loose moral character of the victim').

(b) The accused is 'young and misguided'. (Vinod Kr v. St. of M.P, 1987 Cri LJ 1541).

(c) The victim (a minor) sought to 'satisfy her lust'. (Satish Kumar v. State 1988 Cri LJ 565; Balasahib v. St. of Maharashtra 1994, Cri LJ 3044).

(d) The child (a minor) 'had ceased to be a virgin long ago and was used to sexual intercourse' (Omi alias Om Prakash v. St. of U.P 1994, Cri LJ 135).

(e) The absence of external injuries to the victim implied that she consented to sexual intercourse (Birem Soren v. St. of W. Bengal, 1992 Cri LJ 1666; Dhuli Chand v. St. of Rajasthan, 1992 Cri LJ 3397).

(f) The victim 'did not cry for help' (State of Maharashtra v. Vasant Madhav Deva, 1989 Cri LJ 2004), 'neither blushing nor swaggering, she [the victim] calmly went to the police station 5 km away' (Balia v. St. of Orissa, 1994 Cri LJ 1907). See Sakshi (1996).

5. For me, this is reflected by the fact that I am actually invited to attend workshops to discuss the means by which women can be empowered, on laws relating to crimes against women, to speak on All India Radio about women's issues like reservation, women as guardians, sati, etc. When Nata Duvurry of the ICRW came to Law School and asked me take up the project on domestic violence, I was apprehensive, but hearing that Maja Daruwalla had recommended me was a morale booster.

References

1. Sakshi (1996), *Gender and Judges: A Judicial Point of View.* New Delhi: Sakshi.
2. *The New Indian Express*, 30 December 1999, Bangalore.

16
Full circle

Women's studies sans institutions

Leela Gulati

This chapter traces the path of some issues that have been researched and analysed over a period of time, focusing on questions and features related to women's studies. It also attempts to present certain insights and information gained about the lives and communities researched.

In this effort, we used the case study methodology, which we found especially appropriate for researching various dimensions of the gender issue. This chapter also attempts to articulate efforts to utilise and combine insights from different disciplines such as economics and anthropology in understanding and analysing research questions on women. I would like to think that it also helps to gain a better insight into comprehending families of women belonging to different levels of social status.

Further, it reveals that research questions need not only be esoteric; a small sample, even a family, studied with the right questions, can be meaningful and rewarding. It also tries to shatter the myth that research always requires bulky funds and a large body of data material, expensively collected.

The purpose of writing this paper for this volume is to describe contributions to the development of women's studies in India by women scholars unattached to specific institutions or departments exclusively researching women's issues.

The author would also like to take this opportunity to narrate and share her experience of the transition from being a 'housewife' to becoming a 'research scholar'. The link between the author's personal world of being a woman and the public world of her work is established against the larger perspective of women's studies. This journey traverses the landscape of a very realistic and truthful human experience, that of being caught in the bind of domesticity while at the same time needing and desiring to be involved in something more intellectually stimulating, at a time when it was extremely difficult to find avenues or scope to utilise whatever education or training one had.

By sharing this experience in such detail, it is hoped that women who find themselves similarly placed can take heart and try to open closed doors with perseverance and courage, motivating them to get involved in issues that touch women's lives.

Many married women in our country experience guilt if they are unable to do justice to their career as well as their domestic and family responsibilities. This paper narrates how I came to terms with this problem.

Getting started

Like many other women of my generation, getting married led to my taking a break from my professional career. My husband and I were teaching economics at Baroda University, and when he decided to take a job in the West Indies, I was expected to quit my job and follow. This isn't to say that I questioned the norm. I followed it quite dutifully. Indeed, it wasn't until 1972, when my husband and I moved to Thiruvananthapuram, that the thought of returning to academia struck me. We were in what was, at the time, a quiet and sleepy town, and I wanted to be occupied with something more than childcare and housekeeping. The obvious answer was for me to work at the institute where my husband was working. Unfortunately, this answer was not quite so obvious to those at the institute. I was told (informally, I think) that 'the institute' did not think it was a good idea for both husband and wife to work at the same establishment. The fact that we lived on campus, that I still had childcare responsibilities, and that the only other possible employer was a significant distance away, combined to mean effectively that I would not have a full-time academic position. This did not seem to bother those at the institute who had decided on the 'no husband and wife' policy and it galls me now to recollect that I did not raise a whimper. I was still playing the dutiful wife. After all, my husband worked at the institute and it would not be proper for me to do anything that would undermine *his* position there.

The milieu

Despite the fact that I was not thought 'employable' by the institute, living on campus meant that I was constantly interacting with the academicians there—even if it was predominantly in the role of the wife playing hostess to guests. The institute was young and people there were doing what I perceived as exciting work on questions of poverty, unemployment and development. In particular, a number of people were working on issues such as wage rates and occupational distribution that centred around the labour force participation of men.

Understanding female labour force participation

Why did I decide to work on female labour participation? The obvious reason is that the others (almost all, except me) were ignoring the question. There was data that was available, and this was an issue that I thought was both relevant and important. Significantly, this was a topic that I could work on without threatening the men—after all, I was still conscious that I had to play the 'proper wife'. I think the faculty at the institute found it amusing that there was this housewife working on 'women's issues'! I didn't have any funding, but the fact that my husband was at the institute meant that I had access to a wonderful library. And though many of the men at the institute were fairly disdainful of my work, there were some who were willing to answer my questions.

My final source of inspiration was a book by Ester Boserup[1]. Her book was an account of her observations about female labour participation in Africa and was something she had written while accompanying her diplomat husband on his travels. The book had been given to me by one of my husband's colleagues as an example of something a 'wife' could do. This colleague of my husband thought my two alternatives were either to write something along the lines of Boserup, or to write children's books. I didn't have any inclination towards writing children's books, but Boserup's work was fascinating. Her work also gave me courage. Here was a person who was not working professionally, and yet had made a significant contribution to the understanding of women and work across a multiplicity of countries. It made me feel bad that I had made no attempt to utilise the opportunity I had had to study Trinidadian society. In any event, Boserup and boredom with being a hostess and doing housework, all combined to get me started. I began with the goal of determining the factors that would explain inter-state differences in rates of female labour force participation across India. The International Decade for Women had been announced and it was an opportune time to begin working on a gender-focused issue.

My first publication, *Female Work Participation: A Study of Inter-State Differences*, attracted attention. Initially it was all negative. I had a number of Indian (male) academicians tell me in no uncertain terms that my work was worthless. According to them, not only had I focused on all the wrong factors, but the topic itself was also uninteresting. To say that the comments were rude and mean would be an understatement; I was embarrassed, devastated and generally ready to throw in the towel. But I was lucky. The timing of the article was good, 1975 was the International Women's Year—an accident really. That resulted in international attention. A number of foreign scholars found my work interesting. That, in turn, created excitement within India, among women scholars, and my article got to be the centre of heated debate for almost a year. The people at the institute found all of this quite amusing. As one of them put it (as a compliment), 'the housewife has created a storm in a teacup'.

More papers on women and work

Encouraged by the positive feedback from international scholars and women scholars in India, I continued writing. More papers followed. In some ways, the circumstances were ideal. Secondary data was abundant and easy to use, and the male academicians continued to have little interest in working on the issues I was interested in. From thinking about the occupational distribution of women, I moved on to unemployment rates, urban workers and wage discrimination.

The topics were interesting and kept me occupied. But I found myself becoming increasingly frustrated with the data, which almost made things too easy—one constructed tables, ran a few regressions, and then drew conclusions based on simple stylised models of economic behaviour. I felt as if I was constructing castles in the air, castles that served little more purpose than to become material for more publications to my name. Given that I neither had an academic job, nor appeared to have much hope of getting one anytime soon, I could afford not to be too concerned about the number of publications to my name or the level of prestige of the journals in which these appeared. I began looking for other methods of studying the questions that I was interested in.

A workshop on poverty

It was around this time that there was a major workshop at the institute to look at poverty and related issues. A number of hi-profile scholars attended and I tried to go to as many of the sessions as possible (I had been told that I could attend so long as I was quiet and did not ask any questions). The discussions at the sessions were heated and even emotional, but all I got out of them was the fact that there were sharp disagreements over modelling assumptions (usually having to do with how the utility function was defined) and the use of econometric techniques. The arguments, as I recall, were bitter and heated, all in the name of estimating the number of poor in this country! Those arguments continued late into the evening over food and drink; I got to be privy to a number of them since I was often the one handling the task of providing food and drink.

At the time, what struck me most about the conference was that, despite the good intentions of the scholars, their papers and discussions lacked a human element. There was little or no talk of what it meant to be poor, let alone poor and female. The fact that poor women worked, sustained families and faced periodic unemployment and discrimination, seemed difficult for most of these male scholars to comprehend. To me, it seemed that the majority of these scholars were stuck in their middle-class conception of women as 'non-working' housewives—housework not being considered 'real' work. As scholars competed to display their mastery over the often mathematical and statistical issues relating to the measurement of poverty, questions of how people coped with poverty had receded to the background. None of this is to claim, however, that my understanding of poverty at the time was any better. As for my many criticisms, they were not new, others had said these things before, and said them better.

The housewife fellowship

Around this time, having learnt from friends that the Indian Council of Social Science Research had a small fellowship for housewives, I applied for the same and got it. The grant was small—it was meant for housewives who had an inclination to try their hand at academic work. For me, the grant was vital in that it gave me a small measure of legitimacy within the institute. At the same time, the smallness of the grant and its nature (people referred to it as the 'housewife fellowship') meant that I was able to continue to play the 'non-threatening house-wife' while also doing work that interested me. Looking back, I am incredibly grateful for that fellowship. Without it, I doubt that I could have re-entered academia.

Case study methodology

I was determined to do fieldwork. The smallness of the housewife grant meant that the scope of my research was going to be limited. A large-scale survey, with research assistants and the works, was out of the question. I was on my own and also limited by the fact that I still had to make sure the house was clean, that meals got served, that the kids showed up at school, etc. Given the combination of constraints and what I wanted to do, the one thing that seemed feasible was for me to attempt a few case studies. At that time (as now), the case-study methodology, was not very popular among economists, who preferred rather to construct models with idealised 'rational' or 'reasonable' actors, and was largely the domain of social anthropologists. But it wasn't much of a leap to add a marginalised research methodology to an already marginalised status (the housewife dabbling in academia) and marginalised subject (gender).

Oscar Lewis and Elliot Liebow

The inspiration for using the case study method came from two books. One was a study of five poor families in Mexico by Oscar Lewis and the other was a study of construction workers in New York by Elliot Liebow.[2] These two books appealed to me in a way that nothing in economics ever did. The painstakingly detailed descriptions of daily life that I had expected to be boring and mundane were alive with insights. To me, there seemed to be much to be learned from these rich descriptions of questions of family dynamics, the constraints imposed by poverty, and the construction of preferences. In particular, Lewis' and Liebow's work convinced me that these case studies were a way of demonstrating the need to pay specific attention to issues of gender.

Profiles in female poverty

Taking my cue from Lewis' study of five Mexican families, I decided that I would study the lives of five poor women. Picking five women who would voluntarily give me their time was no trivial job. There were also two additional constraints. First, I wanted each of the women to be from a different occupation because I wanted to be able to draw broader conclusions about the question of the occupational distribution of women in Kerala. Second, I had my household tasks to attend to; duties at breakfast, lunch, and dinner and it was not feasible for me to be off doing research in the evenings (since chores like entertaining guests and getting the kids to do their homework took priority then).

I decided, therefore, to do at least three of the profiles on women who lived nearby. I began with the construction site right next to my home at the institute. It fascinated me that the women seemed to be doing all the hard labour (lifting, carrying, etc.), while the men directed operations and did the 'skilled' tasks (things such as masonry, not to say that carrying 20 bricks on one's head is not a task requiring high skill). I began talking to some of the women construction workers during their tea breaks, asking them questions about wages (they were paid less even when doing identical work as men), promotions to skilled positions (never ever), and sexual harassment (happened all the time). The irony— one that did not strike me until much later—was that all of this was going on at a construction site in a liberal institute dedicated to the study of problems of poverty, development and unemployment. And I regret to say that I did not raise my voice about the treatment of women even when the construction crew was working on my own home. In any event, there was one woman at the site who was especially articulate and receptive to my questions. Eventually, after a number of conversations, the woman, Vijayamma, agreed to be the subject of my first profile. She, in turn, took me to the nearby squatter settlement where she lived and introduced me to other women there. I picked two more women to profile from the squatter colony, one in agriculture, Kalyani, and the other working in the brick industry, Jayamma. I wanted to do a profile each from the fishing and coir industries and for these I went to their work sites to find two women who would be willing to give me their stories. There, I found Kesari and Sara. Though the primary focus of my profiles was the women, my attempt was to capture a broader picture of the economy with the difference that this sketch would be from the perspective of both poverty and gender.

Any hope I might have had of focusing on these five women in isolation quickly disappeared (initially I had tried having them come to my home, so that I could interview them while simultaneously taking care of things at home), for not only was what they were telling me merely part of the picture, but I was also misinterpreting what they said. I began to realise that in order to do these case studies effectively, I needed to get a better grasp of the context. That meant spending time in the communities in which these women lived, and so I began making daily trips to the squatter settlement and to the coir and fishing communities. I also decided to interview the family members of these women, who were willing to talk to me. Finally, I also did interviews of close neighbours and others in the community. Gradually, as I gained the trust and understanding of the communities, the stories began to mesh. None of this is to claim that I fully overcame either my middle-class biases or that I became an insider in these communities. The profiles remained in the voice of an outsider.

All this meant that I ended up with information not only about the lives of the five women, but also about the dynamics of their communities. Since three of the women lived in the nearby squatter settlement, I got to know that community especially well, which resulted in my writing a handful of papers on the squatters as a whole, which among other things, looked at preferences regarding family planning, the effects of government rationing and the problems of widowhood.

Two years after I began my conversations with Vijayamma at the construction site, I published my first book, *Profiles in Female Poverty*.[3] I was worried about how the book would do. I had heard more than a few jokes at the institute about how I had managed to 'dress up' the mundane details of the 'common' woman's life; who really cared about things like what Jayamma ate for breakfast and how she decided to spend the days on which she didn't find work. Fortunately, the book did far better than I could have hoped; reviewers liked the mundane details and even found my simple prose 'refreshing'. A number of foreign women scholars found that the profiles gave them valuable insight and soon I found myself inundated with invitations to speak at conferences and offers of generous grants to do more of this kind of work. I don't think any of this produced any new respect in the minds of the skeptics at the institute, but what it did was to give me confidence. Fifteen years after I began this work, the institute even gave me a job (although the fact that they had taken on a United Nations project, which demanded that there be a gender component, might have had something to do with that!)

Why did the case studies work? I think they demonstrated that detailed studies of individual lives and communities could add to one's understanding of questions of development and poverty. Aggregate data is invaluable. But one can miss the wood for the trees. Case-study data fills in certain crucial gaps. Instead of forcing researchers to hypothesise about the decision-making processes that might explain their large-scale data, case studies provide what can be relatively accurate information about actual decision-making processes. Even more important to me, these micro-studies highlighted the importance of thinking about gender differences and family dynamics. There were everyday decisions about things like who was going to get fed what (men got better and more food even when they earned less), which children got to do homework (boys, of course, while the girls had to do the household chores), and who saved more on the days he or she got work so as to ensure that there would be something on the days when there was no employment (women). All of these were issues that had tended to get ignored in the large-scale studies. Perhaps, most importantly, what case studies can do (and hopefully mine did), is to humanise the subject. They can render uncommon, what we unthinkingly often brush aside as 'common'.

Fertility rates

It was at about this time that researchers at the institute began to notice a drastic drop in the number of kids in primary schools; teachers were afraid that their schools might have to be closed. This, among other things, suggested that something significant was going on in Kerala with respect to fertility rates. As others began to work on the subject, I too decided to do so. Fertility was a question on which I had collected a great deal of information from the squatters, and, I thought that information might now make for an interesting paper. I didn't have any research funding as yet, but my prospects for getting some in the future looked good. Finally, here was an important issue on which the gender aspect was hard to ignore. Two more papers emerged, one, on the age marriage of women in Kerala, and another on the move from a preference for male sterilisation to that for female sterilisation.

The first, in which I looked at the age of marriage in Kerala vis-à-vis the rest of India, gave me a reason to learn about Kerala's history of matriliny. This history (including the practice of women having multiple husbands, which shocked and outraged the British) had by no means equalised things between the sexes, but women in Kerala did seem to be doing significantly better than those in other states. The dynamics of the second question were especially interesting, given the fact that female sterilisation was riskier than its male counterpart and cost more. A rational agent model of the family as a wealth-maximising productive unit might have told one that this was but a natural outcome of the fact that men earned more and hence there was a cogent trade-off made between risk and return, but the story from the squatters was different.

It was not about the risk versus return transaction for the family unit. Indeed, in a number of cases, the women were contributing much more to the family unit. Instead, it was a choice of male versus female, where the female lost because the male was not willing to take the risk that his sexual performance might diminish (or perhaps it was the fear that his male friends would tease him—in any event, the result was the same).

Male migration to the Middle East

Migration of workers to the Middle East was a major feature of the Kerala scene. Though it was an event that affected every aspect of life in the state, it had not been researched sufficiently. Here again, it was important to look at the role women played in these migrant households.

Though migration was exclusively of male workers, the study of these households revealed that women were actively participating in the decision to have the males migrate. My study showed that the decision was made not individually, but collectively; families were pooling their resources, deciding on one person to migrate, and then sharing the benefits. Women played a very crucial role in these decisions, for it was they who mortgaged their land, sold their gold etc., to put together the necessary resources. The impact on the women left behind was enormous, be it economic, cultural or psychological.

Response to study on migration

The response to my work was more than encouraging. My visit to the East West Centre to attend a conference on Asian labour migration was a special opportunity. I went there with a feeling that I had nothing major to contribute and was the last person to make a presentation. The response to my paper was unbelievable. The participants felt that the social and economic impact of Gulf migration on women was tremendous and needed to be studied more extensively for all labour exporting countries. First, the awareness that women were so central to the decision-making process of the migrant worker, the tremendous changes that it brought into the household in terms of its composition, female-centredness, shift in residence pattern and the increasing responsibilities that illiterate poor women took upon themselves for health, education and management of funds was beyond all expectations. The migration process seemed to break down, in particular, the Muslim women's isolation and immobility, bringing them into contact with a wider network of institutions that were hitherto outside their experience.

Women in international migration

My interest in migration continued and I shifted my focus from studying women who were left behind to the study of women who left their husbands behind. Also, I shifted my focus from internal migration to international migration, looking at movements in the entire Asian region. What seemed to be happening was that male migration seemed to have taken a backseat compared to female migration. Women were mostly in the service sector working as domestic help. Also, interestingly, the immigration streams had shifted from the developed countries to within developing countries.

In recent years, my work has been concerned with developing handbooks for development planners. These handbooks were written with the objective of helping to understand the position of women in various sectors as also, to isolate within each of the states, the backward districts which needed to prioritise attention on women's issues.

Ageing and widowhood

Within two decades of my work on the decline in fertility in Kerala, I found that the ageing of the population had already become an important issue. What was happening was that the proportion of women among the elderly was increasing and most of these women were widows. The concentration of these elderly women, particularly in the rural areas, was of great concern. Social security for these widowed and old women became necessary due to the changes in family systems and property rules. Since the state came out with an innovative social security programme for agricultural workers, it became necessary to understand its working among women.

Recent work on narratives

Around the 1980s, a workshop, funded by the Ford Foundation, Women's Development Studies and the Tata Institute of Social Sciences was held, where it was felt that women's identity and life cycle should be researched. The main force behind it was a very eminent psychologist and two social scientists. But I believe the main motivator was Kamala Chowdhary and another person from the Ford Foundation, Carolyn Elliot. We were about 14 women from different disciplines and diverse backgrounds, who had worked on women's issues.

The workshop had a tremendous impact on all the participants but these rich narratives were not recorded or written up and hence did not result in any publication. There was always this nagging feeling that we had lost some valuable material.

So in 1998, we decided to convene another workshop on narratives, which would enable us to come out with a publication. This workshop was naturally structured differently. It included the educated middle class as well as poor, illiterate, working women. The experience of this workshop was very interesting and raised many questions for us to think over.

Revisits and longitudinal studies

While studying the problems of widowhood, we had occasion to go back to one of the five families that had been studied in 1975. We decided to study the life of the brick worker who had recently been widowed. While doing research on Jayamma's life, it became apparent that her story was one of dramatic changes. This inspired us to explore whether there were similar stories of change with each of the other four women, which in turn led to our doing a longitudinal study on the five women earlier studied, of whom Kalyani was one.

In 1998, we invited Kalyani to come and speak at a workshop on 'Context, Gender and Narrative'. When it was her turn, she spoke force-fully and in great anger that she had received no substantial benefit from the women who had spent much time researching her life. Her entitlement to the land she was in occupation of, in the squatter settle-ment, was posing problems, as was the fact that her son's job was not permanent. She went away from the workshop rather disappointed at the callousness and insensitivity to the problems of the poor, even among educated women who claimed to be her well-wishers.

How do we construct 'woman'?

What Kalyani vocalised at this workshop raised important questions about the problematic relationship of middle-class women to poor wo-men, in the context of feminist organising. Kalyani was asked to speak, we could say somewhat cynically, to represent in a tangible fashion the authentic voice of a poor woman; one of the funders of the workshop had been concerned that the list of speakers was entirely made up of highly educated and privileged women and felt that there was a need to diversify this list.

The primary purpose of the workshop was to develop an approach to life history narrative, based on a social psychology of gender. This kind of organising of workshops, and Kalyani's reaction to questions about her daughter Nirmala's suicide show us the limitations of the construction 'woman', when it is presumed that being a 'woman' creates an immediate and strong basis upon which one can find common ground. Here, being a 'woman' was constructed through what one might think was an issue common to all women, the relationship between mothers and daughters. But talking about these relationships may be considered a luxury, and may not be the most pressing issue for many poor women. Constructing 'woman' in this fashion is premised on the idea of a unitary subject created primarily through gender difference from men and not primarily shaped by concerns such as poverty. Kalyani's focus was not on the topic of interest at the workshop but on her financial problems, the question of her entitlement to land and her son's education.

The ethics of fieldwork

What I feel concerned about is the ethics of fieldwork, the relationship between the fieldworker and the field and the relationship of researcher to research subject, especially the ethical and moral issues of the study of very poor people. We had spent years talking to Kalyani about her life, in order to understand how very poor women negotiate their lives. What had Kalyani got out of this? The ethics of such relationships is an issue that all academicians who engage in fieldwork, or who write about the lives of individuals they study, must deal with. Many deal with it by ignoring any problematic dynamics that exist. It is possible that when women academicians study poor women as their subjects, these problematic dynamics are more easily hidden because of the assumption that 'we are all women' and the commonalities that one can feel because of this similarity. But what cannot be ignored are the enormous class and education differentials that do exist within this context.

We found it fascinating that foreign academicians were always much more interested in these very poor women than Indian academicians ever seemed to be. The response of the women we interviewed to the foreigner–researcher was always very good. We wondered to what extent this had to do with a hangover of colonialism or an idealisation of white skin. It could also be due to the fact that foreigners interact with these poor people and situations like squalor and poverty for a very short period of time and hence tended to behave in a much more soothing and appealing way in contrast to the way many Indians react—with an element of contempt and arrogance.

Conclusion

The attempt to go back to the five women in the *Profiles in Female Poverty* for a longitudinal study, has brought my work to a full circle. I am ending where I began. A lot of research has been done and rich insights into issues regarding women and work have been obtained. However, the efforts that have so far been put into research raise many questions; the most important among them being—how does one theorise these findings which have been left at the descriptive level? How does one push the frontiers of work, from the merely descriptive to more analytical levels? I end by saying that these questions can be best answered by new upcoming young scholars who are better qualified and trained and more articulate and sensitive.

Appendix

List of publications

Books and monographs

1. (1981), *Profiles In Female Poverty: A Case Study of Five Working Women in Kerala*, New Delhi: Hindustan Publishing Corporation. (1982), London: Longman.
2. (1984), *Fisherwomen on the Kerala Coast: Demographic and Socio-Economic Impacts of a Fisheries Development Project*, Geneva: Women and Development International Office.
3. (1988), *A Socio-Economic Survey of Scheduled Caste and Tribe Habitats*, Kerala Industrial and Technical Consultancy Organisation.
4. (1992), *Economic And Social Aspects of Population Ageing In Kerala, India*, New York: Department of Economic and Social Development, United Nations.
5. (1993), *In the Absence of their Men: Impact of Male Migration on Families Left Behind*, New Delhi: Sage Publications.
6. (1993), *Asian Women Migrant Workers*, Geneva: Artep, I.L.O.
7. (1994), Leela Gulati and Ramalingam, *Gender Profiles: Kerala*, New Delhi: Royal Netherlands Embassy.
8. (1995), Leela Gulati and Ramalingam, *Poverty and Deprivation: Some Interstate Comparisons*, Bangalore: HIVOS.
9. (1997), Leela Gulati and Hilda Janson, *Gender Profiles: Karnataka*, New Delhi: Royal Netherlands Embassy.
10. (1998), *Poverty and Deprivation: A Socio-Economic Profile of Bihar and Madhya Pradesh*, Bangalore: HIVOS.
11. (1975), 'Female Work Participation: A Study of Interstate Difference' in *Economic and Political Weekly*, Vol. 10 (112).
12. (1976), 'Unemployment among Female Agricultural Labourers' in *Economic and Political Weekly*, Vol. 11 (13).
13. (1976), 'Age of Marriage of Women and Population Growth: The Kerala Experience' in *Economic and Political Weekly*.

14. (1977), 'Rationing And Peri-Urban Community: A Case Study of a Squatter Habitat' in *Economic and Political Weekly.*
15. (1978), 'Profiles of a Female Agricultural Labourer' in *Economic and Political Weekly*, Vol. 13 (12).
16. (1979), 'Female Labour in the Unorganized Sector: Profile of a Brick Worker', in *Economic and Political Weekly*, Vol. 25 (162).
17. (1979), 'Marked Preference for Female Sterilization in a Semi-rural Squatter Settlement: Studies in Family Planning' in *Economic and Political Weekly*, Vol. 10 (11, 12).
18. (1979), 'Child Labour in Kerala's Coir Industry', paper commissioned by the Anti-Slavery Society, London.
19. (1980), 'Family Planning in a Semi-Rural Squatter Settlement in Kerala: Marked Preference for Female Sterilization', in *Economic and Political Weekly*, Vol. 25 (28).
20. (1980), 'Women in the Urban Industrial labour Force in India and, Women on The Move: Contemporary Changes in Family and Society', Paper presented at the UNESCO Meeting of Experts on the Status of Women, Development and Population Trends, Paris.
21. (1983), 'Male Migration to the Middle East and its Impact on the Family: Some Evidence from Kerala' in *Economic and Political Weekly*, Vol. 18 (52853).
22. (1984), 'Agricultural Labourers' in Jouce Lebra, Joy Paulson and Jana Everette (eds.), *Women and Work in India: Continuity and Change*, New Delhi: Pramila Publishers.
23. (1984), 'The Role of Women from Fishing Households: Case Study of a Kerala Fishing Village in Changing South Asia' in *Asian Research Service*, Hong Kong.
24. (1986), 'The Impact on the Family of Male Migration to the Middle East: Some Evidence from Kerala' in Fred Arnold and M. Shah Nasra (eds), *Asian Labour Migration, Pipeline to the Middle East*, London: Boulderwestview (Special Studies in International Migration).
25. (1981), 'Coping with Male Migration' in *Economic and Political Weekly*, Vol. 22 (44).
26. (1988), 'Fisherwomen on the Kerala Coast' in Jana Neidel Hein and Dona Lee Davis (eds), *To Work and To Weep: Women in Fishing Economics*, St. John's Institute of Social and Economic Research, Memorial University of Newfoundland, U.S.A.
27. (1988), Leela Gulati and S.I. Rajan, Population Aspects of Ageing in Kerala: Their Economic and Social Consequence', Working Paper, Centre for Development Studies and United Nations, New York.
28. (1989), 'Women in the Unorganised Sector' in Robin Jeffry (ed.), *The Reader*, Australia: La Trobe University.
29. (1990), 'Agricultural Workers' Pension in Kerala: An Experiment in Social Assistance', *Economic and Political Weekly*, Vol. 25 (37).

30. (1990), Leela Gulati and S.I. Rajan, 'Social and Economic Implications of Population Ageing in Kerala' in *Demography India*, Vol. 19 (2).
31. (1991), 'Women's Role in the Fertility Decline in Kerala State' in *Loyola Journal of Social Sciences*, Vol. 5 (2).
32. (1991), 'Women in the Unorganised Sector in Kerala' in *Indian Journal of Economics*, Vol. 34 (3).
33. (1992), 'Dimension of Female Aging and Widowhood: Insights from Kerala Experience' in *Economic and Political Weekly*, Vol. 27 (43, 44).
34. (1992), 'Migration and Social Change in India' in *Asian Migrant*.
35. (1993), 'Population Ageing and Women in Kerala State' in *Asia Pacific Population Journal*, Vol. 8 (1).
36. (1993), 'Qualitative Research: Case Study as a Research Method', Working Paper, Series No. 3, M.S. University, Baroda.
37. (1993), 'Women and Widowhood', in *Manushi*.
38. (1993), Leela Gulati and Mitu Gulati, 'The Status of Widows in Kerala' in *Manushi*.
39. (1993), 'Widowhood and Aging', in Martha Alter Chen (ed.), *Widows in India: Social Neglect and Public Action*. New Delhi: Sage Publications.
40. (1994), 'Women and Family in India: Continuity and Change' in *Journal of Social Work*, Tata Institute of Social Work.
41. (1995), I.S. Gulati and Leela Gulati, 'Social Security for Widows: Experience in Kerala' in *Economic and Political Weekly*, Vol. 30 (39).
42. (1997), 'Widowhood and Vulnerability in Kerala' in *Loyola Journal of Social Science*, Vol. 11 (2).
43. (1997), 'Women and Work in Kerala: A Comparison of the 1981 and 1991 Censuses' in *Indian Journal of Gender Studies*, Vol. 4 (2).
44. (1997), 'Asian Women in International Migration with Special Reference to Domestic Work and Entertainment' in *Economic and Political Weekly*, Vol. 32 (47).
45. (1997), 'Migration and Social Change in Kerala' in *India International Centre Quarterly*.
46. (1999), 'The Female Poor and Economic Reform in India' in Krishna Ahooja, S. Uma Devi and G.A. Tadas (eds.), *Women and Development*, Council for Social Development.

Notes

1. See Boserup (1970).
2. See Lewis (1959) and Liebow (1967).
3. See Gulati (1981).

References

Ester Boserup (1970), *Women's Role in Economic Development*. New York: St. Martin's Press.

Oscar Lewis (1959), *Five Families: Mexican Case Studies in the Culture of Poverty*. New York: Basic Books.

Elliot Liebow (1967), *Tally's Corners: A Study of Negro Streetcorner Men*. Boston, MA: Little, Brown & Co.

Leela Gulati (1981), *Profiles in Female Poverty: A Study of Five Working Women in Kerala*. New Delhi: Hindustan Publishing Corporation.

17
Oppositional imaginations

Uma Chakravarti

Feminist scholars have been forthright in their criticism of mainstream academia, but have rarely been as forthright in evaluating tendencies manifested within what I would like to call the 'women's studies movement'. Having worked for more than three decades in a women's college which has the unique distinction of having produced a whole generation of feminists in Delhi, often through activism within the college itself, and having watched scores of struggles within the campus on women's issues, I am convinced that the institutional framework of women's studies centres can be both enabling and disabling, depending on the particular configuration of forces operating in universities. The institutional setup of women's studies centres is not necessarily supportive of feminist scholarship, and could actually be obstructive in transforming universities into spaces for women's activism and feminist analyses. It is regrettable, but true, that women's studies centres have functioned within the framework of mainstream patriarchal academia and have often reproduced the imbalances of power operating in universities. Feminist scholars have thus, more often than not, worked outside institutional forums, or sought alternative forums, of which fortunately there are many in a university like that of Delhi, especially because of the vibrancy of its women's colleges; alternatively they have also worked as independent scholars, outside institutional affiliation or special funding of any kind. Some of the most interesting work produced by feminist scholars in Delhi has come from precisely this location—independent of a formal women's studies centre. And yet, neither the range of this work, nor its quality, would have been possible without the impulses and influences which institutions like the University of Delhi provide, as this essay will show. The crucial factor at all times, however, is the vitality of the women's movement in the city, and in the rest of the country, and the issues the movements have thrown up, which feminist scholarship has had to address. It is from this location that the finest work—on sati, on women and the right-wing communal mobilisation, on land rights for women, on the experience of communal violence during Partition, on women's participation in production without access to the income generated by their labour, and on a score of other issues—has come.

The university as a reflection of the wider universe

It was in 1966 that I joined Miranda House, a women's college set up in 1948, immediately after Independence, as a training ground for the new women of India.[1] At the time, Miranda House was still the premier women's institution in University of Delhi , with a faculty drawn from all over India, who were fiercely individualist and feminist in their lives, without formally or self-consciously ever being part of such a formation. Being located on the campus meant that they were involved in both the academic and the political life of the university—indeed of the wider universe of the nation; one of our senior faculty members even stood for the parliamentary elections of 1952. Politics was thus clearly not a male preserve and was as much shaped by women as by men. Our students vigorously translated this into action within the college itself in the late 1960s and the early 1970s, and channelised their political understanding into two campaigns—democratising the university and introducing the gender question in the campus. But before I proceed to outline the atmosphere in the campus, let me delineate, in broad outline, the wider universe of the nation, which is the proper context of the university in which I have spent my entire working career.

When I joined the community at the University of Delhi, it was, like the nation, going through the first period of crisis and questioning that India witnessed in the post-Independent era. Between 1967 and 1975, there were agrarian struggles, tribal movements, workers' movements, student movements, anti-corruption movements and anti-price rise movements in different parts of the country. Student unrest on the campuses of Bihar and Gujarat in particular, had their repercussions in the University of Delhi. These movements linked the problem of unemployment with corruption, authoritarian governance, lack of accountability and a fall in the living standards of the middle classes because of inflation. At the same time, the Naxalite movement of the late 1960s shook the complacency of the middle classes as it dramatically focused, through a recourse to violence, on the unresolved land question; it pointed to the failure of land reforms, and therefore, to the long-standing structural contradictions that persisted in the Indian countryside, despite the 'successes' of the Green Revolution and the launching of several rural development programmes. The continuing oppression of large sections of the rural population, most of whom were landless and Dalit, in particular, made an impression on the idealistic sections of students; Naxalbari touched a chord in many of the students of the University of Delhi, some of whom went off to live and work with the 'people in the countryside'.

Student unrest in the University of Delhi was more generally expressed through a broadly socialist/leftist agenda in the 1960s and early 1970s. Within the campus, the first campaign I can recall was about the language issue, since teaching was up until then primarily, or solely conducted in English. The student movement succeeded in introducing the Hindi medium in the university. More widespread, sustained and perhaps more volatile was the demand for democratising the campus to include student participation in decision-making. Miranda House was the scene of much student activity in foregrounding these campaigns and it was the first women's college to join the students' union at a time when other women's institutions had isolated themselves from the domain of 'politics' as the place occupied by 'lumpenised' youth. This was a classist position that Miranda House was a pioneer in rejecting. Things have come full circle with women demanding to be part of that very space and hoping to transform it through their presence—arguments that we hear routinely now over the women's reservation debate. Gheraos and demonstrations outside the vice-chancellor's office in the university and similar demonstrations outside the principal's office in Miranda House were a common feature of those days, generating great outrage amongst the senior faculty. Some of us younger teachers could and did, however, empathise with the spirit of the times and the fundamental questions they were raising.

Where the fiery students of my college went far beyond us and taught us a thing or two was in their gut sentiments on the stereotyping of women as women—feminine tropes that required them to be beautiful and virtuous products of the 'male gaze', as it is now termed. Miranda House, as the most trendy and elite women's college in the University of Delhi, had for many years crowned its most 'attractive' fresher with the title of Miss Miranda. In the new atmosphere of the late 1960s, where elitism had become an embarrassment which was not totally unacceptable, and Miranda itself was seeking to bridge the gap between what was dismissively termed its 'behenji' constituency and its elite students, the Miss Miranda contest stood out as a regressive, elitist and anti-woman practice which the democratic student body voted to end. At a hotly debated general body meeting, speakers argued against the commodification and objectification of women in a contest that measured beauty by extremely narrow criteria, and by only one standard, that of physical appearance. The women who got to become Miss Mirandas were 'beautiful' by upper class standards—beauty contests could never capture the beauty of other women who might be engaged in hard manual labour which put lines on their faces and cracks on their hands. In any case why create one standard for an institution like Miranda House, which drew its students from a whole range of segments of society, with a range of capabilities and talents? Beauty contests, even when they were sought to be linked with other criteria like 'talent' or 'personality', were just not acceptable to the spirited young women of the early 1970s and so they were voted out. Today it is the teachers, whose own ideas were revolutionised in those years, who have worked to keep that rebel tradition alive in the new era of liberalisation, privatisation and the market economy, which puts a high premium on Indian girls being crowned Miss World and Miss Universe and thereby turning India into a 'beauty superpower'.

This early expression of feminism long predated the beginnings of the women's movement in Delhi. What was significant was that a series of women students of Miranda House, who were all active in various campaigns in the college, have gone on to become central figures in campaigns for gender equality: R. Geetha works with unorganised labour in Tamil Nadu and pursues women's issues relentlessly; Nandita Haksar constantly reminds the legal system of its gender bias and its anti-people bias; Akhila Ramachandran lobbies persistently for women's issues in the media; Anuradha Kapur, Maya Rao and Tripurari Sharma have introduced the subtleties of women's psyches on the stage; Chandita Mukherjee makes sensitive documentaries on important issues including gender, while Urvashi Butalia, Radha Kumar, Kirti Singh, Ruth Vanita and Madhu Kishwar have all been an integral part of the women's movement. Others like Brinda Karat and Ritu Menon, who were in Miranda House before these turbulent times began, have also made a mark in the feminist world. Brinda has gone on to become a well-known feminist-activist in a political party and Ritu is equally well known as a feminist publisher, along with Urvashi Butalia. The point I want to emphasise is that these 'girls' actually introduced some of their teachers to feminism and led them into the movement—a debt that needs to be acknowledged in print. We grew because of them, not the other way around. Classroom and corridor interaction is a dialogic process which works in very complicated ways, and the university is a very important place for such interactions to germinate and flower. I am convinced that I would not have gone on to address the issues that I have in my academic work, had it not been for three inputs—the experience of teaching in Miranda House during the 1960s, 1970s and 1980s; being a part of the women's movement in the city of Delhi; and being a part of the democratic struggles on the campus and the more general democratic rights movement in the last three decades.

During the first half of the 1970s, a series of wider events forced their presence on the campus. One of the early demonstrations in the city on the Bangladesh issue was organised by Nandita Haksar who was then my subsidiary student in a history class and who dragged me off to march down Daryaganj and donate blood in a camp she organised in the university. Other students took me along to anti-price rise demonstrations, organised by left-wing women's groups in the city. By 1974, the campus was seething with anti-establishment politics; student leaders were, on the one hand, tearing up their degrees as valueless pieces of paper, since no jobs were available, and on the other, were inviting leaders like Jayprakash Narayan, among others, to speak to huge student audiences on the campus. The crisis of state legitimacy had repercussions everywhere—in trade unions, in the fields, in public sector institutions and on the campuses. The reaction of the state was swift and shocking—the imposition of the Emergency in June 1975.

The Emergency was experienced with a peculiar intensity in the University of Delhi, unparalleled in terms of university experience, leaving a legacy of teacher and student activism for many years thereafter.

Since the University of Delhi, with its constituent colleges, has a very large faculty, many of who shared anti-authoritarian and/or anti-Congress views, about 200 teachers were initially picked up by the police and detained on false charges. Six of them remained in jail for the entire period of the 19 months of the Emergency. A senior and well-loved teacher of my college and my own department had to go underground in order to escape imprisonment, and was never able to recover her health and well-being. Students, some of whom we knew had protested against the authoritarian actions of the state, were held by the police and even tortured. When the Emergency was lifted, the campus became the scene of heightened political activity, much of it focused on the need to protect the civil rights of citizens against the onslaught of an authoritarian state. As part of this mobilisation, films such as Anand Patwardhan's 'Prisoners of Conscience' were shown in Miranda House and other colleges of the campus. Later, a largely attended All India Civil Rights Convention was held in Delhi and 1977 marked the beginning of the civil and democratic rights movement in the city, as also in the rest of the country. These groups have been the conscience keepers of the city and have investigated civil rights erosions both here and in other states, providing a forum for teachers (like me), lawyers, students and other professionals to be part of a political process in civil society, without being affiliated to any political party. Over the years, women's groups have often worked in conjunction with them on various issues, beyond the specific ambit of gender.

Against the grain: Women in the eye of a storm

The political and social experiences of the late 1960s and the 1970s, and, in particular, the Emergency and post-Emergency periods, provided the space for the appearance of many kinds of movements, of which the women's movements have had the most visible impact on contemporary Indian society.

Across the country, political sensibilities had been sharpened, but women had also found that their presence in political movements and the issues raised by them within these movements did not always find satisfactory responses. Women's wings of political parties were expected to mobilise women on issues identified by the parties or political groups rather than on issues raised by women themselves. By the second half of the 1970s, this conjuncture provided the context for the birth of what is now termed 'autonomous women's groups' (AWG). Other more explicitly party-linked women's organisations, some of which had a long history of existence, were energised and recharged by the questions raised by these AWGs, which, for the first time, explicitly confronted the institution of 'patriarchy'; together, they constituted a formidable force that burst upon the post-Emergency scene as they took up the protest against the specific forms of violence against women in India, such as dowry murders and custodial rape. Discussions in women's organisations in Delhi such as Samata and Stree Sangharsh, and in the Forum Against Rape in Bombay, sharpened the understanding of the ways in which a wholly 'indigenous' set of patriarchal practices was operating; this understanding provided the basis of the earliest campaigns and it might be useful to remind ourselves, as well as others who will inherit our legacies, that from the very beginning the women's movement in India has been organically linked to the contradictions emerging *in India itself*—it is not an imitation of the western women's movement as some people have alleged. Such a charge is motivated and is intended to deflect from the very solidly based foundations and workings of gender inequality on our home ground.

By the late 1970s, the emergence of women's groups across the country made it possible for the first countrywide campaign to be launched against the sexist and classist judgement in the Mathura rape case where a young tribal girl had been raped in police custody. Outraged by the assumptions of a judiciary steeped in upper caste, patriarchal norms, women's groups lobbied for a retrial using very creative forms to mobilise public opinion. Earlier the rape of Rameeza Bee in police custody in Hyderabad had also resulted in spontaneous protests when women's groups and civil rights groups had worked together to demand action against the guilty policemen. The 8 March 1981 campaign was inevitably focused on the issue of custodial rape. I can still recall the occasion when the street play on custodial rape was performed in Ajmal Khan Park in Delhi and the police watched the searing indictment of their institution with grim expressions on their faces.

Over the next few years, the women's movement took off in all directions and in a variety of locations. No one who had even the slightest concern about social and political issues could stand outside the force generated by the movement. Being a teacher in a lively women's college gave others and me the unique location of being 'facilitators', working to provide a means by which women's organisations in Delhi could bring their campaigns to the campus through discussions, workshops, and the performance of street plays. Among the plays performed were 'Om Swaha', 'Roshni', 'Aurat', and 'Ahsas' and a host of others, all dealing with the multiple dimensions of women's oppression. Each play would conclude with some kind of a formulation that the women's movements were seeking to provide in order to end these oppressions. Of particular concern to us was that cases of domestic violence were being brought to light even within the community of teachers and the task then was to have the teacher's union, for example, discuss forms of patriarchal violence prevalent amongst its own members.

At the same time, the university itself was generating its own set of contradictions; University of Delhi has been among the most unsafe of campuses thanks to the culture of machismo and street aggression that the city has allowed to flourish and which the authorities within the university have never seriously tried to tackle. Given the lumpeni-sation and goondaism of some sections of the male component in the student community, whom the authorities do not want to take on, it is the university's women students who have had to pay the price. Women students have been molested in 'student specials', the buses that carry students to and from the university, on the streets of the campus and even inside their classrooms. Spontaneous protests by women students after each such shocking incident has had to be more sustainedly fol-lowed up by women teachers, given the transitory nature of the stu-dent community. The molestation of women students of St. Stephen's College on the days preceding the festival of Holi some years ago, did, however, arouse the ire of a whole new generation of feminists, who have gone on to become activists in other fields as well.

An early attempt to address and resist the culture of violence against women students was made in the mid-1980s through the setting up of the 'Goonda Virodhi Abhiyan', a loose organisation of teachers, both men and women, students and karamcharis. Later, the Gender Studies Group pioneered the first report on the nature and extent of violence against women in the form of sexual harassment in the University of Delhi. Apart from getting the university community, its authorities, and the general public to recognise the term 'sexual harassment' rather than 'eve teasing' (the trivialised form used by the media), the report docu-mented and provided an understanding of what it meant to be sexually harassed, and how women dealt with it in their student lives. Its findings were shocking because 92 per cent of the women informants reported that they had been sexually harassed at some point or other in their student years.

The report of the study on sexual harassment had been preceded and followed by at least two prominent cases in the University of Delhi where women employees had been sexually harassed by their male 'colleagues' who were placed in positions of authority over them. The cases acted as eye-openers for those who had campaigned to demand action against the offenders, as the university system closed its ranks to protect the men charged with sexual assaults and went so far as to initiate action against the protestors in one of the cases.

Building on these experiences, students and teachers on the campus have, in the last three years, worked to formulate a comprehensive policy to deal with sexual harassment, which still awaits being accepted or taken seriously as a base document. What is regrettable is that far from working with students and teachers who are actively raising issues of sexual harassment on the campus, the officially constituted women's development centres have never actively taken up complaints of sexual molestation by male teachers or administrative staff when the offender is a university employee. That women's studies centres can and have played an active role in addressing and dealing with sexual harassment, even within the framework of university power structures, is evidenced by the example of the women's studies centre at Pune University, which ensured action against a university professor who was regarded as being too eminent a scientist to be indicted.

Participating in many of the campaigns mentioned above, and others that have erupted at various points, has often been frustrating and time-consuming, but also rewarding; the university is a crucial arena for the intersection of activism, awareness and scholarship. It is also a cross-section of many strands of people, ideas and issues and so it is amongst the most fertile of places to generate discussions both within the classroom and in other forums. And so, I have, over the years, been enriched by drawing from these discussions and experiences whether it was about beauty contests, hostel rules for women (where the hostel functions in loco parentis), the screening of the film 'Fire' for an all-female audience or incorporation of gender into courses that had hitherto left it out of its frame.

Other journeys: The struggle to build a critique of patriarchies

It should be clear from the long preamble in the preceding sections of this essay that I regard the activism of the women's movement, as well as other democratic movements, to be a necessary and contingent factor in the birth and growth of the 'field' of women's studies. The women's movement of the last two decades has provided context and impetus for the emergence of women's studies in India because many, if not all the feminist scholars of our time, have been involved in the movements against rape, dowry, sati and domestic violence, amongst a host of other campaigns. It was here that the multiple forms and structures of patriarchies and the cultural practices associated with them began to be outlined through the experiences of women on the ground. The explicitly political women's movement, and the insights derived therein, provided feminist scholars with the experimental material on the basis of which they formulated gender as a category of analysis.

For the first few years of the women's movement, almost all the energies of women, including those of us who were formally in the university, were spent in 'fire-fighting' operations, planning demonstrations and participating in them, thinking about issues like dowry murders, trying to understand what went on 'inside the family' and working out strategies for handling the enormity of the problems we were dealing with. Among the most difficult questions we had to address was the classic and still-repeated formulation that it was not men who oppressed women but women themselves who oppressed other women, as evident from the participation of mothers-in-law in dowry murders; equally difficult to take in was the evidence of many wives, unable to name their husbands in dying declarations, who had been set on fire by their in-laws and husbands. At least in Delhi, women's studies was spearheaded by these and other questions that acted like a blow in the stomach; by the early 1980s it became imperative for us to look at history, traditions and 'culture' as they worked in India, from a feminist standpoint.

In November 1981, teachers who were involved with the women's movement, or who were close to it such as Sudesh Vaid, Kumkum Sangari and Neeraj Malik of the Indraprastha College for Women, organised a seminar on 'Women in myth and literature', and I was invited to chair a session. I had till then not worked specifically on gender, since like many of the women scholars of the time, I had chosen a completely mainstream theme for my Ph.D thesis. While my concerns were already working in the direction of looking at the past from the point of view of alternative traditions in India, especially those that had appealed to oppressed peoples, as Buddhism certainly had to the Dalits, I was not sufficiently sensitive to issues of gender. While looking at the sources, I had noticed the uneven way in which women were featured in the Buddhist texts, which led me to include a few pages on this theme but I was unable to build gender centrally into my research on the social dimensions of Buddhism[2]. Nevertheless, because I had looked at a body of ancient texts, I found that I became useful to those who were exploring tradition from a feminist standpoint, such as the organisers of the seminar at Indraprastha College. This seminar turned out to be very stimulating; though it was still too early to come up with a full or complex understanding of culture and its relationship to gender, it was rich and varied in its explorations and my own work on issues of gender dates back to this seminar.

Sometime thereafter, a chance encounter with the Pali Jataka stories turned out to be a revelation: in the Pali account of the story of Rama, Sita is described as Rama's sister. I was struck by the variations in narratives, which had ultimately culminated in the production of the epics, the *Ramayana* in particular. Curious about these narrative variations, I looked for the account of key episodes such as Sita's abduction, her *agni pariksha*, her abandonment and her final descent into the earth. Among these key moments was also the drawing of the *lakshman rekha*, a metaphor that resonates in the life of every Indian woman. How often fathers or brothers have evoked its imagery to create boundaries around us, as my own brother had done, in my adolescent years. To my utter surprise, the *lakshman rekha* episode did not feature in the Valmiki version. Astounded, I looked at the *Ramacharitamanasa* of Tulsidas and found it missing there too. Finally, it became clear that the *Ramayana* was as much a construct as any other narrative which had changed over the centuries, and that it was crafted with an ideological coherence that made the concept of *pativrata*—chastity—the most effective means by which women could become complicit in their own subordination. Once the norm was in place, women aspired to be like Sita, even if they were required to obliterate themselves in the process. When I wrote up these 'discoveries' and went on to present them in colleges, workshops and before women's groups, I could immediately create a rapport with my audience; this was because while almost everyone knew the story, very few people knew about the variations and everyone was fascinated by the twists and turns in the development of the narrative.

Exploring the variations in the narrative of the *Ramayana* was like unravelling a mystery, since a parallel narrative about the relationship between text and context began to emerge. At the same time the multiplicity of our traditions, many of which were now lost to us, needed to be unearthed and this led to my looking at the *Therigatha*, a compilation of the verses of Buddhist *bhikkhunis*. The *Therigatha* was unique in two ways: it was the earliest evidence of women's voices that we had access to in India, or perhaps anywhere in the world; and the verses clearly indicated that women had felt oppressed by the drudgery entailed in domestic labour, which was their lot in life, and aspired to a more meaningful existence. The search for dignity and identity expressed in the verses of the *Therigatha* also made it clear that women's quest for a life of their own, beyond husband and kin, went very far back into the past and was not an artificial creation of westernised feminism but the very indigenous aspiration of women oppressed by specific indigenous forms of domination, created by our own societies.

The importance of looking at tradition has also surfaced from the point of view of trying to locate enabling aspects of our past; since the dominant culture upheld hierarchies of caste, class and gender, women have searched the past for dissident traditions and figures who had critiqued and resisted the oppressive, dominant culture. Almost naturally, therefore, the Bhakti movement became a focus of feminist attention. Over the years, an impressive body of writing on various aspects of bhakti has fine-tuned our understanding of the spaces religious movements have provided for women to express themselves but they have also shown us the limits of those spaces. However strong or radical some of these movements were, though the experience of bhakti was deeply gendered, and while men and women bhaktas did succeed in democratising access to God, the movements were unable to transform social relations, whether in the spheres of caste, class or gender. Thus the difficulties of using bhakti as a resource for struggles today, especially in the field of gender, have been fairly sharply brought out by the furore created by present-day Lingayats, who have sought and succeeded in having a ban imposed on a scholarly book with a 'radical' interpretation of the content of the movement. The Lingayats, as follow-ers of Basaveshwara who was against caste, and whose movement provided the space for Akka Mahadevi's uninhibited verse, should have been our allies in battling all forms of caste and gender oppression, rather than reflecting the prejudices of the dominant traditions. It ap-pears to me that unless social relations are transformed, radical ideologies get blunted. This is what has happened to the ideological potential of bhakti, as it has been sanitised and accommodated within a larger frame-work of hierarchical structures; all that is left of the radical edge of bhakti is a residue of humanitarian impulses and even those are sometimes difficult to claim as outlined above.

In a different register, throughout the decade of the 1980s, feminist scholars, particularly historians, felt the need to explore the historio-graphy of the women's question in the writing of mainstream history and especially the construction of a 'golden age', when women were suppo-sedly free and were said to have occupied a high pedestal in Indian society. What was notable is that whereas in the West, women were virtually absent from history in works published in the 19th and the first half of the 20th centuries, in India they were a key component of a carefully crafted script for the past put together by 19th century Hindu intelligentsia. Examining the historiography of the women's question here has meant looking closely at why women's 'high' status in ancient India was so central to the self-image of the 19th century intelligentsia. For feminist scholars, it was imperative to disseminate the limitations of this way of looking at the women's question and thereby put aside the ghost of what I have described as the Altekarian paradigm.

These early forays into history, mythology and tradition helped us to understand, to an extent, our past and our present as a product of the past, but it did not help us to analyse the complex formations in which both our past and present were embedded. By the end of the 1980s, a whole series of complex questions on the caste, class and regional aspects of the working of patriarchies had come up both in the women's movements and in women's studies. That women experienced subordination in very different ways according to where they were located, was clear to those who were involved with grass-roots work. As movements such as Shahada, Bodh Gaya and Chipko became well-known (through rather delayed attention in the feminist media), the linkages between patriarchies, class and the state as they worked in the present were also becoming evident to scholars working in the area of women's studies. These sharpened sensibilities coincided with the appearance of important feminist theoretical works. A work that I was fascinated by was Gerda Lerner's *The Creation of Patriarchy*, which Gail Omvedt's stimulating review in *The Economic and Political Weekly* brought to my attention. The most significant aspect of this work, from my point of view, was that it dealt with the early historic period in Mesopotamia, a region not too far from India, and Lerner had both provided a hypothesis linking together class, patriarchy and the state, as well as a methodology for a rigorous analysis of the formation of patriarchy. By the end of the 1980s, I managed to have a series of face-to-face interactions with her and found her comments on my work insightful. I had already tried to link class and gender together in an essay I wrote on women who formed the underclass in ancient India. Since I was concerned about the internal stratification *within* women, who have never constituted a homogenised category for me (sisterhood is not a given; it has to be forged as a conscious political affiliation which refuses to be complicit in any oppressive arrangement—this is the only way in which the material differences between women can be erased), I tried to link caste (a uniquely indigenous institution), class, gender, the state and ideology together in the context of ancient India. As of now, I have only managed to lay out a design for a larger and more detailed work on the contours of the early formation of patriarchy/patriarchies in ancient India, which I hope I can do in the near future. Making use of the more readily available source material necessary for such an analysis, I decided to first explore the connections between class formation, caste contestations, nationalism, changing gender norms and the transformation of legal processes in the context of 19th-century Maharashtra. This has enabled me to outline linkages between various institutions that have a bearing on the formation of patriarchies.

Living in dark times has thrown up its own set of imperatives; we could not easily stick to our specialised academic training. Becoming involved in the women's movement took us along in a certain direction, but it is impossible to function within discrete and closed units in India of today. From 1984 onwards, growing majoritarianist tendencies in the state and communal violence have impinged more and more on our lives. While many of my friends have produced very fine studies on women and communalism, including addressing the very difficult question of women's agency and participation in right-wing mobilisation, I have not done any work in this field on my own. But, inescapably, I have been drawn into joint work, first with a much-loved erstwhile student, then with a democratic rights organisation and more informally with friends and like-minded scholars. This is an important part of my life, giving me a sense of support since shared concerns and shared work make it easier to live through trying times. Bolstered thus, we may be able to bring about better days in the future.

Where do we stand today and what should our agenda be? On the women's studies front, we have taken great strides (enough to begin a review!), though there is much to be done yet. We have pioneered certain areas of research, sometimes leading to takeover bids by mainstream academics. We have also put gender on the map of serious scholarship, although it remains an arena still largely worked on by women. We have a number of diehard opponents and quite often our work is trivialised. At the same time, we have a number of sympathisers among male scholars, but given the new variant of the traditional division of labour, I suspect that we are leaving men behind, who are often unable to understand the complexities of our formulations. Other undesirable developments following from gender, regarded now as upbeat, especially by the mainstream publishing market, are that studies on class are being marginalised. Perhaps what needs to be done is to mainstream gender, making it impossible for anyone to study anything without exploring its gender dimensions. We have shown quite unequivocally that when we explore gender we do so in its wider caste and class setting. Mainstream scholars, especially those studying stratification, need to show us that they can do the same when they are writing about caste and class. That will end this new division of labour and make for better scholarship all around, and thereby a more holistic understanding of our society.

Notes

1. For a rich account of the history of Miranda House, see Chakravarti, Singha and Srinivasan (eds.) (1998).
2. It took almost a decade before the first and perhaps only work, which has succeeded in building gender centrally into exploring a mainstream issue, could appear. See Roy (1994).

References

Uma Chakravarti, Radhika Singha and Ramya Srinivasan (eds) (1998), *Reliving Miranda*, New Delhi: Miranda House.

Kumkum Roy (1994), *The Emergence of Monarchy in Northern India*, New Delhi: Oxford University Press.

About the editors

Pam Rajput is Professor of political science and the Founder-Director of the Centre for Women's Studies and Development at Panjab University, Chandigarh, where she teaches political science, human rights and gender studies. As Indo-Shastri Fellow and recipient of Commonwealth Association of Universities Exchange Fellowship, she visited and lectured at various universities in Canada and South Africa and was a Visiting Professor at Hiroshima University, Japan. She is elected (four times) Chair of Research Committee on Women, Politics and Developing Nations of the International Political Science Association. Currently, she is also Convenor of the Women's Studies Collective in India. She has previously been member of the UGC's Standing Committee on Women's Studies for eight years.

Devaki Jain graduated from Oxford, and taught economics at the University of Delhi. She was the Founder-Director of Institute of Social Studies Trust (ISST) till 1994. She received an Honorary Doctorate (1999) from the University of Durban, Westville, Republic of South Africa and was awarded the Bradford Morse Memorial Award (1995) by UNDP at the Beijing World Conference. She was a visiting Fellow at Institute of Development Studies, University of Sussex (1993), and a Fulbright Senior Fellow attached both to Harvard University and Boston University (1984). She was also a Fellow at the Scandinavian Institute of Asian Studies, Copenhagen (1983).

She has been a member of the Government of Karnataka's State Planning Board a member of the UGC's Standing Committee on Women's Studies and of the South Commission chaired by the late Dr. Julius Nyerere. She has authored and edited many publications both jointly and singly, such as *Vocabulary of Women's Politics* (2001), *Minds, Bodies and Exemplars: Reflections at Beijing and Beyond* (1996),

Speaking of Faith: Cross Cultural Perspectives on Women, Religion and Social Change (1986), *Tyranny of the Household: Investigative Essays on Women's Work* (1985), *Women's Quest for Power: Five Case Studies* (1979) and *Indian Women* (1975).

About the contributors

The **Anveshi Research Centre for Women's Studies**, Hyderabad, founded in 1985, supports political thinking about gender, caste and community through its women's studies library, documentation on contemporary subjects, discussion forums and multidisciplinary research initiatives.

Jasodhara Bagchi is the Founder-Director of the School of Women's Studies, Jadavpur University, Kolkata. She is currently its Adviser.

Kamalini Bhansali retired as vice-chancellor of SNDT University in 1989, after serving it in various capacities for nearly three decades.

Uma Chakravarti has been teaching history at Miranda House, University of Delhi since 1966.

Chaya Datar is Chairperson of the Women's Studies Unit, Tata Institute of Social Sciences, and founder of Stree Mukti Sangathana and Forum Against Rape.

Neera Desai is a former Professor of sociology and Founder-Director of the Research Centre for Women's Studies at SNDT University, Mumbai.

V.S. Elizabeth is Associate Professor at National Law School of India University and Co-ordinator of the Centre for Women and Law.

Leela Gulati is an Associate Fellow at the Centre for Development Studies, Thiruvananthapuram.

Devaki Jain is former Director of the Institute of Social Studies Trust.

Surinder Jetley is a former Professor of women's studies, Director of the Centre for Women's Studies and Development, and Head of Department of Sociology at the Banaras Hindu University.

Susheela Kaushik teaches political science at the University of Delhi and was till recently the Director of the Women's Studies and Development Centre, University of Delhi.

Maithreyi Krishnaraj is a former Professor and Director, Research Centre for Women's Studies, SNDT University.

Vina Mazumdar is Chairperson of the Centre for Women's Development Studies, New Delhi.

Regina Papa is Professor and Head of the Department of Women's Studies, and Director of the Centre for Women's Studies, Alagappa University, Karaikudi.

Pam Rajput is Professor of Political Science and Director, Centre for Women's Studies and Development, Panjab University, Chandigarh.

Bharati Ray is the Founder-Director of the Women's Studies Research Centre, Calcutta University.

Kumud Sharma is a former Director of the Centre for Women's Development Studies, New Delhi.

Rameshwari Varma is a former Director of the Women's Studies Centre, University of Mysore.

Amita Verma is a former Director of Women's Studies Research Centre, M.S. University of Baroda and a former Professor of human development and family studies.

Index

382 ✽ Index